T0290043

Organising Responses to Climate Change

Climate change is the most important issue now facing humanity. As global temperatures increase, floods, fires and storms are becoming both more intense and frequent. People are suffering. And yet, emissions continue to rise. This book unpacks the activities of the key actors which have organised past and present climate responses – specifically, corporations, governments, and civil society organisations. Analysing three elements of climate change – mitigation, adaptation and suffering – the authors show how exponential growth of the capitalist system has allowed the fossil fuel industry to maintain its dominance. However, this hegemonic position is now coming under threat as new and innovative social movements have emerged, including the fossil fuel divestment movement, Fridays for Future, Extinction Rebellion and others. In exposing the inadequacies of current climate policies and pointing to the possibilities of new social and economic systems, this book highlights how the worst impacts of climate change can be avoided.

DANIEL NYBERG is a professor of management at the University of Newcastle Business School and an honorary professor at the University of Sydney. He has published widely in journals including *Academy of Management Journal*, *British Journal of Sociology*, *Environment and Planning: A*, and *Organization Studies*, and he is the co-author of *Climate Change, Capitalism and Corporations: Processes of Creative Self-Destruction* (Cambridge University Press, 2015, with Christopher Wright). He is currently a Chief Investigator on an Australian Research Council Discovery project (2022–2024) on climate change adaptation in Australian industries.

CHRISTOPHER WRIGHT is a professor of organisational studies at the University of Sydney Business School and key researcher at the Sydney Environment Institute. He has published in many of the leading management journals including the *Academy of Management Journal*, *Journal of Management Studies*, *Research Policy*, *British Journal of*

Management and *Human Relations*. He is the author of several books including *Management as Consultancy: Neo-Bureaucracy and the Consultant Manager* (Cambridge University Press, 2015, with Andrew Sturdy and Nick Wylie) and *Climate Change, Capitalism and Corporations* (Cambridge University Press, 2015 with Daniel Nyberg).

VANESSA BOWDEN is a lecturer in sociology at the University of Newcastle. She has published in journals including *Global Environmental Change, Environmental Politics,* and the *Journal of Sociology.* She is currently working on research projects exploring the social dynamics of climate adaptation amongst coastal communities and the role of the fossil fuel sector in shaping energy transition in Australia.

Organising Responses to Climate Change

The Politics of Mitigation, Adaptation and Suffering

DANIEL NYBERG
University of Newcastle, New South Wales
CHRISTOPHER WRIGHT
University of Sydney
VANESSA BOWDEN
University of Newcastle, New South Wales

CAMBRIDGE
UNIVERSITY PRESS

CAMBRIDGE
UNIVERSITY PRESS

University Printing House, Cambridge CB2 8BS, United Kingdom

One Liberty Plaza, 20th Floor, New York, NY 10006, USA

477 Williamstown Road, Port Melbourne, VIC 3207, Australia

314–321, 3rd Floor, Plot 3, Splendor Forum, Jasola District Centre, New Delhi – 110025, India

103 Penang Road, #05–06/07, Visioncrest Commercial, Singapore 238467

Cambridge University Press is part of the University of Cambridge.

It furthers the University's mission by disseminating knowledge in the pursuit of education, learning, and research at the highest international levels of excellence.

www.cambridge.org
Information on this title: www.cambridge.org/9781009266949
DOI: 10.1017/9781009266901

First published 2023

A catalogue record for this publication is available from the British Library.

ISBN 978-1-009-26694-9 Hardback
ISBN 978-1-009-26693-2 Paperback

Contents

Part V   The Politics of Climate Futures

Figures

Tables

Acknowledgements

This book is what is sure to be one of many 'COVID-19' babies. Begun when the pandemic was first coming to light, we had little sense of the extraordinary events we would witness, mostly from our homes. While much of the book was written in isolation, the assistance and feedback we have received while writing and thinking through our ideas belies this context. We are ever grateful for the professional and personal support we have received in this process. Firstly, a special thanks to Randi Irwin and Liv Hamilton for their invaluable research assistance and to Neil Robinson who helped us sharpen our writing, as well as Valerie Appleby and the team at Cambridge University Press. Thank you also to Dan Cass, Christian De Cock, George Ferns, Jean-Pascal Gond, Michael Mann, Ivy Scurr and Sheena Vachhani and all of those from whom we received feedback and comments on early chapter drafts, papers and conference presentations. Funding for our research into business responses to climate change and low carbon transition was provided by the Australian Research Council under its Discovery program (DP180102064), and without this funding, this book would not have eventuated. Lastly, we would like to thank our partners Katie, Denise and Steve who provided so much support, advice and encouragement, and our children Isla and Millie, Genevieve and Alexander, and Melody who remind us of the importance of not giving up. This book is for those who continue to fight for the future. While much of the book outlines what a difficult task this is, we are inspired by the resistance and creativity of those in the various movements holding the line. We hope this book can play a part, however small, in that process.

PART I

The Politics of Climate Change

1 | *Organising Climate Change*

The alarm bells are deafening, and the evidence is irrefutable: greenhouse gas emissions from fossil fuel burning and deforestation are choking our planet and putting billions of people at immediate risk.

António Guterres, United Nations Secretary-General
(quoted in Harvey, 2021b)

As unprecedented heatwaves, fires and floods wracked North America, Europe and Asia during the northern hemisphere summer of 2021, the United Nations Intergovernmental Panel on Climate Change (IPCC) released its long-awaited Sixth Assessment Report (IPCC, 2021). The frankness of the document stunned the world's media. Summarising tens of thousands of scientific papers, the report found that our planet is now experiencing warming unseen in 125,000 years and that atmospheric carbon levels are at their highest in 2 million years. It warned that global warming could exceed 1.5 degrees Celsius (°C) above preindustrial levels in around a decade unless truly rapid, large-scale and immediate reductions in greenhouse gas emissions are made. The bleak truth is that our world is currently on track for between 2.1°C and 3.5° C of warming by the end of the century. In the context of the unprecedented climate impacts experienced at just over 1°C of warming, a rise of 2°C, 3°C or even 4°C presents a genuinely apocalyptic future. As United Nations (UN) Secretary-General António Guterres grimly declared in response to the IPCC's report, this is nothing less than 'a code red for humanity'.

Human-induced climate disruption is the most pressing issue facing our species, yet the ineffectiveness of the political response becomes ever more apparent in the face of the escalating crisis. Even as scientific projections re-emphasise the magnitude of the problem, the world's addiction to economic growth and the fossil energy that fuels it continues to expand – and, as a result, so do carbon emissions.

While governments and corporations make soothing noises about the 'grand challenge' of climate change, tangible action in the form of dramatic reductions in carbon emissions has remained illusory. There is much busyness in the halls of power in terms of commitments to future action, appeals to 'sustainability' and the building of processes of carbon accounting and certification, yet the crucial metrics of aggregate carbon emissions and atmospheric concentrations of greenhouse gases still worsen.

This book is about unpacking that fundamental conundrum. Why are meaningful actions to avert catastrophe still so few and so limited, despite the clear scientific evidence that human activities now threaten the future viability of much of life on this planet? To paraphrase journalist Elizabeth Kolbert (2006), how is it that a technologically advanced society could choose, in essence, to destroy itself?

This is the question we seek to address. Specifically, we explore how corporate and political leaders have sought to *organise* climate change – that is, how existing economic and political frameworks have not only produced an all-encompassing environmental crisis but sought to shape the response to it in ways that ensure nothing substantial should change. We seek to lay bare the creation and maintenance of a ruling order of economic and political activity – one that refuses to bend even when confronted by the destruction of our planet's life-support systems.

In this opening chapter, we outline the broader context of this issue and set out our central argument – that the climate crisis is the product of a specific political economy: global capitalism. This is a model of economic and social development that has become so fundamental to political understanding that it is rarely questioned, let alone challenged. Overall, while it takes various context-dependent forms, capitalism relies on the fervent pursuit of continued economic growth and fossil energy consumption on a compound basis ad infinitum. The key actors in this process are global corporations, state-owned enterprises, allied governments and political parties, along with the supporting institutional apparatus of think tanks, consultancies and media whose power and finances depend on a perpetuation of economic growth at all costs.

Although the catastrophic environmental consequences of this trajectory have long been sidelined and ignored, the debt now falls due: this is the age of consequences. As climate change and associated environmental crises demonstrate, a focus on growth and consumption disproportionally benefits the wealthy within the Global North and advanced economies and has resulted in a fundamental shift in the basic Earth system. The dramatic economic change that has accelerated over the two centuries since the first Industrial Revolution has upended the stable climate of the past 12,000 years of the Holocene. Humanity has now engineered a new and much more unstable geological epoch: the Anthropocene (Steffen et al., 2015). This has become a very different planet – one that climate scientists argue will likely challenge the continued existence of organised human society.

We begin this chapter by reflecting on the recent pandemic and how it revealed the underlying vulnerability of a globalised, interconnected economy to the disruptions of the natural world. COVID-19 offered a chance to question the 'business-as-usual' trajectory of infinite growth and fossil energy – a 'fork in the road', as it were – but it also highlighted how corporate and political leaders defend and reassert this model as the only logical path that can be followed. We then outline the historical context of fossil fuel energy, climate change and political responses to the worsening climate crisis. Finally, we re-emphasise the potential for a fundamental reimagining of the climate crisis and set out the structure of the book to follow.

1.1 2020: A Fork in the Road?

The IPCC's sombre review of climate science captured headlines around the globe in mid-2021, but it was not long before media attention refocused on the other immediate crisis gripping the world's nations. The COVID-19 pandemic had toppled many of the comfortable assumptions of the global economy during the preceding two years, with unemployment queues growing in the face of near-shutdown and governments taking extraordinary measures to protect their economies by borrowing money at levels previously unimaginable. Lockdowns and restrictions meant energy demand plummeted. Greenhouse gas emissions declined in tandem (Le Quéré et al., 2020). Crucially, the new willingness for government spending reinvigorated campaigns for a 'Green New Deal' or at the very least a green-led recovery (Mock, 2020).

Such programmes had already been proposed as a means of mitigating climate change while attempting to protect jobs by reorienting economies away from fossil fuels and towards more sustainable industries. This would involve injecting funds into renewable energy infrastructure, investing in energy efficiency and more sustainable forms of transport and, importantly, providing support for communities reliant on fossil fuel industries to develop new industries as the economy transitioned. Calls for such measures came not only from environmentalists: the Organisation for Economic Co-operation and Development (OECD) and the International Energy Agency (IEA) were also among those urging governments to phase out their support for fossil fuels (OECD, 2020).

As a result, as the pace and intensity of the global economy were exposed as unsustainable, there was a glimpse of how things might be different. Newspapers around the world reported on the rewilding of urban spaces. Goats were reportedly on the streets in Wales. Peacocks were wandering around Ronda in Spain. Even a puma was photographed next to parked cars on a road in Chile (Newburger & Jeffery, 2020). This was by no means a reversal of the Sixth Great Extinction, but the possibility of cohabitation and scaling back the old habits of humans as masters of the world was at least teased. Could the speed of business as usual be slowed enough to make time for other priorities? Was this an opportunity to put climate change commitments into action?

Apparently not. By 2021, it was clear that existing business practices would not be challenged. As countries rolled out stimulus packages aimed at kick-starting economic growth, there was little consideration of environmental issues. By August 2021, of the US\$1,950 billion spent by OECD countries on recovery, only US\$336 billion was assessed as having a positive environmental impact (OECD, 2021). A Vivid Economics analysis (2020) comparing the policies and the financial contributions of governments in the G20 – the twenty largest economies in the world – found sixteen of the twenty stimulus packages would 'have a net negative environmental impact'; this was particularly the case for the United States (US), Canada, Australia, Saudi Arabia, China, Russia, India, Mexico and other nations with pre-existing carbon-intensive industries.

In establishing a path towards recovery, certain trajectories were depicted as 'natural' or self-evident. Others were presented as utopian or risky. Despite rhetorical statements of a 'green recovery' during the first year of the pandemic, policies still stressed traditional patterns of investment, consumption and job creation. Unsurprisingly, this response was marked by a rebound in global carbon emissions (Le Quéré et al., 2021). Rather than taking the fork in the road towards an alternative future, the world merely glimpsed the possibility of a positive rerouting as it continued to accelerate down a highway dangerously potholed by fossil-fuelled consumption and an escalating climate crisis.

1.2 How Did We Get Here?

The polarised political debate that has raged during the past several decades suggests the basic science of human-induced climate change is both complex and controversial. It is not. It is actually relatively simple.

Concentrations of greenhouse gases such as carbon dioxide (CO_2), methane (CH_4) and nitrous oxide (N_2O) absorb and re-emit infrared radiation from the Earth's surface. They thus play a critical role in ensuring a balance in our planet's energy budget, resulting in stable climatic conditions for the existence of life. However, industrialisation and economic growth have relied on the ever-increasing use of fossil fuels for energy, manufacturing and transport, as well as the depletion of carbon sinks such as forests, mangroves and peatlands. This human disruption of the carbon cycle has resulted in steadily increasing atmospheric concentrations of greenhouse gases and a warming of the planet above pre-industrial levels (see Figures 1.1 and 1.2).

Drawing on the latest peer-reviewed scientific papers, the IPCC's *Sixth Assessment Report* found current carbon dioxide levels of 415 parts per million (ppm) to be the highest in around 2 million years. It also found global average warming of 1.09°C to be the highest in more than 125,000 years. Importantly, the speed of this change is unprecedented and heralds climate impacts such as the disintegration of the Greenland and West Antarctic ice sheets and glaciers – a process that is likely irreversible and which will play out over centuries (IPCC, 2021).

Continuing increases in global greenhouse gas emissions are a direct result of more than 200 years of economic development reliant on the use of fossil fuel energy – primarily coal, oil and gas. This trajectory, which has now brought the world to the brink of environmental collapse, can be traced back to the first Industrial Revolution, which unfolded in Britain during the late eighteenth and nineteenth centuries.

It was coal power that provided the basis for rapid industrialisation across manufacturing and expanded global markets through the

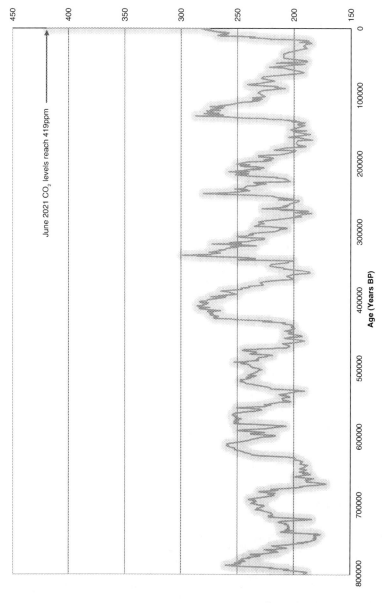

Figure 1.1 Atmospheric CO_2 concentrations for the past 800,000 years
Source: Bereiter et al. (2015); NOAA. (2021).

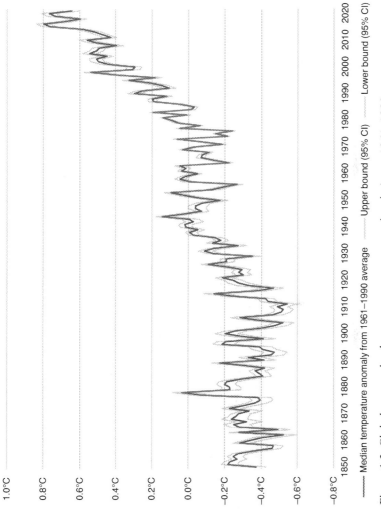

Figure 1.2 Global average land–sea temperature anomaly relative to 1961–1990 average

Source: Morice et al. (2012); Met Office Hadley Centre. (2021).

1850 1860 1870 1880 1890 1900 1910 1920 1930 1940 1950 1960 1970 1980 1990 2000 2010 2020

—— Median temperature anomaly from 1961–1990 average ⋯⋯ Upper bound (95% CI) —— Lower bound (95% CI)

1.0°C

0.8°C

0.6°C

0.4°C

0.2°C

0.0°C

−0.2°C

−0.4°C

−0.6°C

−0.8°C

transformation of transport (e.g., the development of railways and steam shipping). Industrialists were no longer tied to a specific geographic location, and shipping lines and navies were no longer limited by the direction of the wind. Coal-fired steam engines freed up capitalist endeavour, facilitating not only industrialisation but access to new sources of materials, labour and markets under colonial empires (Klein, 2014; Malm, 2016).

By the twentieth century, oil emerged as another key fossil fuel for expansion. The power of the fossil fuel industry grew dramatically during the decades after World War II, driving economic growth and underpinning the emergence of Western consumer lifestyles. Fossil energy was closely protected by national governments keen to build their economic power (Mitchell, 2013), and corporations such as the 'Seven Sisters' – British Petroleum, Royal Dutch Shell, Gulf Oil, Standard Oil of California, Standard Oil of New Jersey, Standard Oil of New York and Texaco – became the most wealthy and powerful companies in the world (Stevens, 2013).

Amid the globalisation and continued growth of economic activity, the ever-increasing consumption of the world's fossil fuel reserves has accelerated during the past fifty years (see Figure 1.3). The rise of Asian economic powerhouses such as Japan, South Korea and, more recently, China and India has broadened the scale of consumption. Beyond Western majors such as ExxonMobil, BP and Chevron, state-owned fossil fuel enterprises – for example, Saudi Aramco in Saudi Arabia, Gazprom and Rosneft in Russia, Kuwait Petroleum, National Iranian Oil Company, China National Petroleum Company, Pemex in Mexico and Petrobras in Brazil – have joined the ranks of the world's largest producers of oil and gas (Victor et al., 2012; Luciani, 2013). Integrated global distribution networks of pipelines, tankers, refineries, ports and rail systems have further reinforced fossil fuel investment and path dependency. National governments continue to strongly support the expansion of fossil energy through public financing of infrastructure, subsidies, discounted royalties and favourable tax regimes – a system critics have labelled 'fossil fuel welfare' (Lenferna, 2019). Global fossil fuel subsidies alone are conservatively estimated at around US$330 billion per annum (Coady et al., 2017), with the International Monetary Fund (IMF) suggesting the true amount could be closer to US$5 trillion (Skovgaard & van Asselt, 2019).

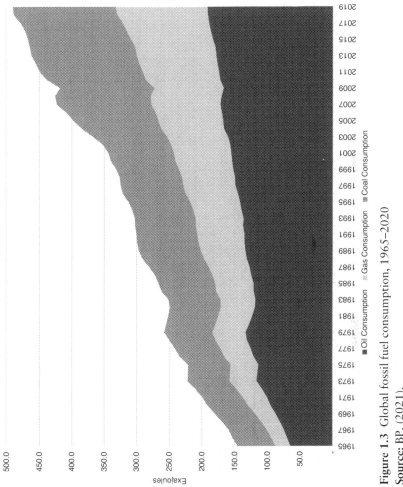

Figure 1.3 Global fossil fuel consumption, 1965–2020
Source: BP. (2021).

Today fossil fuels provide more than 80 per cent of the world's total primary energy supply. They underpin the global financial system not only as the most heavily capitalised sector but also as a dominant source of finance and investment for the world's banks, insurance companies and pension funds (RAN, 2020). Particularly in the Global North, fossil energy buttresses economic and social life through the provision of energy, transportation, trade, consumption and standards of living. Yet this 'petro-market civilization' (DiMuzio, 2012) comes at a huge environmental cost: a fundamental disruption of the Earth system, resulting in an existential threat to much of life on our planet.

1.3 Magical Thinking: The Failure of Climate Governance

In 2015, under the Paris Agreement, 195 nations brokered history's most inclusive commitment to curb greenhouse gas emissions. This not only sought to limit global warming to 'well below' 2°C beyond pre-industrial levels but also sought to 'pursue efforts' to limit the global temperature increase to 1.5°C. This suggested the world's political leaders had seen the light and meaningful action to reduce carbon emissions was at last in train. The media reiterated an upbeat message, with the front page of the *New York Times* declaring: 'The deal, which was met with an eruption of cheers and ovations from thousands of delegates gathered from around the world, represents a historic breakthrough on an issue that has foiled decades of international efforts to address climate change' (Davenport, 2015).

However, despite the Paris Agreement, tangible climate action has remained elusive (Spash, 2016; van Renssen, 2018). By relying on voluntary national commitments for emissions reductions – which were themselves inadequate to achieve the 2°C target – the accord lacked a clear plan of action or an enforceable means of compliance, instead leaving individual nations to determine how emissions reductions might be achieved. To date, no major economy is on track to meet its Paris commitments, let alone the more ambitious 1.5°C goal.

This failure was echoed during the most recent UN Conference of the Parties, COP26, held in Glasgow in November 2021. Billed as humanity's 'last chance' to avoid catastrophe, the event boasted the tagline '1.5 to stay alive', yet the resulting national pledges on emissions cuts, announced after two weeks of political wrangling, fell well short of this target and are instead likely to deliver between 2°C and 2.7°C of warming this century. In addition, commitments to phase out fossil fuels or provide financial support to developing economies for climate 'loss and damage' were sidestepped (Climate Action Tracker, 2021; Harvey et al., 2021). While the conference's organisers sought to put a positive spin on the outcome, it was later revealed that the largest contingent of delegates hailed from the fossil fuel sector (McGrath, 2021b).

Thus, despite three decades of international negotiations, the global economy remains addicted to continued economic growth and ever-increasing carbon emissions (Weart, 2011; Stoddard et al., 2021). National governments, especially historically large emitters such as the US, have resisted hard regulatory measures limiting or prohibiting the use of fossil fuels. The short-term economic and political advantage for individual countries and industries has invariably trumped the long-term needs of environmental well-being and a habitable climate.

In seeking to paper over this contradiction, governments and corporations have increasingly proclaimed long-term goals to reach carbon neutrality or 'net zero'. For instance, the European Union (EU) has committed to achieving carbon neutrality by 2050, while the United Kingdom (UK), France and Germany have made their own pledges to realise the same objective. Finland has committed to hitting 'net zero' by 2035; Sweden by 2045. Most of the major tech corporations, including Facebook, Google, Amazon and Apple, have ambitious targets, as do several major oil companies (see Chapter 3).

This focus on net zero became something akin to a stampede during 2021, with more nations and companies proclaiming their commitments. Yet what is often lacking in these plans is any detail of how such lofty goals will actually be met. The preferred but blurred route for most fossil fuel companies and countries dependent on fossil energy appears to be carbon offsets and still-unproven technologies for carbon capture and sequestration.

This creates the appearance of action while facilitating a continuation of fossil fuel extraction and use (Black et al., 2021). Public statements seem to indicate that the momentum for change is growing, but they can just as easily be viewed as a means of pushing back the urgently required shift. American futurist Alex Steffen (2016) has termed this process 'predatory delay'. A key factor has been the way in which businesses and governments have framed climate change as an

issue that can be accommodated within existing assumptions of economic growth and market capitalism.

For instance, one of the first economic policy responses to climate
change was led by British economist Sir Nicholas Stern, who famously
declared that 'climate change is the greatest market failure the world
has ever seen' (Stern, 2007: viii). Rather than representing it as an
existential threat to the future of human society and the functioning
of planetary ecosystems, Stern's review – along with similar economic
analyses (see, e.g., Garnaut, 2008) – interpreted climate change as
a policy challenge that could be dealt with through the use of judicious
market mechanisms.

From this perspective, 'carbon pricing' – that is, the costing of each
tonne of carbon pollution produced – would internalise a market
'externality' and drive change and innovation throughout national
and global economies. Despite early opposition, the fossil fuel sector
has been largely supportive of such mechanisms and has in fact been
planning for their implementation for some time: Rio Tinto has had an
internal price on carbon in place since 1998, Shell since 2000 (World
Bank, 2015a) and BHP Billiton since 2004 (BHP Billiton, 2015). With
Joe Biden's advocacy of climate action key to his US presidential
election victory in 2020, even the American Petroleum Institute –
a long-time opponent of emissions regulation – has announced its
support for carbon pricing (Mann & Puko, 2021).

Yet it is unlikely that such moves are genuinely altruistic. Chief
Executive Officers (CEOs) and managers of corporations know that
by being involved in the implementation of pricing mechanisms, they
can limit their impact – and, by extension, they can limit climate
mitigation as well. In the EU, for instance, business groups lobbied
for the free allocation of permits during the implementation of carbon
pricing, resulting in a dramatic drop in the price per tonne of carbon
emissions and thereby diminishing the effectiveness of such measures
(Hanoteau, 2014; Pearse, 2016). ExxonMobil, BP and Total have all
supported a carbon price of US$40 per ton in the US while at the same
time planning to increase oil output – prompting commentators to
suggest this is merely a means of avoiding stronger legislation such as
a ban on internal combustion engines, which is being proposed in
European nations (Collins, 2019).

Moreover, it is fair to say that governments have been hesitant to
implement carbon trading. The introduction of such schemes, along

with carbon taxes, has often been thwarted in increasingly polarised national political debates (Carattini et al., 2018); there are also several cases of governments pushing ahead with schemes and then seeing them repealed when a nation's leadership changes (Crowley, 2017; Raymond, 2020). In Australia, the issue has been credited with the removal of two prime ministers and an opposition leader. This suggests that while many may claim to be supportive of measures to mitigate climate change, businesses frequently use their political power and incumbency to limit such actions.

Small wonder that despite growing recognition of a worsening climate crisis, the political and economic dominance of fossil energy can be seen in ongoing increases in extraction, consumption and investment. Even though it became comparatively cheaper during the years between 2010 and 2020 and grew as a result, renewable energy is not replacing fossil fuels. Between 2010 and 2019, for instance, primary direct energy consumption in coal, oil and gas collectively grew from 121,691 TWh (terawatt-hours) to 136,761 TWh; renewables went from 761 TWh to 2,806 TWh (BP, 2020b) – a larger proportional increase yet still a very small percentage of total use.

These statistics underline that a hard and fast break from the current fossil energy addiction is needed to truly decarbonise the global economy. Unfortunately, rather than stepping back from the abyss, much of the innovative capacity of corporate and political leaders has focused on deepening the crisis by identifying new sources of fossil energy – the so-called unconventional fossil fuels, such as fracked gas, tar sands, mega-coal mines and deep water and Arctic oil. For now, alarmingly, the world remains locked in a process of 'creative self-destruction' (Wright & Nyberg, 2015).

1.4 Geopolitical Antagonism

The need to dramatically reduce carbon emissions has re-emphasised divisions between so-called developed and developing economies. The vast bulk of historical emissions is the result of the rich world's wealth, while many poorer economies – which are most exposed to future climate change impacts – are yet to enjoy similar gains. The geopolitical splits over decarbonisation are becoming ever more pronounced, with economies such as China and India now among the world's largest carbon emitters as they push for economic development (Wang & Yang, 2020).

As we outline in greater detail in Chapter 5, the key impacts of climate disruption are likely to be both numerous and catastrophic. They are expected to include more intense and frequent extreme weather events such as hurricanes, floods, droughts and wildfires (National Academies of Sciences Engineering and Medicine, 2016); the transformation of ecosystems and widespread species extinction (Kolbert, 2014); crop failures and threats to food supplies (IPCC, 2019); sea-level rises of a metre or more, rendering cities and coastal regions uninhabitable (Hansen et al., 2016); the movement of large volumes of people from climate-threatened regions (Berchin et al., 2017) and climate change as a 'threat multiplier', leading to heightened geopolitical conflict and wars (Dyer, 2010; CNA Military Advisory Board, 2014).

These devastating consequences will not be borne equally around the globe. It has long been recognised that those nations and citizens with the smallest carbon footprints will be most affected. This brings up the issue of differentiated responsibility both within and between nations. For instance, by 2017, the US, China and the EU had produced more than 50 per cent (25, 12.7 and 22, respectively) of global cumulative emissions (Ritchie, 2019). On an individual level, the super-rich are in the top 10 per cent of emitters: they account for 45 per cent of global emissions and are distributed around the globe, with one-third living in emerging economies (Chancel & Piketty, 2015).

As noted by Mann and Wainwright (2018: 55), this knowledge necessarily brings 'an explicitly moral element to our decisions'. Already the impacts of climate change are being felt in poorer nations, with one study showing a ~25 per cent increase in inequality between poorer and wealthier countries as a result of global warming (Diffenbaugh & Burke, 2019). Sea-level rises and storm surges are already threatening food supplies in the Pacific Islands and will eventually make many areas there uninhabitable; the latter prospect, along with its related 'climate refugee' discourse, further embeds the inequalities of climate change by depicting citizens of these states as passive victims (Perumal, 2018).

Such narratives feed into the view that current dominant economic structures will continue to dictate the future. They may also suggest the time frame for acting on climate change has already passed. The impossibility of imagining a future without compounding economic growth further entrenches existing power relations.

It is now more than a decade since Thompson (2010) outlined three choices for countering the climate crisis: mitigation, adaptation and suffering. However, the present situation might be beyond this triumvirate. Mitigation has been delayed; adaptation is responsive rather than proactive; and suffering is present.

1.5 Book Structure

As activist and journalist Naomi Klein argued more than a decade and a half ago in *The Shock Doctrine*, governments often use crises brought about by wars, terrorist attacks, market crashes or natural disasters as opportunities to push through neoliberal policies that further enrich elites at the expense of other citizens (Klein, 2007). As populations everywhere witness a procession of ever-worsening storms, droughts and fires on daily newsfeeds, it is pertinent to ask whether an alternative politics can be fashioned on a sufficient scale and in enough time to reduce the harm of a climate catastrophe. In this book, we argue that unless there is a dramatic turnaround in the politics of climate change, the current catastrophe will only worsen.

Having set out some of the basic parameters of the current climate crisis and its economic and political underpinnings in this chapter, in Chapter 2, we develop our ideas theoretically through reference to the concept of *hegemony*. We use this to explore how corporate and political rulers establish – and re-establish – corporate capitalism as the only permittable solution to the crisis while at the same time incorporating or dismissing alternatives. As we note, despite the existential threat that climate change poses to human civilisation, it appears the only responses that can be entertained require the continuation of the system that caused the problem in the first place.

In Part 2 of the book, we turn our focus to *the politics of mitigation*. In Chapter 3, we explore how the fossil fuel industry has maintained a hegemonic position in climate policy by emphasising and even exaggerating the links between the industry's ongoing expansion and the economy. We show how the industry has attempted to assuage concerns about climate change by seeding denial and doubt and exploiting its extensive relationships with the political elite and conservative media. We also explain how, by employing long-term emissions-reducing

targets that are unlikely to be met, it has attempted to hold off policy
responses that would impact profits in the short term and convinced
governments to support its quest for technological solutions that have
been promised for decades yet are still to be delivered.

These ploys have not gone unnoticed, and in Chapter 4, we outline
the new social and environmental movements that have arisen in the
wake of decades of climate inaction. Following on from the Paris
Agreement, these grassroots bodies represent a transformation of an
environmental lobby traditionally led by non-government organisations (NGOs). They have engaged in a targeted, counter-hegemonic
strategy of working with a diverse coalition of social actors in preventing new fossil fuel projects and building divisions between fractions of
capital. We show how, although the extent of their influence on climate
policy remains unclear, they have been effective in raising public awareness of a worsening crisis and challenging the current trajectory.

In the third part of the book, which examines *the politics of adaptation*, we ask whether the time frames for creating broader structural
change have in many cases run out. In Chapter 5, we consider the
various attempts at managing climate impacts and argue that these
responses have so far been dominated by the existing framework of
corporate capitalism, which suggests the best means of solving problems is through subsidising corporate activity rather than government
or community intervention. We show how government approaches to
climate adaptation in various localities have favoured the protection of
industry and the funding of corporate emergency responses. We also
explore the preference among policy elites for technological fixes and
still-unproven – not to mention potentially dangerous – attempts at
geoengineering, which we see as a perpetuation of corporate activity at
the expense of local communities and the climate.

Chapter 6 examines how the broader climate discourse impacts
communities at the forefront of climate risk and how this affects
what is regarded as possible when attempting to adapt. We argue that
the polarisation of the issue has resulted in communities potentially
closing off climate change as a concern, with government representatives and community members alike hesitant to acknowledge it as
a cause of extreme weather events such as wildfires, flooding, erosion
and so on. This form of blinkeredness is often linked to economic
priorities and is yet another example of how particular notions of the
economy are able to supersede the consequences of climate disruption.

We posit that many of the ways in which climate adaptation is framed, in particular around notions of 'resilience', feed into the existing corporate hegemony; that the link between climate change and its impacts threatens the status quo and that the issue is therefore politically avoided. This raises an uncomfortable question: if communities are unable to talk about climate change, even when it is already impacting them, what does this mean for those who suffer the impacts the most?

In the fourth part of the book, we focus on *the politics of suffering*. Here, we argue that climate change threatens to further entrench and exacerbate existing suffering, which will be as unevenly distributed as established inequalities. We show that while the fossil fuel industry has long raised the spectre of 'energy poverty' in order to contend it is not possible to shift towards renewable energy, the very countries the industry is claiming to help are among the worst affected.

In Chapter 7, we examine the ways in which the existing discourse of climate change, as propagated by corporations and politicians, in particular, displaces the suffering already being experienced by those in poorer nations. We explain how these impacts are represented as a spectacle while at the same time separated as distant realities for those benefiting from fossil fuel expansion.

In Chapter 8, we consider the political resistance to this narrative and look at how those experiencing the impacts engage in international advocacy to resist the idea that they are passive victims. We unpack the ways in which the 'distant other' can be made present in challenging the prevailing hegemony; we investigate how this form of agonistic politics refuses the hegemonic incorporation of critique that attempts to push climate action into the future; and we explain how suffering, by being framed in the present, becomes a counter-hegemonic force.

In the final part of the book, we focus on the *politics of climate futures*. In Chapter 9, we provide some tentative political solutions for addressing climate change. With renewable energy in many instances cheaper than fossil fuels and with a majority of people around the world supporting meaningful climate action, the solutions we propose are not foremost technological or even educational: rather, they are about politics. We promote 'the three Ds': urgent *decarbonisation*, to render fossil fuels stranded assets; *degrowth*, to ensure humanity stays within planetary boundaries; and increased *democracy*, to loosen the grip of fossil fuel industries.

Finally, in Chapter 10, we argue that the climate crisis can be seen as a symptom of the breakdown or suspension of the prevailing capitalist order; an interregnum. Here, we provide three possible future trajectories in response to the social disruptions resulting from climate change that extend from a continuation of the current path to more extreme as well as hopeful possibilities.

2 | The Hegemony of Corporate Capitalism

Did we aggressively fight against some of the science? Yes ... Did we join some of these 'shadow groups' to work against some of the early efforts? Yes, that's true. But there's nothing illegal about that. You know, we were looking out for our investments. We were looking out for our shareholders.

Keith McCoy, ExxonMobil lobbyist (quoted in Egan, 2021)

For several years now, oil giant ExxonMobil has trumpeted its recognition of the risks posed by climate change. In tandem, it has proclaimed its support for climate action. Its declarations to this effect followed embarrassing revelations that for decades, the corporation had concealed its own scientists' warnings of the catastrophic implications of continued fossil fuel extraction. In 2018, in its annual Sustainability Report, the company informed investors and the general public that it was taking a multipronged approach to addressing climate change. Yet these claims were recently exposed as hollow when Keith McCoy, an ExxonMobil lobbyist, outlined the business' enduring determination to 'look out' for its investments and shareholders. While the corporation's public pronouncements on the need for climate action provided a 'great talking point' on Capitol Hill, explained McCoy, he and his fellow lobbyists were working hard to scupper lower emissions targets and increased carbon taxes. The reality, it turned out, was that ExxonMobil was secretly seeking to dismantle the very same alternative futures with which it had supposedly aligned itself. Behind all the grandiose talk of corporate social responsibility, the pursuit of profit still held sway.

Dominant for more than 200 years, capitalism's assumption of endless compound economic growth and consumption fuelled by fossil energy has produced the rapidly increasing greenhouse gas emissions driving the climate crisis today. Yet the politically proffered 'solution' to climate change in almost all nations appears to be *more* capitalism, and the favoured solution to overconsumption, by extension, is *more* consumption.

Even though this contradiction is glaringly obvious, challenges to the ascendency of corporate capitalism are routinely met with scepticism. They are labelled naive or unrealistic. They are accused of threatening to drag humanity 'back to the dark ages' (Neubacher, 2012). This is especially evident in the ongoing promotion by government and industry of the exploration, production and consumption of fossil fuels. The tension between corporate capitalism and the future of a habitable climate for humanity and much of life on the planet has shaped the ideas in this book. Considering this situation, what theoretical explanation can we offer?

It is in answer to this question that we focus on the concept of hegemony. In this chapter, we discuss the hegemonic configuration of corporate capitalism as 'the natural order' and explore how an incapacity or unwillingness to see alternatives – including *existing* alternatives – hinders action on climate change. We conceptualise hegemony to explain the vice-like grip corporate capitalism exerts on most nations, as well as the possibilities of at last loosening it.

If industrial corporations are able to lure much of the global population into a planetary suicide pact, then surely new dynamics and novel ways of organising society should be possible. After all, there is ample evidence that the hegemonic configuration around fossil fuels and corporate capitalism has been *fought for* by vested interests: if ExxonMobil's executives did not see the need to address climate change as a threat to their business, for example, then why did they send their lobbyists to 'aggressively' work against it? Our position is therefore political, in so far as we believe the current hegemony can – and must – change.

In the following pages, we explain how hegemony works in establishing corporate capitalism as the only permittable solution to a problem *caused by* capitalism. We then make an analytical distinction between the strategies, practices and discourses of everyday 'politics' and the broader antagonism that constitutes society – what is termed 'the political' (Laclau & Mouffe, 1985).

Especially with its global reach, corporate capitalism projects a particular temporal linearity in engaging with climate change. This leads to responses that focus on carbon neutrality and a singular, calculable future. Sold as 'progress', the present path is constructed as inevitable. This 'business-as-usual' framing results in the ongoing delay of tangible climate action, prioritises short-term interests and ignores the places and people already experiencing the impacts of climate change.

As we have noted, human-induced climate disruption is not something that will happen in the future. It has already happened and is still happening now. Unpacking the temporal assumptions of hegemony is important in understanding the influence it exercises in undermining the urgency of a rapidly worsening crisis.

2.1 Fossil Fuel Hegemony

The key reference in formulating and popularising the concept of hegemony is Italian Marxist Antonio Gramsci (1891–1937). Written partly in code to evade censorship, his *Prison Notebooks* (1971) developed groundbreaking insights into the crushing defeat of worker revolts in Europe during the 1920s and 1930s (Jones, 2006) – failures Gramsci attributed to the inability of the working class to form alliances with other groups, such as peasants and intellectuals.

Gramsci argued that to win a political contest without overwhelming force and coercion requires concessions and compromises to create a system of class alliances capable of mobilising the majority of the population. The political aim in constructing hegemony is therefore to gain consensus by providing 'intellectual and moral leadership' throughout society (Gramsci, 1971: 57). This is not simply a coalition of the willing: hegemony is a continuous process of winning the active and passive consent of key actors in forming a ruling bloc – one that circulates a formal conception of the world so that societal classes and groups come to share certain political objectives. Hegemonic practices forge a 'collective will' (Gramsci, 1971: 125).

The contemporary applicability and usefulness of Gramsci's ideas can be illustrated in explaining the business sphere's inordinate influence on climate policy in a range of different nations. Analysis shows how 'fossil fuel hegemony' in countries such as Australia, Canada and the US comprises a coalition of actors with aligned interests supporting carbon-dependent economic growth and constraining legislation around emissions mitigation (Wright et al., 2021).

For instance, the US oil and automotive industries defended their hegemonic position against the regulation of greenhouse gas emissions during the 1990s by building a dominant coalition within the business sector and challenging the science of climate change (Levy & Egan, 2003). These industries have since shifted emphasis towards a discursive approach that promotes a 'win-win' stance aligned with the prevailing market ideology and so achieving an even broader hegemonic alliance – resulting in very modest emissions targets in the US. Fossil-fuel-dependent industries have thus fortified a 'historical bloc' of consensual legitimacy, supported by government and political allies.

More recent research on fossil fuel hegemony has explored how the sector has gained and maintained the consent of key actors in securing continued dependence on coal, oil and gas (Bell et al., 2019; LeQuesne, 2019; Kraushaar-Friesen & Busch, 2020). Studies have outlined a range of political activities that preserve fossil energy's near stranglehold on public policy, including using political campaigns to outflank arguments for renewable energy (Wright et al., 2021), discrediting opponents (Bell et al., 2019), lobbying and funding politicians (Brulle, 2018) and founding conservative think tanks and social movements supportive of the industry (Dunlap & McCright, 2011). Overall, such activities have encapsulated major political parties in a potent nexus that promotes the expansion of fossil fuels (Mitchell, 2013).

Fossil fuel companies owned and controlled by states also feed into globally connected forms of capitalist exchange, driving ever-increasing levels of greenhouse gases worldwide. This further ensures a seemingly relentless reliance on fossil energy is articulated as the 'collective will' and 'common sense' (Gramsci, 1971). As a result, the obvious position of reducing fossil fuel use is dismissed as unrealistic or unduly simplistic.

Viewed through the prism of Gramsci, the concept of fossil fuel hegemony explains the historical process of political strategies leading to the long-standing impasse on climate change. The percentage of people literally denying the physical reality of global warming may be diminishing, yet there is no meaningful slowdown in investment in and extraction of fossil fuels. The strength of this hegemony is underscored by the fact that people recognise the link between fossil fuels and climate change yet still fail to mobilise enough support for alternatives.

The passive compliance of populations is crucial to preserving the status quo. For example, a recent BloombergNEF (2021) report detailed how subsidies actually increased in seven of the G20 countries between 2015 and 2019, with US$636 billion provided in direct support for fossil fuels in the last of those years. While money is poured into the destruction of the planet, politics deftly stifles dissent.

Lobbying is central to this feat. ExxonMobil is by no means alone in having a public-facing commitment to addressing climate change while quietly endeavouring to derail relevant policies. A report by InfluenceMap (2019) showed the five largest publicly traded oil and gas companies spent over US$1 billion on misleading climate-related branding and lobbying during the three years after the Paris Agreement. Financial donations to politicians ensure limited legislation. Meanwhile, political messaging aimed at consumers seeds confusion and complacency. By promising future emissions targets, encouraging doubt about alternatives and dressing political subsidies in technocratic language, the state-capital nexus ensures there is no broad mobilisation against fossil fuels' continued use.

Ernesto Laclau and Chantal Mouffe's (1985) reworking of hegemony can be especially useful in understanding the dismal contradiction between recognising fossil fuels as the engine of climate change and nonetheless relying on them in perpetuity. Building on Gramsci's legacy, Laclau and Mouffe developed the underlying 'logic' of the social and contingent constitution of hegemony. By updating Gramsci's conceptualisation of hegemony for complex and pluralistic societies, Laclau and Mouffe left behind the primacy of fundamental classes in bringing about radical social change.

Laclau and Mouffe argued that a revolutionary overthrow of the dominant hegemony through unity of class purpose is not possible, since there is no structural system per se to depose. Classes and interests may appear relatively entrenched, yet the very possibility of mobility – however rare – suggests they are not predetermined. Laclau and Mouffe therefore replaced Gramsci's 'positive' essence of social totality with a 'negative' emphasis on antagonism. This means it is not *commonality* of, say, class interests that holds together hegemonic projects in changing the economic structure: it is instead *difference*.

2.2 The Hegemonic Projects of Global Capitalism

Laclau and Mouffe (1985) advanced the concept of hegemony by detailing the practices and processes underlying hegemonic projects. Hegemony can be seen as 'a practice of linking together contingent demands and identities into more universal projects' (Laclau &

Mouffe, 1985: 118). This entails making particular social demands universal by constructing them as objective or natural.

Corporations and capitalism provide compelling illustrations of this phenomenon. Through decades of anthropomorphising, corporations are now often regarded as natural entities that have their own cultures and even their own personalities (Bakan, 2004). Capitalism – ultimately no more than a form of exchanging goods and services – has essentially come to be accepted as the bedrock of society in the space of a little over 200 years. In the 2010 ruling in the case of *Citizens United* v. *FEC*, the US Supreme Court even gave the contractual networks of a corporation the right to free speech!

Expanding the hegemony of corporate capitalism requires the recruitment and integration of an array of political forces and social actors. For example, the formation of business schools in US and European universities during the twentieth century sought to professionalise the roles of managerial elites and legitimise the goals of economic efficiency and profitability (Khurana, 2007; Nyberg & Wright, 2022): the hegemony of corporate capitalism joined forces with the increasing demands of tertiary education to promote companies as the primary form of exchanging goods and services and to project CEOs as heroic figures worthy of admiration and identification.

The constructed forms of corporate capitalism that business schools and other institutions naturalise are based on continued capital accumulation and economic growth, as enabled by an expansion of markets dominated by large corporations that subsume all other kinds of relations – including the delivery of public goods and services (Nyberg, 2021) – as monetary exchange (Streeck, 2016). At the core of corporate capitalist expansion is a set of political practices aimed at imposing the rule of the market – deregulation and privatisation – and 'limiting the role of the state to the protection of private property rights, free markets and free trade' (Mouffe, 2018: 12). The dominance of this philosophy was perhaps most cogently expressed in former UK Prime Minister Margaret Thatcher's famous doctrine of TINA – 'There is no alternative'.

As convincingly demonstrated by Boltanski and Chiapello (2005), even critiques of capitalism can be employed to maintain and expand corporate hegemony. This involves negating or incorporating oppositional forces and demands – as illustrated, for example, by recent legislative frameworks' inclusion of nature within carbon accounting and ecosystem services methodologies (Böhm et al., 2012). This particular turnaround typified the necessary process. Dissenting voices' criticism of escalating carbon emissions was modified by applying a financial value to environmental damage and linking it back to the basis of capitalist relations. Emissions were effectively turned into a commodity to be bought and sold within a market; destruction and inequality were transformed into a 'win-win' outcome; and the message that somehow emerged was that what is good for capitalism is also good for the environment, communities and workers.

It is important to stress at this stage that we are not implying that a cabal of actors at the heart of capitalism is orchestrating these practices. While there are obviously strategic alliances between political parties, corporate-funded lobbyists and industry associations promoting these hegemonic formations, there is no 'structural centre'. The system is evidently incomplete; otherwise, it would not need to be maintained and reinforced.

The formations of corporate capitalism are instead simply achieving what they were designed to do: generate wealth for shareholders and senior managers. They are supported by a state-capital nexus manifest in how political leaders sell insider knowledge to private consulting, lobbying and financial firms, as well as in how an increasing number of governmental functions are outsourced and led by industry actors (Nyberg, 2021). None of these practices is 'natural', but they are routinely depicted and viewed as such. With the state functioning as a weakened regulator that rarely punishes corporations or executives for abuses such as insider trading, money laundering and rate fixing (Streeck, 2016), the task of preserving hegemony becomes ever easier.

2.3 Constructing a Political Frontier

One of the greatest achievements of global capitalism is its own reification. There is no 'real' objective structure upholding the market, the economy or corporations as actors within the political formation. What is habitually referred to as 'the market' or 'the economy' is held together through their difference from the Other – that is, those constructed as oppositional forces.

It makes sense to promote what we call 'fossil fuel energy' only if there are *alternative* sources of energy. We would otherwise simply speak of 'energy'. This illustrates why the political practice of building hegemony can be seen as based on (i) construction of equivalence between heterogeneous demands and interests and (ii) the exclusion of different or competing demands and interests (Laclau & Mouffe, 1985). As noted earlier, the key to understanding the political boundaries that temporally stabilise hegemonic formations is *difference*.

Hegemonic projects connect heterogeneous demands and interests in continuously changing formations. For example, Nyberg et al. (2018) show how the fossil fuel industry and the UK government linked together different demands and interests of employment, cheaper energy, secure energy supply and even emissions reductions in support of shale gas fracking. There was no common ground for these demands; they were of a very different nature. This illustrates how the logic of equivalence involves the construction of a chain of equivalence between different political demands. Constructing equivalence between such disparate demands and interests changes both the formation of the hegemonic project and the basis of the demands and interests themselves. For the very reason that it requires difference, it is an ongoing and relative process that cannot be completed or closed and that allows for groups and social actors holding contradictory outlooks.

Consider, for instance, people who are concerned about climate change. They would generally like to see 100 per cent renewable energy, but – as members of households with budgetary constraints – they would also like energy to be cheap in order to keep costs down. If the fossil fuel hegemony were to successfully link the different elements of cheap energy and fossil fuels, then the resulting formation could include actors concerned about climate change, yet if demands around renewables and cheap energy were instead linked, then the very same actors could be included in another formation – one opposing the expansion of fossil energy.

To be meaningful, a hegemonic project of constructing equivalence also requires a limit. In other words, the differences within the project require a negation or another difference that is not within the relation of equivalence (Marchart, 2018). This underlines the significance of the Other. We can illustrate this point by returning to the example of shale gas fracking in the UK. Here, the demands of employment, cheaper energy, secure supply and emissions reductions were held together by a difference with opponents – such as environmentalists (Nyberg et al., 2020) – that served as a common and 'outside' reference point in establishing a political frontier. It is this kind of designation of an adversary that separates the 'we' from the 'they', divides the 'us' from the 'them' and supplies the necessary Other.

By way of further illustration, we can examine corporate capitalism itself. We might note, for example, that even within the fossil fuel sector, there are many rival industries and firms promoting different sources of energy and so competing with each other for production and consumption. Take a recent report from APPEA, an oil and gas industry association in Australia, describing gas as 'integral to a low-carbon Australian economy'. This argument was advanced on the basis that 'natural gas is a lower-carbon form of energy suitable for electricity generation, industry and households' (APPEA, 2020: 4). Meanwhile, coal served throughout the report as the unnamed spectre in the country's fight against climate change – showing how the Other can frequently shift or even be reconstructed.

The groups on either side of the political frontier, as well as the frontier itself, are constructed through struggle. The political subjects and identities do not pre-exist: they are instead formed through the construction of hegemonic projects and conflicts (Howarth, 2013), and the key is then to develop discourses with which people can identify. For example, as we discuss further in Chapter 3, fossil fuel corporations such as BP and Shell have recently committed to achieving net-zero emissions by 2050. In doing so, they have aligned their interests with those of people anxious about climate change, especially those who want to see a 'gradual' or 'sensible' transition (Wright et al., 2021). The mobilisation in this instance is designed to convince those worried about the threat of environmental disaster, not to act on their concerns 'just yet' – and the result is that stronger action is delayed.

The political frontier is thus used to include an expanding number of demands and interests while excluding the Other – or Others. Another notable example in recent years has been refugees, who in many Western democracies have been constructed as extremists or even terrorists (Barlai et al., 2017). In the politics of climate change, the political opponents of corporate capitalism are connected to these threatening Others through articulations of green 'extremist' or 'eco-terrorist' figures (Potter, 2011; Irwin et al., 2022).

For instance, describing the actions of Dakota Access Pipeline opponents in the US, a senior manager of Energy Transfer Partners used the issue of citizenship to equate environmental protests with terror campaigns (Daly, 2017). The implication is clear: on one side of the political frontier are 'sensible' people who support fossil energy – or who are at least in favour of a managed transition and the marketisation of climate action – and on the other are dangerous 'greenies' and 'eco-terrorists' committed to wrecking the economy and wreaking havoc. However, there is no inherent logic underlying this beyond the constructed difference, some of which are linked together in a logic of equivalence (the 'sensible') and some of which are used for division of the social space ('greenies'). It is this incorporation of critique and the marginalisation of others that sustains dominant hegemonic formations.

This is how the politics of different political forces plays out within a social context that favours some actors, interests and 'facts' over others. Recognising this, we next explore the distinction between politics and the constituted ground upon which it is played out – that is, the political – in an effort to better understand the strength of hegemonic formations and the possibility to promote alternatives through counter-hegemony.

2.4 Counter-Hegemony: Politics and the Political

In the previous section, we outlined how the politics of equivalence and difference establishes hegemonic formations. There are two analytical sides of hegemony that account for the dominance of certain actors in society: (i) practices of a regime or policy holding sway over social actors and groups through consent, compliance and, at times, coercion and (ii) practices linking together separate demands and differentiating them from the Other (Howarth, 2015).

The first of these explains the dominance, while the latter explains how the dominance is established and maintained. We have illustrated this through examples of how the fossil fuel industry, in concert with state actors in developed economies such as the UK and Australia, has preserved its hegemony by linking demands for cheap energy with social identities built on nationalism in opposition to climate science and green alternatives.

At this point, to understand both the context in which this occurs and the possibility of challenging the hegemonic formation, we need to clarify the ontological foundations of politics. In order to do this, as we will now explain, it is necessary to separate *politics* from *the political*.

Politics encapsulates the actors, institutions and functions of political governance. It can be observed in words and images, as well as in material practices (Laclau, 2005). For example, when politicians introduce a policy, it is possible to see the actor (politicians), the supportive institutions (political party, form of governance and so on) and the potential material effects (economic, political and social implications).

What we have defined as hegemony is the practice of politics for maintaining dominance by, for instance, announcing fossil fuel subsidies, supporting new fossil fuel infrastructure and changing environmental legislation in favour of fossil fuel industries. The politics of these hegemonic practices produces a given order, and the meaning of the social institutions supporting it becomes temporarily fixed (Mouffe, 2018).

The sedimentation of practices over time results in a perceived social 'reality' (Laclau, 1990). This can be seen in diverse aspects of everyday life – from cultural rituals and family relations to economic exchanges and political formalities. These practices gain assumed objectivity through the possibility to anticipate what will happen when conducting quotidian activities. For example, we expect to exchange economic value for food when grocery shopping, or we expect to exchange it for household goods, clothes or other items when visiting department stores. Most everyday activities are conducted in this way – that is, with certain anticipation – otherwise, the social world would be completely chaotic and unliveable. It is important to note, though, how the political nature of this constructed reality is concealed through the taken-for-grantedness of day-to-day life's flow.

It is only when this flow is interrupted that *the political* shines through. For instance, the everyday activity of consuming goods can be turned into politics by revealing that much of this consumption contributes to increasing carbon emissions and climate change and that the taken-for-granted and seemingly natural practice of shopping is therefore linked to environmental disaster and the ongoing suffering of people.

However, there is a difference between arguing for the politics of consumption – that is, asking consumers to shop in a more environmentally friendly way – and making consumption itself political. The latter challenges convention and frames consumption as an antagonistic activity, revealing the economic basis of most Western societies as neither neutral nor evident. It is the lack of a natural foundation or ground that constitutes 'the political', and it is antagonism, the organising logic of the political, that ensures politics can surface in any social relation or situation.

Perhaps more than any previous issue, climate change exposes the antagonism underlying society. As we have already stated, this stems from the naturalisation of endless economic growth based on fossil energy over the past two centuries. There is no firm ground on which this growth can continue without avoiding further and more severe impacts, and current dominant representations of the crisis are clearly not sufficient for dealing with the situation.

Instead, to meaningfully address climate change, the prevailing practices of economic and political institutions need to be dislocated. Such a change is possible precisely because there is no firm ground – which is to say the 'reality' can always be otherwise. Not everything is political, but all sedimented forms of social interaction can be *made* political by showing their lack of foundation and identifying opportunities for alternatives.

With no conceptual distinction between various social actors in hegemonic politics, counter-hegemony is a matter of dislocating taken-for-granted assumptions. It is about challenging the appearance of political stability that conceals contradictions and differences. For example, by laying bare, the capitalism-versus-climate-change paradox that underlies market societies – in other words, by questioning the instituted reality – the antagonism can become visible and opened up for political debate, rendering alternative paths possible.

Theoretically, the antagonistic politics of counter-hegemony can be based on (i) a lack of completeness due to difference and (ii) an inability to entirely represent or signify the empirical world. The contingent and temporarily stabilised foundations can thus be reactivated by linking different demands in pluralistic societies or by universalising particular experiences that are not yet instituted. Let us briefly examine this process more closely.

First, it is vital to acknowledge that in pluralistic societies, there is no single political frontier. There are instead multiple ongoing disputes and debates, with the possibility for politics to construct social demands that alter allegiances or create new ones. For example, the climate protest movement Fridays for Future constructs an equivalence based mainly on age. It links heterogeneous classes and cultural backgrounds across and within many different nations. On 25 September 2019, on its day of global action, it encompassed around 6,000 protests in 185 countries, with the constructed Other including mainstream political parties, individual politicians and older generations blamed for the situation younger people face today. With many participants involving themselves in social demands and a political movement for the first time, Fridays for Future can be said to have challenged the sedimented social practices of schoolchildren in the politics of climate change.

Second, climate change itself can be seen as counter-hegemonic, in so far as the materiality of environmental impacts disrupts the sedimented practices that hide the contradictions of compound economic growth (Nyberg & Wright, 2016). Unprecedented heatwaves, fires and floods are becoming harder to incorporate within the dominant economic system as either 'natural' or justifiable. In the face of extreme weather events and other devastating corollaries, the hegemonic projects reinforcing the instituted reality are subject to ever-greater challenges and increasingly difficult to maintain.

Ultimately, the politics of constructing both equivalence and difference is possible because of the political. Since there is no complete representation, new groups can be established. Because no total identification exists, other types of demands can be linked to climate action. This is why, for example, many climate protests now entail similar demands from seasoned environmentalists and schoolchildren alike. The constructed difference here is not only the articulated 'enemy' of fossil fuel corporations: it is also the baby boomers who refuse to change their consumption patterns and who persistently vote for politicians who will not act.

Moreover, the urgency of these new social demands is increasingly driven by irrefutable evidence of unfolding environmental collapse. Today, as the climate crisis intensifies, even the most long-standing trope – that of a passive, caring Mother Earth – no longer applies. Like a growing number of the people who inhabit it, even the planet itself is fighting back.

2.5 A Time and Space for Climate Action?

One other feature of the current climate crisis is how corporate promises to deal with climate change prioritise time over space, with commitments to 'carbon neutrality' expressed in years and decades within assigned future milestones. For instance, as noted previously, major fossil fuel corporations such as BP and Shell have committed to achieving net-zero emissions by 2050. Similarly, future commitments to 2050 are also made by political leaders in petrostates such as Australia and the US. These timelines come with assumed technological investments and innovations that will lower emissions, increase natural carbon sequestration or even capture and store emissions (see Chapter 3 for further details).

However, these temporal nominations and solutions are void of actual places; they lack spatial embeddedness. This absence of a direct location for change is not surprising since change is generally associated with time. Yet, change is also a temporal movement through space. Change happens to places such as a country, a power plant or a technological device. Analytically, this implies a dualistic distinction where space is a static location or the structural repetition of practice, and time is the intervention that interrupts the place or repetition.

However, by prioritizing time, these corporate articulations further maintain the hegemonic regime. This contributes to a deferral of time, including substantive climate action, since the measure or experience of time has no visible present within an identifiable place. This 'placelessness' of corporate climate pledges also enables a disregard for current and coming impacts of climate change experienced in different geographic locations (see Chapter 5). Climate change pledges and commitments are generally vague on details of 'how', 'where' and 'who' will be changed beyond that change will happen. It is obvious that practices informing energy production, transportation and agriculture will need to change, but firms or actual places are rarely mentioned in these future imaginings.

Thus, spatial politics is hidden. The fossil fuels assumed to be left in the ground to reach future targets are not assigned. The underlying agency of change is projected and delayed to temporal structures of 'the future' or '2050'. The difference here is temporal in that change means something different from the previous instance or time. However, the difference is also necessarily spatial in that the repetition itself is different. Otherwise, it would be identical and closed – it is not possible to repeat something without the possibility of change. Even what is seen as identical replication of practice happens in a different time and space. A theorization of hegemony based on difference thus requires a co-implication of time and space or 'space-time' (Derrida, 1976). In understanding climate change, this means that there is no temporality of climate change without spatiality of its effects and no spatiality of events without the inscription of temporality.

However, by focusing on temporal aspects, the hegemony reinforces spatial repetition. The current practices of consumer capitalism can be repeated ad infinitum. The future is constructed as a repetition of the past into the future – there is no difference and, hence, time stands still.

This impossibility is achieved by constructing a temporal singularity and linearity. A dominant past is naturalized as the only past that is determining the present as well as providing directions for the future (Nyberg et al., 2020). For example, political leaders in oil and coal states in the US, such as Texas and Alabama, construct fossil fuels as a 'God given' right and 'our way of life', a position reinforced by former Vice President Pence who promised that 'developing the vast, natural, God-given resources that we have' would make America great again (Dochuk, 2019). The past is naturalized and must necessarily continue into the future.

The future is thus seen as the repetition of what has been, with commitments to a projected future in which decarbonisation has already happened. Capitalism as the taken-for-granted system is repeated and anticipated to continue. For instance, it is assumed that 2050 targets will be met within existing economic models and practices. Hegemony thus acts to repress alternatives and frame them as unworkable in, for example, suggesting that relying on renewable energy is unrealistic – with actual changes pushed into the future, a not yet.

However, every temporal demarcation is also spatial. Drawing a line or building a wall happens in time *and* space. That is, temporal succession is marked by the *spacing* of a *temporal* interval separating past from future. Politically, borders and walls are different in both time and space – space-time. Exclusions of Others are spatial and temporal.

To visualize the conceptualization of space-time and show the implications for climate change, we can draw on the logical structure of 'the trace' (Derrida, 1982). A trace refers to a visible material marker that exists independently of subjective consciousness and individual experience. Traces show the co-implication and movement of space over time – for example, paw prints in the snow or a dotted line on a piece of paper. The physical marks left behind by a trace are not identical as they are spaced and separated. This is a repetition that changes the previous meaning of the mark in the trace. As such, the trace is always in deferral to the next sign or clue. Examples such as ice cores and coral reef degradation are compelling examples of material traces that are used to signify temporal shifts and transitions in accounting for climate change (Nyberg et al., 2022). Thus, emphasising the traces or spacing of time helps create an affirmative succession of time (Derrida, 1976).

This does not mean succession in chronological linear time, but rather the trace shows the constative delay or deferral inherent in temporality. By spacing the temporal constructs in decades, rather than months or years, actions are delayed. Turning to traces or impacts by firms and industries places them in a spatially grounded timespan that foregrounds the politics of climate change. The traces – borders, drilling sites, emissions and so forth – show their marks on the planet and impacts on both humans and non-humans. Examining the traces of climate change can thus locate the impacts of climate change in space-time and help hold dominant actors to account in addressing climate change. There are traces of the fossil fuel hegemony to make visible in displaying the antagonism between capitalism and the climate.

2.6 Defending the Hegemony

Climate change highlights the fundamental contradiction between corporate capitalism and the maintenance of our planet's life-support systems (Wright & Nyberg, 2015). In this chapter, we have shown how the concept of hegemony can explain the ability of corporate capitalism – especially the fossil fuel sector – to paper over this critical paradox and preserve a firm grip on political and organisational climate responses. By employing Laclau and Mouffe's (1985) post-foundational theory, we have illustrated how hegemonic regimes hold sway through the logics of equivalence and difference.

Corporate capitalism constructs climate change in a particular way: a generalised issue that can best be dealt with via market mechanisms, the innovative capacity of companies and the march of technological progress. Yet the contingency of the political ensures there is always more than one possibility, and this provides the potential for counter-hegemonic forces to reactivate the underlying potential for change.

Climate change is often framed as an external enemy – an Other that needs to be kept at bay – but this approach in itself conceals the political underlying the construct. It is the political that can overthrow corporate capitalism's narrow conceptualisation through, for example, activists' politics or climate change's material impacts. The fact is that there are alternatives that have been excluded rather than actualised – which is to say there are roads not yet taken.

As we have noted, it is too late to prevent climate change. It is already unfolding. What remains is a window for avoiding increasingly catastrophic consequences, and even this is closing rapidly. While most institutions now acknowledge the importance of addressing the crisis, the necessary responses are consistently pushed into a particular future that is assumed to be a continuation of the present. The idea that a dollar today is somehow worth more than a dollar tomorrow is central to the hegemonic project of corporate capitalism. Escalating short-termism, together with increasing trading in futures and options, has cemented assumptions of a linear and progressive way ahead defined by the ever-greater capitalisation of fictitious commodities.

This priority of time over place disregards the current and coming impacts of climate change experienced in different locations. As we have seen, prevailing responses to the crisis prioritise the rights of those living today over those of the generations still to come and value the wealth of the Global North over the well-being of populations in the Global South. As Mohamed Adow, director of Power Shift Africa, declared at the end of COP26: 'The needs of the world's vulnerable people have been sacrificed on the altar of the rich world's selfishness' (Harvey et al., 2021).

In organising climate change, corporate and political leaders are obfuscating the deep ethical and moral issue of rising global and intergenerational inequality and the theft of a viable future for much of the world's population. As we will show in the following chapters, climate change as a material reality involves both time and space, not to mention momentous decisions about who and what are prioritised in reacting to the gravest threat to the future of our species.

PART II

The Politics of Climate Mitigation

3 | Fossil Fuel Hegemony, Green Business and Growth

Bernard Looney ... understands the frustration and anger of protesters ... He shares their deep concern about climate change and will set out his low-carbon ambition for the company next week. He hopes that what he has to say then will give people a sense that we get it and are very serious about working to address the problem.

BP statement (BP, 2020a)

In early 2020, on his first day as the new CEO of BP, Bernard Looney learnt Greenpeace protesters had shut down the London headquarters of the world's fifth-largest oil company. Visiting employees in Germany at the time, he responded by publicly announcing he would strive to make BP a net-zero carbon emitter by 2050 – a commitment that would include reductions in direct and embedded emissions. Aligning himself with the activists, Looney insisted he understood the protesters' anger and shared their concerns. Of course, such claims from the fossil fuel industry were nothing new, with the most famous example arguably being the rebranding of BP as 'Beyond Petroleum' twenty years earlier. Today, in the face of growing demands for meaningful climate action, such forward-looking pledges and declarations of sympathy are becoming increasingly common. More than ever before, the fossil fuel industry is seeking to align itself with the moral high ground and incorporate the growing social critique. But what is the real motivation here?

A key challenge to fossil fuel hegemony is the recognition that responding to the existential threat of human-induced climate disruption requires a dramatic reduction in the amount of carbon emissions produced by the global economy. Climate science presents a stark choice in this regard.

The first option is to continue the current trajectory of dangerous levels of climate change that will make further regions of the planet uninhabitable for humans and other species. The second is to

41

dramatically decarbonise the worldwide economy at an unprecedented pace: IPCC (2018) modelling suggests emissions need to decline by around 45 per cent by 2030 to limit warming to 1.5°C.

The strategy of decarbonisation, often referred to as climate mitigation, will necessitate the reduction of emissions not only in energy production but also in transportation, manufacturing, industrial processes, agriculture and food production. It will also require the end of both deforestation and the destruction of other critical carbon sinks (IPCC, 2018). All this will have to occur at a speed and scale unseen in history – potentially entailing what some have characterised as a globally coordinated emergency wartime response (Delina & Diesendorf, 2013).

Given the current reliance on fossil fuels, as outlined in Chapter 1, it should be apparent that such a transformation demands a fundamental reshaping of existing economic relations. The threat of climate change therefore applies not only to human existence but also to the fossil fuel hegemony that has underpinned the global capitalist economy.

Despite this, the global fossil fuel burn has continued to increase year by year. In 2019, it hit an all-time high of 11.7 Gtoe (billion tonnes of oil equivalent) – up from 7.1 Gtoe in 1990 (Saxifrage, 2020). One recent study of global energy utilities found only 10 per cent of companies had expanded their renewable energy capacity at a faster rate than their gas- or coal-fired capacity, with ongoing construction of new coal and gas infrastructure during the past decade likely to lock most into continued use of fossil fuel energy generation (Alova, 2020).

In fact, notwithstanding the attention given to emissions reduction through various international climate agreements and dramatic rises in renewable energy investment – especially wind and solar – more than half of all cumulative global fossil fuel consumption has occurred since 1990 (Saxifrage, 2019). To put it another way: most global fossil fuels have been produced and consumed *after* the scientific consensus on anthropogenic climate change was established.

In this chapter, we outline how, in spite of overwhelming evidence of carbon pollution's central role in a worsening climate catastrophe, key corporate interests around the world have maintained political coalitions that defend the hegemony of fossil energy. While there have been marked variations in corporate responses to climate change – including the greater adoption of sustainability and decarbonisation commitments – the economic system remains rooted in a dependency on fossil fuels and economic growth, thereby ensuring a continued increase in atmospheric greenhouse gas concentrations.

The politics underlying the fossil fuel hegemony is not only about constructing equivalence between social demands and the interests of the fossil fuel industry but also about repressing cleaner and often cheaper energy alternatives. The industry has shifted from denying climate change to a form of 'predatory delay' in defending the current carbon-dependent economic system for as long as possible (Steffen, 2016). We argue that the failure of climate change mitigation can be attributed both to the corporate-orchestrated delay in transition and, ultimately, to the defence of the hegemony.

3.1 The Fossil Fuel Industry and the Reframing of Climate Politics

One of the key factors shaping the limited response to climate change and the need for emissions mitigation has been the strong political resistance of the fossil fuel industry to decarbonisation. This can be seen throughout the history of the corporate organisation of climate change denial, which has been extensively documented (Oreskes & Conway, 2010).

The fossil fuel industry's approach during the 1990s and the early years of this millennium focused on seeding doubt about the scientific consensus on the causes and severity of climate change. All that was needed to ensure people continued increasing consumption based on relatively cheap energy was to undermine 'global warming' or 'climate change' as a mobilising signifier. This was an intentional and successful strategy that resulted from the industry's economic and political power. An equivalence of social demands promoted by industry associations, related sectors (e.g. automotive and chemical manufacturers), politicians and media was constructed over the course of several decades. This hegemony reinforced the perceived 'reality' of the necessity of ongoing fossil fuel expansion.

Growing political recognition of climate change first began to emerge in the late 1980s. The founding of the IPCC in 1988 was a particularly notable landmark in this respect. Yet this served only to prompt major US corporations in fossil fuels, energy and manufacturing to join forces and push back against proposals for the regulation of carbon emissions (Levy & Egan, 1998). Through financial contributions to political parties, funding for advertising campaigns and appeals to broader conservative values via right-wing media – most notably Fox News – these groups created a 'climate change denial industry'. They transformed policy debate in the US from a bipartisan issue into a source of ideological divide – a clear political frontier (Dunlap & McCright, 2011; Brulle, 2014). This strategy established a hegemonic formation in which conservatives, fossil fuel executives and blue-collar workers supported the industry's expansion and determinedly differentiated their 'historical bloc' from others – for example, environmentalists – who sought to reduce emissions.

Corporations such as ExxonMobil continued to cast doubt on climate science by emphasising uncertainties in projections and highlighting claims that reducing emissions could result in huge economic costs (Supran & Oreskes, 2017). Initially set up to encourage *literal* denial – that is, to insist climate change was not real (Norgaard, 2011) – this proliferation of arguments could be reworked to suggest responding to the crisis would prove too expensive. For instance, organisations such as the American Energy Alliance – set up by former fossil fuel lobbyist and Republican staffer Thomas Pyle – lobbied against a carbon tax by stating it 'damages American economic competitiveness' (AEA, 2015).

Opponents thus amplified the potential short-term economic impacts of putting a price on carbon while at the same time edging the issue of climate change out of the discussion. As a result, climate change became an empty signifier. Rather than representing a substantive shift in the planetary system and a potential threat to life on Earth, the term 'climate change' was subsumed by other concerns such as 'the economy', 'free enterprise' and employment, and weaponised as an ideological symbol (Antonio & Brulle, 2011).

This was not a uniquely American response. Fossil fuel interests in other countries also politically mobilised against policy proposals for climate mitigation. Another nation at the forefront of fossil fuel expansion was Australia, which has now become one of the world's largest exporters of coal and gas (Moss, 2020). Australia's growth in this regard has relied on a close nexus between coal and gas companies, industry associations and bipartisan political support for extractive industries. Denial of climate change has been pronounced among conservative politicians, business-sponsored think tanks and major media outlets since the mid-1990s (Pearse, 2007; Wilkinson, 2020). This is just one more illustration of the construction of political frontiers that equate alarm over climate change and wanting action to mitigate its effects with naivety and economic risk.

3.2 Predatory Delay

The realisation of the magnitude of human-induced climate disruption represented an existential threat to the business model of the fossil fuel industry during the 2000s and growing support for action forced the industry and its allies to change tack. While continuing to seed doubt over climate science, fossil fuel interests argued for the need to delay any mitigation initiatives that would slow economic growth.

In the ensuing years, the industry proved to be highly successful in constructing an equivalence between fossil energy and economic welfare. Even as the pushback on climate denial has occurred – to the extent that most people in a variety of nations now accept the reality of the crisis (Shwom et al., 2015) – doubts about specific impacts and timing have been pitted against the potential costs of mitigation policies, resulting in the effective deferment of such initiatives.

Institutionalised through decades of collaboration with political leaders, the significant power of the fossil fuel industry has represented such a dominant order that challenges to its role have been considered fanciful (Coll, 2012; Mitchell, 2013). The industry exists at the heart of a hegemonic coalition of political and economic interests that is perhaps unassailable even in the face of the existential threat it poses to the future of human civilisation. As Levy and Egan (2003) have argued, the continued dominance of the industry has been based on its capacity to defend its position within the global economy. The historic bloc it established so early has continued to adapt and defend ongoing growth, even as apparent agreement about the need to act on climate change has become stronger.

Beyond political lobbying, fossil fuel corporations have sought to sway public opinion through marketing and advertising campaigns (Brulle et al., 2020). These efforts have stressed doubt about climate science and promoted the economic and even 'moral' benefits of fossil fuel expansion in ways that obfuscate the role of the industry in causing and exacerbating the crisis (Lamb et al., 2020). For instance, ExxonMobil's (2013) advertising campaign, featuring the trademark 'Energy Lives Here', emphasised the pervasiveness of oil both in individuals' everyday lives and in the economy. Asking consumers what they would see if they could 'see energy', the advertisement showed various uses of fossil fuels – transportation, mobile phones, medical procedures, concerts and so on – and highlighted how many jobs such activities produce.

In late 2020, in a similar vein, Shell tweeted a survey that asked people: 'What are you willing to change to help reduce emissions?' 'Offset emissions', 'Stop flying', 'Buy [an] electric vehicle' and 'Renewable electricity' were offered as possible answers. It is through this kind of technique that the fossil fuel industry has attempted to transfer any blame or concern for climate change onto the individual, suggesting it is the responsibility of end-use customers to reduce demand.

Fossil fuel companies also sought to promote the moral worthiness of their activities by showcasing the social benefits they provide to impoverished and marginalised communities. For example, US coal giant Peabody Energy's public relations (PR) campaigns have stressed how its products can deliver affordable electricity to so-called developing nations (Goldenberg, 2015), while Canada's tar sands industry has promoted its products as 'ethical oil' in contrast to oil produced under more authoritarian regimes (Levant, 2010; Laurie, 2019). Fossil fuel majors use such PR and marketing efforts to present themselves as concerned 'corporate citizens' that side with good causes and oppose what are depicted as tyrannies.

These articulations construct an equivalence between the industry, citizens and the community. The corollary of fossil fuels being part of people's everyday lives is that it is seen as irrational to curb the industry – the argument being that you, as a citizen, are at fault for wanting the energy it provides. This strategy sits well with the increasing neo-liberalisation of politics around the world, with citizens constructed as consumers and individual self-interest presented as leading to the greatest public good (Lammi et al., 2012).

This also makes it possible to portray any mobilisation around climate change as against citizens and contrary to the collective good. Here, the construct is that societies will ultimately suffer the impacts of increased prices and unreliable provision. Although well aware of the looming impacts that might turn public opinion, the hegemony continues to work to delay any shift – no doubt all too conscious that every additional year spent extracting fossil fuels will mean further revenues and profit.

3.3 Solutions and Transition Energy

With social movements applying growing pressure to transform, the fossil fuel industry has also continued a long tradition of depicting itself as taking the lead on environmental concerns. In the face of increasingly dire scientific projections, corporations have begrudgingly acknowledged the science of climate change, but they have also pivoted to a message that technological solutions are possible while continuing to rely on fossil energy. As it insists it has 'solutions', the industry incorporates widely held concerns into its own rhetoric. This suggests either that climate change requires industry funding for new technologies that will prolong the use of fossil fuels or, in the case of gas, that it requires a move to a *different* fossil fuel.

In the UK, for example, Norwegian-owned resources company Equinor attempted to promote the gas it produces as a low-carbon energy source (Dempsey, 2019). While regulators issued a warning for misleading advertising in this case, such rhetoric functions alongside existing doubts about climate science. The objective of efforts like these is to downplay the urgency of the crisis and imply the industry is already taking steps to solve the problem.

Key among industry-promoted solutions has been the discourse of 'clean coal'. This rests on the assertion that more efficient technology in the sphere of coal-fired electricity production can dramatically reduce the industry's climate impacts. Examples include the promotion of 'high-efficiency, low-emissions' (HELE) coal-fired power plants and carbon capture and storage (CCS) technologies. The coal industry in Australia has long promoted these ideas as silver bullets for ever-increasing carbon emissions. As critics have pointed out, however, HELE technology is neither new nor particularly less polluting, and despite a billion dollars' worth of government and levy funding, no commercial-scale CCS project has yet emerged (Hudson, 2017).

Considering the limited emissions capture and additional cost, coal-fired power with CCS can be seen as far less attractive than existing renewable energy options (Holmes à Court, 2018). Indeed, internationally only a small number of functioning CCS plants are in operation, most of which have failed to deliver the scale of emissions capture that has been promoted (Garcia-Freites & Jones, 2020). For instance, while global oil giant ExxonMobil continues to promote the promise of CCS in its public climate communications, to date, it has captured less than 6 per cent of its operational emissions (Scope 1 and 2) and less than 1 per cent of its total emissions (including Scope 3) since 2004 (ExxonMobil, 2022).

The declining cost of renewable energy in comparison to coal-fired electricity has led some market analysts to conclude thermal coal is now in structural decline (Surane, 2020). In response, fossil fuel advocates have promoted the potential of methane – dubbed 'natural gas' – as an alternative energy source and a 'transition fuel' in the move towards future decarbonisation. In the UK, for instance, energy companies and sympathetic conservative politicians campaigned vociferously during the 2010s for the opening up of a new shale gas industry that would use the controversial technique of hydraulic fracturing – better known as fracking (Nyberg et al., 2018, 2020). This process was originally developed as an unconventional means of accessing oil and gas in the US, where its widespread adoption during the 2000s resulted in a massive increase in domestic production and led to the country becoming a net energy exporter. According to its advocates, fracking ushered in a global energy revolution (Gold, 2014; Downie, 2019). While significant protests in the UK resulted in regulatory limits on the fledgling industry and restricted its feasibility, gas fracking has expanded across Europe, Asia and North America. It is now widely promoted as a 'cleaner' fossil fuel for electricity production and heating (Bomberg, 2017).

Australia has gone even further, proposing the rapid expansion of gas extraction and export as a means of global emissions mitigation. The country is home to some of the world's largest gas-processing facilities, including the enormous Chevron Gorgon liquefied natural gas (LNG) project. Despite its role in dramatically *increasing* Australia's domestic carbon emissions, industry leaders have promoted the expansion of gas extraction as 'the best thing we can do to reduce global emissions by displacing coal and dirty fuels in Asia' (Santos, 2019: 5). The 'transition fuel' argument has been echoed by government ministers keen to talk up the industry's growth (Macdonald, 2019).

However, research suggests such 'transition fuel' claims neglect significant fugitive emissions within the supply chain, as well as the more potent warming impact of methane as a greenhouse gas (Schwietzke et al., 2014). The marginal benefit of gas over coal or oil as a source of energy is still debated. Leakages and the release of methane as part of the extraction and distribution process are rarely detailed in public strategies (Howarth et al., 2011). Investment in gas can also be seen as an opportunity cost for investing in climate friendlier and often cheaper renewable energy solutions (Parkinson, 2018). In addition, gas pipelines and infrastructures are built to last for more than fifty years, meaning investment in such schemes also significantly extends the timescale of reliance on fossil fuel. Dominant players within the industry can therefore be seen as prepared to cast aside its dirtiest offspring – coal – in order to strengthen the hegemonic project for the longer term.

Beyond its impact within national political arenas, the fossil fuel industry's activities extend into international negotiations on climate change. Fossil fuel companies and industry associations have for years been regular attendees at and sponsors of the annual United Nations Framework Convention on Climate Change (UNFCCC) Conference of the Parties – better known as COP (CIC, 2019) – enjoying enhanced access to government leaders and decision-makers through networking and via presentations promoting 'clean coal' and gas expansion as a 'transition fuel' (Henn, 2017). US officials at UN Climate Change Conferences have even staged events advocating the increased use of fossil fuels, proclaiming: 'No country should have to sacrifice economic prosperity or energy security in pursuit of environmental sustainability' (Witte & Dennis, 2018).

COP26, the most recent event, proved no exception, with the Australian government hosting a 'CCS' display by oil and gas company Santos at the front of its pavilion (Morton, 2021). This showed once again that despite the worsening scientific assessment of the climate crisis, the fossil fuel industry continues to defend its dominant role in global energy production. The political vision that 'business as usual' can continue without consequence – what some have described as a 'fossil fuels forever' imaginary (Levy & Spicer, 2013) – remains paramount.

3.4 Fractions of Capital: The Promise of Corporate Decarbonisation

However, it is important to note that we do not suggest *all* businesses support fossil fuels. Nor do we suggest that those who *do* support fossil fuels are identical in their objectives and actions. Rather, we argue that those that support fossil fuels have an interest in defending the existing hegemony while often still competing to be at the forefront of energy solutions. It is also important to note that corporations in other sectors are arguably less threatened by climate change as a signifier. For them, it could represent new, environmentally friendly markets to which they can align their products and services. They might even be able to create entirely novel markets and find new sources of profit as a consequence of the phenomenon (Funk, 2014).

As a result, while there is a capitalist hegemony that endorses corporate solutions, there is also the existence within this hegemony of fractions with competing interests. Indeed, the corporate response to climate change has been far from homogenous, with differences emerging as the scientific and social implications of the crisis have become more urgent.

Thus, in contrast to the fossil fuel sector's early denial and subsequent obfuscation of climate science, other industries and corporations have in the last decade or more engaged with the issue and even advocated for more meaningful action. For instance, many corporations have established sustainability functions that emphasise climate change as a strategic concern for their operations in terms of risk and opportunity (Hoffman, 2005; Lash & Wellington, 2007). This has included the *market risk* of new competitors and new 'green' technologies and products, the *reputational risk* of consumers and employees shifting their allegiance from environmentally destructive activities towards what are perceived as 'greener' businesses and industries, *regulatory risk* from potential government regulation and pricing of GHG emissions and 'carbon taxes' and finally the *physical risk* of climate-induced extreme weather events threatening operations and infrastructure (see Chapter 5; Nyberg & Wright, 2016). More generally, a discourse of 'corporate environmentalism' – in which businesses promote their role in benefiting both their shareholders *and* the environment (Jermier et al., 2006) – has gained momentum, often resulting in corporate eco-efficiency initiatives aimed at reducing carbon emissions while improving costs and profitability (Dauvergne & Lister, 2013).

Promoted by a growing range of businesses, this 'win-win' philosophy is linked to a broader theory of 'ecological modernisation' in which increased economic development is seen not only as improving social outcomes but also as benefiting the environment through technological innovation (Mol & Spaargaren, 2000). In an assumed equal valuation of the economy and the planet, corporations and their executives are presented as key actors in the societal response to climate change – epitomised in billionaire businessman Sir Richard Branson's claim that 'our only option to stop climate change is for industry to make money from it' (Neubacher, 2012).

As set out in Table 3.1, climate-aware businesses have implemented a broad range of business activities that respond to these various climate risks and opportunities. These have included the traditional 'business case' for emissions cuts and renewable uptake delivering cost reductions and efficiency improvement, through to innovation and the development of new 'green' products and markets, as well as culture change programs aimed at engaging employees in a culture of environmental activities (Wright & Nyberg, 2017). Beyond these internally facing initiatives, many corporations have also sought to head off reputational and regulatory risks through external strategies of 'green' marketing and PR (Brulle et al., 2020), corporate lobbying and building political coalitions with industry associations and the media to push back against undesired regulatory change (Brulle, 2018; Wright et al., 2021).

Businesses are also increasingly participating in voluntary reporting and public ranking of their environmental performance through schemes such as CDP (formerly the Carbon Disclosure Project) and the Dow Jones Sustainability Index (Knox-Hayes & Levy, 2011). These companies have sought to engage politically in advocating for policy interventions for emissions reduction and building alliances with environmental NGOs in order to project an environmentally responsible image as well as anticipate future reputational risks (Ceres, 2019).

Such initiatives often form part of a wider corporate social responsibility agenda in which companies attempt to create both shareholder value and 'shared value' (Porter & Kramer, 2011). This perspective has found institutional form in groups such as the B-Team and the World Business Council for Sustainable Development. These have contributed to the creation of the UN Sustainable Development Goals, in which economic development and business growth are presented as vital responses to climate change and other societal 'grand challenges' (Najam, 1999; Bothello & Salles-Djelic, 2018).

Table 3.1 *Examples of corporate climate responses*

Motivations	Examples of corporate responses
Improved efficiency and reduced costs	Reduced energy expenditure through production improvements and supply chain analysis
	Adoption of cheaper renewable energy
	Change in car/truck fleet to electric vehicles
	Reduction and recycling of waste (e.g. changes in building and production design)
Competitive threat of new 'green' technologies and products	R&D investment to identify and create 'green' products and services ahead of competitors
	Market scanning for competitive threats and mimicking new technologies and products
	Buy into 'green' technologies through take-overs and acquisitions
Reputation amongst consumers and employees	'Green' marketing and branding of products and services
	Developing alliances with environmental NGOs to pre-empt reputational shocks
	Promotion as a 'responsible' corporate citizen and 'green' business
Government regulation of carbon emissions	Lobbying against carbon pollution regulation
	Building coalitions with opponents of action on climate change (e.g. free-market think tanks, conservative political parties)
	Investing in low-carbon technologies and renewable energy to reduce carbon emissions intensity
	Incorporating carbon pricing in investment decisions
	Adopting a 'leadership' position advocating market forms of carbon regulation
	Voluntary reporting of carbon emissions to avoid mandatory requirements

Table 3.1 (*cont.*)

Motivations	Examples of corporate responses
Physical damage to operations and infrastructure from extreme weather (see Chapter 5)	Climate modelling Scenario planning for physical events Safeguarding or relocation of physical infrastructure Developing emergency strategies for extreme weather events Selling off physically vulnerable activities Supply chain collaboration

However, these interventions have also consistently emphasised the benefits of business self-regulation and presented market-based approaches – for example, carbon pricing and emissions trading – as the most efficient response to the crisis. Perhaps tellingly, governments and international bodies have been relegated to obligingly providing supportive legal and administrative structures for these new markets (Böhm et al., 2012; Wright & Nyberg, 2015).

3.5 Towards Low-Carbon Economies?

Although superficially positive, these sustainability initiatives are put in place as a means of defending current practices from critique or the threat of regulation. It is the incorporation of critique and the staving off of regulation that ensure the maintenance of economic growth based on unlimited consumption and increased energy use. That said, recent developments in energy and financial markets indicate some gradual shifts in the world's energy production.

For instance, the rapidly declining cost curve of renewable energy sources such as solar and wind, along with technological innovations in battery storage, has dramatically exceeded market forecasts and made traditional options far less price competitive (Jacobson, 2020). This has resulted in a steady decline in demand for thermal coal in different markets. Governments in countries such as the UK, Germany and South Korea are reconsidering their reliance on coal-fired electricity production and announcing the mothballing of new plants and the accelerated closure of older facilities in favour of wind and solar investment (BP, 2020b).

These changes have led some technology analysts to estimate as much as half of the world's electricity production will come from renewable energy sources by 2050 (BloombergNEF, 2019). Such a transformation would likely crowd out coal, oil and gas as primary energy sources. However, it is worth remarking that in many countries – the US foremost among them – declines in coal consumption are a result of a transition to gas and therefore not necessarily illustrative of a shift to renewables. At least for now, renewables are being added to the mix but are not replacing fossil fuels per se – which is why emissions continue to rise.

Changes in energy production are also being driven by new thinking in financial markets, as encapsulated in recent statements and actions by major investors and central banks. For instance, in 2015, in a widely publicised speech delivered at the headquarters of insurance giant Lloyd's of London, Mark Carney, the then Governor of the Bank of England (2015), cited extreme weather events and the prospect of stranded carbon assets as evidence of the threat climate change could pose to the insurance industry. Following this, the G20 Financial Stability Board published recommendations for the disclosure of climate risk in corporate financial reporting (TFCD, 2017). Major institutional investors such as BlackRock, HSBC and the Norwegian Sovereign Wealth Fund have since announced plans to reduce their exposure to fossil fuel stocks and instead focus on 'green' investment opportunities (Holter & Sleire, 2019). The IEA, a long-time advocate of fossil energy, recently called for the cessation of all new fossil fuel projects and an accelerated phase-out of unabated coal and oil power plants in order to achieve a net-zero carbon economy by 2050 (IEA, 2021a).

Major resource corporations are already factoring the relevant risks into their strategic planning. Mining giants Rio Tinto and BHP Billiton, for example, have signalled their respective exits from the thermal coal market and outlined a focus on other resources as inputs into a future lower-carbon economy (Parkinson & Mazengarb, 2019). However, as we explain further in the following chapter, such apparent changes in direction are not always indicative of new priorities for companies: after all, it is persistent campaigning by environmental NGOs, not positive action by businesses themselves, that has more often than not forced change.

Similarly, more companies have publicly announced goals to reduce emissions by signing up for initiatives such as Science Based Targets or the RE100, which commits to the adoption of 100 per cent renewable electricity by 2050 (Walenta, 2020). Declaring plans to dramatically reduce their carbon footprints, leading technology businesses such as Microsoft, Apple, Facebook, Amazon and Google are at the forefront of such moves.

For instance, Microsoft recently pledged to radically cut its emissions and be carbon negative by 2030. It also said it would 'remove' all the carbon ever produced by the company – founded in 1975 – by 2050 (Smith, 2020). Practically, this has involved Microsoft investing in hydrogen fuel cell technology to replace diesel generators as backup power for the business's massive data centres, implement an internal carbon tax to fund sustainability initiatives, carry out a detailed analysis of supply chains and invest in power purchase agreements with renewable energy providers (Roberts, 2020).

Analogously, Apple – long criticised for the disconnect between its marketing image of 'cool' design and the reality of sweatshop labour and a reliance on fossil-fuel-generated power – has announced its aim to be completely carbon neutral by 2030. This will apply across all its business operations, its supply chain and its products' life cycles. The company has channelled significant investment into renewable energy for its direct operations and has made a commitment that all product suppliers will eventually run on renewables (Apple, 2020).

Claims of an environmentally focused approach have also extended to sections of the fossil fuel sector. With increasing competition from renewable energy and the risk of emissions regulation, it has become commonplace – especially for some of the more diversified companies – to announce limitations on coal and oil investments and to declare targets for reducing emissions. As observed at the beginning of this chapter, BP was early out of the gate; Shell and Total declared their own 2050 net-zero emissions goals just months later; and even US oil titans ExxonMobil and Chevron duly joined the fray – albeit in a relatively subdued manner.

Thus, in contrast to the general reticence businesses had adopted towards the topic of climate change a decade ago, in the years since the Paris Agreement, climate change has become an increasingly central component of companies' sustainability declarations. For instance, as set out in Table 3.2 below, a growing range of major corporations around the world now devote significant attention to their climate commitments on websites and media releases.

Yet such goals are invariably framed within particular boundaries. For example, while BP's recent announcement went further than many others in acknowledging a need to reduce emissions, close scrutiny of the company's pledge revealed that it excluded the partnership with Russian oil and gas giant Rosneft – which accounts for 40 per cent of BP's oil production – and that the plan would depend on offsets and CCS. Both the environmental and economic values of offsets are notoriously challenging to calculate. Determining the 'permanence' of emissions avoided is difficult, as is assessing whether emissions are 'additional' (Sedjo & Sohngen, 2012). It is also common for companies in richer nations to purchase offsets from operators in developing countries in order to avoid actually reducing emissions themselves (Böhm et al., 2012). Meanwhile, as discussed earlier, the potential of CCS is equally problematic.

These issues suggest BP's plan, while arguably quite ambitious, is likely to fall short of its claims, but what it *does* do, of course, is help the company stand out from the rest of the industry as a leader in taking action on climate change. In addition – and perhaps more importantly – it implies that governments need not intervene in the market and that companies are more than able to assume this responsibility themselves. Announcements of carbon-neutrality goals are thus aimed less at making a positive difference and more at responding to critique and defending fossil fuel hegemony. The same can be said of claims that solutions are imminent, which present an alluring response to the growing public concern about the worsening climate crisis. Here, the argument presented is that there is no need for alarm, that corporate ingenuity and innovation will solve the 'grand challenge' of climate change and that all will be well if we trust businesses and markets to continue maximising shareholder wealth.

3.6 No Time or Place for Carbon Mitigation

Corporate pledges of future carbon neutrality and imminent climate solutions are thus, we argue, less aimed at making a positive difference and more at responding to critique and defending fossil fuel hegemony.

Table 3.2 *Examples of corporate climate commitments*

Company	Description
Asia Pulp & Paper (Indonesia)	One of the world's largest paper producers, Asia Pulp & Paper's 'Vision 2020' included the following goals: >10 per cent reduction in the carbon intensity of operations (2012 baseline), implementation of peatland best practice management programme, zero-paper fibre from high conservation forests and support the national target for the identification and protection of high conservation value and High Carbon Stock forests.
FedEx (US)	FedEx recently announced its 'Priority Earth' sustainability initiative with a goal to have carbon-neutral operations by 2040. It focuses on electrification of its pickup and delivery vehicle fleet by 2030, invests in biofuels and improved fuel efficiency for its airline fleet, improves eco-efficiency in its 5,000 facilities worldwide and provides funding for research into 'natural carbon sequestration solutions' to reduce its aircraft emissions.
Gazprom (Russia)	The world's third-largest emitter of industrial GHG emissions, Gazprom adopted an Environmental Policy in 1995 and Comprehensive Environmental Program in 2011. Through improved eco-efficiency, the company claims to have reduced operational GHG emissions by 14 per cent in the past two years and saved over 3 billion tons of fugitive methane. It aims to reduce gross pollutant emissions and contaminated effluents in surface water and has introduced an ISO 14001-compliant environmental management system.
Google (US)	Google claims to have been carbon neutral since 2007 and aims to be carbon-free by 2030, matching its energy use with 100 per cent renewable energy. Key initiatives include developing 'carbon-free' energy

Table 3.2 (*cont.*)

Company	Description
	and storage facilities and helping deployment across cities, procuring carbon offsets for historical emissions, issuing sustainability bonds valued at $5.75 billion to encourage green energy, sponsoring a €10 million challenge to fund climate innovation and investing in carbon capture and reafforestation.
HSBC (UK)	Europe's second-largest fossil fuel financier, HSBC released its 2020 climate plan with the goal of becoming the leading bank supporting the transition to net-zero. Its goals include using the Paris Agreement Capital Transition Assessment tool to develop ways to achieve net-zero emissions in direct operations and supply chain by 2030, help develop a functioning global carbon offset market and provide financial support (estimated between $750 billion and $1 trillion over the next ten years to support heavy-emitting companies to progressively decarbonise.
Ikea (Netherlands)	Ikea aims to be 'climate positive' by reducing carbon emissions across its value chain, halving GHG emissions by 2030 and becoming 'net-zero' by 2050. Specific strategies include improving eco-efficiency and seeking 100 per cent renewable energy in its operations; sourcing cotton, timber and other products from sustainably certified suppliers and increasing the recycled content in products.
Sony (Japan)	Launched in 2010, Sony's long-term goal under its 'Road to Zero' plan is to have a zero environmental footprint in its business activities and through the life cycle of its products and services by 2050. The 2025 targets include 5 per cent reduction in annual energy consumption of products (baseline 2018), 15 per cent or more conversion of facilities to renewable energy and collaborating with supply vendors to reduce environmental impact.
Toyota (Japan)	The world's largest auto company, Toyota has stated that it supports the Paris Agreement and is committed to action in line with its requirements. This includes the goal of carbon neutrality for all

global plants by 2035; expansion of investment and production of electric vehicle models including global sales of 3.5 million battery electric vehicles by 2030 and accelerated development of hydrogen and biofuel technologies.

Vale (Brazil)	The company's latest climate change goals include reducing operational emissions (Scope 1 and 2) by 33 per cent by 2030 and net-zero by 2050, adopting 100 per cent renewable energy in Brazil by 2025 and globally by 2030 and reducing net Scope 3 emissions by 15 per cent by 2035. Key strategies include improved eco-efficiency, carbon offsets, adoption of renewable energy (hydroelectric) and carbon sequestration via reafforestation and forest conservation. To date, the company claims 25 per cent of its direct energy use comes from renewable sources and 1 million hectares of forest have been protected through the Vale fund.
Walmart (US)	The world's largest retailer, Walmart has committed to science based targets for emissions reduction, including achieving zero emissions across global operations by 2040 and engaging suppliers to reduce supply chain emissions by 1 billion metric tons by 2030. The company aims to power up to 50 per cent of its operations with renewable energy by 2025 rising to 100 per cent by 2035.

They are a delaying strategy aimed at pushing much-needed decarbonisation into a distant future where future innovations and technologies are presented as solving the conflict between endless economic growth and the destruction of a habitable climate. Such tactics work by appealing to the idea that people can continue unlimited consumption, that government intervention is not required and that companies can be trusted to do the heavy lifting of reducing emissions. The long-term time frames of these purported commitments, as well as the lack of detail that tends to characterise them, indicate such tactics are principally geared towards delaying the transition science tells us is imperative.

Thus, a key limitation of much business engagement with climate change is the dominantly short-term focus on financial performance, evident in the focus on quarterly and semi-annual financial reporting (Slawinski et al., 2017). Climate change, as an ongoing phenomenon spanning decades and generations, exceeds the capacity of most corporations (and governments) to conceptualise and respond to it. This business and governmental short-termism also results in a paradoxical distancing of climate change as a risk or threat located somewhere in the future, a concern that business and political leaders will need to confront but not yet, and perhaps not for some decades. Time here is conceived as a continuous deferral without any clear passage or temporal markers for how these commitments are related to the present.

Added to this, corporations are also curiously divorced from the spatial realities of climate change. While there is significant attention by businesses to the physical risks of extreme weather events on operational activities and infrastructure (see Chapter 5), much corporate climate response occurs in the globalised non-spaces of financial markets, media, sustainability ratings and political lobbying. There is thus often little tangible experience with local manifestations of climate change and the natural and social systems that are most adversely affected. Firms can, after all, relocate their operations in response to climatic impacts, and this is one way in which companies appear to be responding to the physical risks of worsening climate disruptions (Nyberg & Wright, 2016).

Indeed, case studies of corporate climate responses have highlighted how such initiatives are often subject to significant change over time, including the diminution of earlier ambitious goals and a return to traditional 'core' business concerns following changes in corporate leadership or a decline in profitability (Wright & Nyberg, 2017). There is thus no guarantee that corporations will actually deliver on their climate pledges, nor any broader systemic commitment to meaningful emissions mitigation in a political context of laissez-faire corporate voluntarism.

3.7 An Age of Faux Decarbonisation

Despite fanciful announcements, many corporations continue to invest in the industries they claim to be shifting away from. For example, activists gave a cautious welcome when BlackRock, the world's largest asset manager, declared it would divest US$500 million from its coal-related businesses (Helmore, 2020). In his communication to the CEOs of BlackRock's investee companies, founder and chairman Larry Fink encouraged businesses to disclose their climate-related risks. As ever, though, the devil was in the detail: the divestment did not include oil and gas – industries in which BlackRock has significant investments (Helmore, 2020). Moreover, BlackRock's commitment to withdraw funds was restricted to companies gaining more than a quarter of their income from thermal coal – meaning several larger, more diversified corporations were unaffected. These included mining giants Glencore (of which BlackRock owns 6 per cent), Anglo American plc and BHP Billiton (Biesheuvel, 2020). Like BP, BlackRock might reasonably portray itself as a leader in its field – but only in the context of ongoing fossil fuel use (Stockholm Environment Institute et al., 2020).

Indeed, while some see these corporate announcements as signs of a sea change in the global business response to the climate crisis, analysis of the practice and policy of the major oil corporations during the past fifteen years has found no evidence of operational decarbonisation. Furthermore, while the public discourse has moved towards a more climate-focused stance, researchers have argued that even the more progressive European-based oil companies have merely been hedging their bets through limited diversification and risk mitigation (Green et al., 2021). Viewed from this perspective, any apparent conversion on the issue of climate change appears more part of a longer-term pattern of skilful marketing and defensive justification in the face of growing social and political critique (Brulle et al., 2020).

It is worth examining the tangible evidence – or, more accurately, the lack of it – that decarbonisation is actually under way. First, the emissions mitigation commitments of many companies stress a reduction in emissions *intensity* rather than a reduction in absolute numbers; second, like much of the tech industry, decarbonisation relies on future investment in unproven technologies; third, net-zero goals depend on dubious offsetting purchases and also often neglect to include the Scope 3 emissions that result from consumers' use of businesses' products (e.g. the fuel burned around the world in cars, trucks and planes). It soon becomes painfully obvious that many of these declarations fail to align with the Paris Agreement's target of limiting global warming to less than 2°C above pre-industrial levels.

Little wonder, then, that carbon emissions have continued to rise. There was a brief lull in their growth in 2020 as the world reeled from the impact of the COVID-19 pandemic, but the respite was short-lived. In carbon-intensive economies – the US, China, Russia, India, Brazil, Canada, Australia and Saudi Arabia among them – the fossil fuel industry is still expanding, assisted by government subsidies and financial incentives (BloombergNEF, 2021).

The so-called fracking revolution has led to the US becoming the world's biggest producer of oil and gas (Downie, 2019). China is now the largest producer of coal; it also accounts for more than half of all consumption globally; it is making significant investments in new fossil fuel projects in developing economies through its Belt and Road initiative; and it is constructing new coal-fired power plants as part of its post-pandemic recovery (Umbach & Yu, 2016; Standaert, 2021). Expansion of fossil fuel extraction has led to dramatic growth in energy exports for Canada and Australia, with the former's Alberta tar sands delivering oil to the US and China (Bloomberg, 2019) and the latter – as stated previously – now among the world's largest exporters of coal and gas (Kilvert, 2019). Yes, renewable energy is also growing; but it is not necessarily displacing fossil fuel energy sources (Carbon Tracker Initiative, 2021). In an era of growing social and political conflict over the climate crisis, global capitalism's addiction to fossil fuels appears as strong as ever.

In the next chapter, we explore how climate change re-emerged as a dominant political issue around the world. We reflect on how business leaders have come under mounting pressure to defend their actions in the face of fossil fuel divestment movements, re-energised social demands for positive action and lawsuits targeting companies for their historical deceptions over climate change. We consider how new forms of grassroots organising have sought to draw the links between intergenerational equality, protection of the environment and climate change. Finally, we argue that the success of such movements is evident in the ways in which corporate executives and governments have attempted to label environmentalists as the Other and resist moves to decarbonise the economy.

4 | *Challenging Fossil Fuel Expansion*

This is not a political text. Our school strike has nothing to do with party politics, because the climate and the biosphere don't care about our politics and our empty words for a single second.

(Thunberg, 2019b: 1–2)

In 2018 and 2019, unable to vote yet increasingly aware of the grim legacy being left to them, millions of young people followed the lead of Swedish student Greta Thunberg, who had started skipping school on Fridays to protest alone outside her country's parliament. These activists were vocal, accusing the fossil fuel industry and prior generations of stealing their futures; and they were bold, abandoning their classrooms to make their feelings known and demand government action. Thunberg herself was invited to the UN Climate Action Summit in September 2019. The speech she delivered there was characteristically blunt. She admonished the event's participants for repeatedly failing to act on climate change and famously declared: 'How dare you?' As she spoke, millions of like-minded souls engaged in 'climate strikes' around the globe. Taking to the streets in more than 160 countries, they marched under the Fridays for Future banner. Thunberg had clearly had an impact: the would-be inheritors of a climate catastrophe were suddenly in revolt.

Just as it seemed 'climate fatigue' (Kerr, 2009) had become entrenched, the fossil fuel industry found itself confronted by new, vibrant and diverse adversaries. Locally organised, internationally connected and arguably more strident than any of their predecessors, these fast-emerging environmental movements disrupted everyday practices and called for ever-stronger action from governments.

The industry was clearly concerned. Mohammed Barkindo, general secretary of the Organisation of the Petroleum Exporting Countries (OPEC), described young people as 'perhaps the greatest threat to our industry going forward' and acknowledged that 'there is a growing mass mobilisation of world opinion ... against oil' (Snaith, 2019). Along with conservative politicians who had until then held off meaningful action on climate change, fossil fuel businesses suddenly needed new strategies to maintain the hegemony.

In this chapter, we detail the varied responses from environmental movements in their engagement with climate change politics in the years after the Paris Agreement of 2015. The accord was greeted with widespread relief when it was adopted at the eleventh hour, but it soon became apparent that even its most unambitious targets were unlikely to be met (Leahy, 2019) – prompting more radical, grassroots organisations to take the lead in addressing the climate crisis.

Recognising the 'old politics' of consensus had failed, global social movements such as Fridays for Future and Extinction Rebellion became prominent. Meanwhile, other elements attempted to mobilise the law and finance as a means of slowing the growth of the fossil fuel industry and accelerating government action. While each brought its own programme of change, the movements constructed a political frontier in which concerns for the environment and future generations would be pitted against corporations and policymakers supporting the ongoing use of fossil energy.

Our outline of environmental movements' different approaches is followed by an analysis of the reactions they triggered. We show how politicians and fossil-fuel-dependent entities firmly backed the status quo, with only minor tweaking to accommodate aspects of the environmental critique. These strategies incorporated the interests of opposition movements within the hegemonic project while at the same time promoting a more confrontational politics of difference by demonising environmental actors as extremists or even terrorists. As highlighted in the previous chapter, lowering greenhouse gas emissions entails the difficult tasks of breaking up the fossil fuel hegemony and challenging the pervasiveness of consumption-driven economic growth. This, we argue, demands nothing less than a broad mobilisation against dominant forms of corporate capitalism.

4.1 Green Governmentality

The potential for negotiations to enact a global turnaround in the trajectory of the climate crisis has long been a strong focus of the environmental movement. The assumption underlying this strategy is that the scale of the transformation required demands an international agreement that can facilitate the transition towards a decarbonised world economy.

This perspective of 'green governmentality' (Bäckstrand & Lövbrand, 2007) puts faith in the notion that shared responsibility for the environment, guided by science, will lead to a just outcome in managing the crisis. In practice, this process has been facilitated by the annual COP events, held since 1995, at which NGOs from environmental and social justice movements have had a growing presence. While NGOs do not have decision-making powers within the COP process, they have at least used their attendance to track how the climate policy debate is progressing and to pressure nations to adopt more ambitious policies (Rosewarne et al., 2013).

After the disappointment of the Copenhagen negotiations in 2009, for example, NGOs emphasised the need for more meaningful dialogue to continue in the lead up to the 2015 conference in Paris. Seen as the last chance for serious global climate action, the Paris Agreement both instilled hope and provoked dismay. While more conservative environmental organisations such as the World Wide Fund for Nature (WWF) and the Sierra Club celebrated the deal, claiming there was a new consensus on the urgency of mitigating climate change, groups with stronger commitments to social justice and grassroots practice – Friends of the Earth and the Indigenous Environmental Network among them – declared the outcome an outright failure (Chivers & Worth, 2015). The agreement was criticised by some as 'a laissez-faire accord among nations that leaves the content of domestic policy to governments' (Dimitrov, 2016: 2). Subsequent COPs have underlined how hard it is to maintain pressure on individual countries, especially petrostates with prominent fossil fuel industries (Harvey, 2021a).

The inadequacy of international negotiations in delivering a sufficient response to the crisis has led environmental groups to react in different ways. Some have attempted to work with industries and businesses in advancing decarbonisation, while others have developed campaigns aimed at using the system to slow the growth of fossil fuels; these latter efforts have included the divestment drive spearheaded by international NGO 350.org, as well as a dramatic rise in litigation.

As noted earlier, there has also been an emergence of a new breed of climate movements. These are more forthright in both their tactics and their demands for positive action. Crucially, they go beyond merely advocating for governments to demonstrate climate leadership: they instead seek to disrupt incremental responses through large-scale protest and civil disobedience (see Table 4.1).

Table 4.1 *Demands and tactics of climate movement organisations*

Organisation	Key Demands	Tactics
Fridays for Future	Keep the global temperature rise below 1.5°C compared to pre-industrial levels Ensure climate justice and equity Listen to the best-united science currently available	'Global Day of Climate Action': mass 'strikes' led by students and young people Locally organised mobilisations around international negotiations Campaign to end fossil fuel subsidies
Extinction Rebellion	Tell the truth Act now Go beyond politics	Non-violent, disruptive civil disobedience Actions have included physically blocking fossil fuel infrastructure, traffic disruption, theatrics including 'die-ins', awareness-raising signage in strategic public locations
350.org	A fast and just transition to 100 per cent renewable energy for all No new fossil fuel projects anywhere 'Not a penny more for dirty energy'	Fossil fuel-free campaign: lobbying councils, education institutions, faith organisations, pension funds and more to divest from fossil fuel companies. Locally organised independent groups work on different campaigns, mostly aimed at national governments.
WWF	Create a climate-resilient and zero-carbon world, powered by renewable energy	Working with partners in Colombia, Kyrgyzstan and Tajikistan, Paraguay and

Table 4.1 (*cont.*)

Organisation	Key Demands	Tactics
		Bolivia to help communities adapt to climate change.
		Supporting the Green Climate Fund and Global Environment Facility
		Working with companies to help reduce their emissions
Sierra Club	Move beyond coal 100 per cent clean energy	Locally organised campaign for US city- and state-based governments to sign up for 100 per cent renewable electricity by 2035 and other sectors by 2050
		Regulation focused campaigns to close coal, oil and gas
		Promotion of electric vehicles and stricter car emission standards
		Student coalition currently working on promoting a 'Green New Deal'

4.2 New Frontiers

There is a classic observation that environmentalism comes in waves. The first focuses on conservation and preservation; the second is centred on regulation and litigation; and the third is 'based on economics' (Van Huijstee et al., 2011: 45). Such an outline follows the 'ecological modernisation' discourse, which attempts to argue that there is no tension between economic growth and environmental protection and that the two simply need to be 'decoupled'. While this perspective has been thoroughly critiqued, the appeal to the dominant economic system – together with a lack of criticism of current political arrangements – has kept the notion popular.

This 'win-win' rhetoric is particularly attractive for environmental groups. Such arguments can be seen in the growing prevalence of NGOs and others using the courts to pursue positive climate outcomes, and they can also be seen in widespread efforts to encourage investors to withdraw their money from entities involved in fossil fuels. By avoiding direct conflict with the forces of capitalism, groups can promote a shared interest in protecting the environment and suggest that rather than being threatened, governance and economic systems need only to be better managed.

Litigation focuses on a range of climate-related issues, including disaster management, responsibility for global warming and accusations of companies making false claims. Many cases are increasingly linked to violations of international human rights – such as those related to a healthy environment – and rely on the idea of what are often considered universal 'rights'. In 2020, for example, a group of young German citizens filed a lawsuit against their government. They alleged existing legislation violated the right to life and physical integrity, as well as responsibility for future generations, under Germany's constitution. While some aspects of the case were rejected, the Federal Constitutional Court ruled that the government's commitment to reduce greenhouse gas emissions by 55 per cent by 2030 disproportionately placed a burden on future generations; it further ruled that clearer targets for 2031 and thereafter should be set. The government quickly announced it would comply with the judgment (AP News, 2021).

In the same year, in another landmark case, a group of NGOs and Dutch citizens took oil giant Shell to court, arguing that its policies should be in line with the Paris Agreement. The court found in the activists' favour, stating that by 2030, the company should reduce its carbon dioxide emissions by 45 per cent of 2019 levels (McGrath, 2021a). While Shell declared its intention to appeal against the decision, such cases are increasing in number and are expected to continue to do so (UN Environment Programme, 2020).

These successes bring to light the potential for NGOs and others to use the courts to push for climate action and ensure compliance with international agreements (Beauregard et al., 2021). A database of more than 1,800 cases filed globally since 1986 has revealed 58 per cent had positive outcomes for climate action, 32 per cent were unfavourable and 10 per cent had 'no discernible likely impact' (Setzer & Higham, 2021: 5).

There are difficulties, however, in tracing the efficacy of such tactics. Climate litigation remains a challenge, with issues over attribution of responsibility and the jurisdiction of particular courts hard to demonstrate (Stuart-Smith et al., 2021). There is also a growing trend of 'counter-litigation' – including opposition to renewable energy schemes or challenges to rulings seen as impinging on rights such as property development – as a result of which recourse to the legal system can ultimately work *against* climate action in some instances (Setzer & Higham, 2021).

In addition, groups can find themselves caught up in lengthy appeals processes. There is even scope for governments to simply change laws that might force them to take stronger action on the climate crisis. There are numerous limitations inherent in trying to use legal systems to bring about positive change: while there may be potential to slow the growth of the fossil fuel industry, 'carbon-intensive corporations have been and are currently doing precisely what they are supposed to – accumulating capital – [and that] is the condition that must be addressed' (Gunderson & Fyock, 2021: 2).

It is also worth remarking that the enormous wealth of fossil fuel firms can be brought to bear in fighting legal battles. This implies there will be an unequal playing field until the industry's bottom line is finally impacted – which brings us to the key question of whether the accumulation of capital can continue *without* the fossil fuel industry.

The divestment movement seeks to answer this question. Its strategy emphasises the role of institutional investors in funding coal, oil and gas businesses and argues that they have a moral responsibility to shift their money towards more sustainable sectors. Inspired by the divestment drives witnessed during the anti-apartheid struggle in the 1970s and 1980s, the movement aims to have key investors remove their financial support for fossil fuels in order to make the construction of new projects unviable.

Taking its lead from ethical investment campaigns in the UK and the US, the divestment movement began on university campuses and was popularised when 350.org launched its 'Go Fossil-Free' initiative in 2012 (Hestres & Hopke, 2020). A two-pronged approach soon emerged. On the one hand, a 'moral call to action' stressed that investment in fossil fuels was unethical and that companies wishing to be seen as socially responsible should remove their support for the industry; on the other, attempts to erode fossil fuels' financial basis centred on the escalation of regulatory and reputational risks.

The response from investors has been mixed. The targets of campaigns are often organisations within communities that are more likely to accept calls for investment to be based on ethical principles. Faith-based organisations, educational institutions, governments and investment funds are among those to have reacted positively. Many have seized on divestment as an opportunity to proclaim their own values: for example, Bill de Blasio, the Mayor of New York City, spoke of 'standing up for future generations by becoming the first major US city to divest our pension funds from fossil fuels' (Millman, 2018).

Although the campaign has led to 1,497 institutions shifting their finances away from fossil fuels at the time of writing (Global Divestment Commitments Database, 2021), a criticism of the movement has been that it has 'failed to resonate with political conservatives or moderates' (Hestres & Hopke, 2020: 375). Like the climate movement more generally, proponents of divestment have been accused of being 'utopian' or 'unrealistic'.

As Healy and Barry (2017) have noted, however, such an interpretation frequently represents an attempt to avoid the politics of the situation. Seen another way, attacking environmentalists for wanting improvements reveals a lack of ambition – if not outright denial – on the part of incumbent industry leaders. By enabling small groups to take action in their own communities, the divestment campaign can be viewed as strengthening the climate movement as a whole at a time when many governments remain steadfastly opposed to meaningful action.

As a preference for renewable energy over fossil fuels continues to develop, the divestment drive has contributed to undermining the public image of fossil fuel corporations in terms of their moral culpability and heightened investment risk (Hestres & Hopke, 2020). It has thus impacted the wider discourse about the future of energy sources and, as discussed later in the text, furthered divisions not only between industries but also between some of the larger, diversified resource corporations and 'pure play' coal and oil companies. In tandem, litigation attempts have advanced the vital argument that governments and companies have broken not only the law but also the social contract that assumes they should protect current and future citizens alike.

The politics here is clear: the ills of certain corporations are separated from the good of capitalism in general. This differentiation paints fossil fuels as a 'sin' industry. By decoupling capitalism's continuation of wealth creation from the 'sin' of ongoing reliance on fossil fuels, the movement aims to build a wide-ranging coalition in support of decarbonisation.

Both litigation and divestment have sought to push the moral implications of climate change into pre-existing social structures that are more often used to support, not challenge, the status quo. Moreover, both have sought to draw an equivalence with the broader moral values and expectations of social systems. For others, meanwhile, moving away from discussions about climate change and instead emphasising an alignment between concern for land and water has proven more fruitful.

4.3 Unusual Friends

For the broader environmental movement, both on local and national levels, the competing economic interests of communities reliant on extractive industries often represent a significant challenge. Large fossil fuel corporations consistently emphasise their own contributions to economic well-being and the employment opportunities they provide. In promoting new carbon frontiers, the hegemony frames economic growth, jobs and royalties as essential in funding public services.

The political debate over fracking in the UK offers a classic illustration. While opponents warned the environmental costs would be borne by local communities, advocates championed the economic and employment benefits this new means of extraction would supposedly bring (Nyberg et al., 2018). The fossil fuel industry was quick to call attention to its shared interests 'with energy consumers, landholders and workers by appealing to their interests in jobs, cheaper energy and financial incentives' (Nyberg et al., 2018: 247).

The aim in such instances is to determinedly steer away from the potentially radical implications of climate change by feeding into existing political frameworks that prioritise concern for the economy. This helps explain why, for instance, the Australian Manufacturing Workers' Union claimed the Australian Labor Party (ALP) was losing elections by allowing 'the bosses to turn the workers and environmentalists against each other to their own benefit' (quoted in O'Malley,

2020). A 'jobs and growth' strategy has been noticeably successful around the world in regions facing ongoing encroachment from activities such as mining and fracking.

Crucially, some environmental organisations have also deliberately turned away from discussing climate change directly – and not just because of the difficulties that can surround communicating the phenomenon. They instead focus either on positive 'low hanging fruit' campaigns like increasing renewable energy and energy efficiency or on local impacts – for example, conflicts over land use, threats to waterways and aquifers, destruction of biodiversity, toxic pollution and so on. Environmentalists are thus themselves able to emphasise equivalent interests within communities, building what are often unlikely coalitions.

For instance, the Australian NGO Lock the Gate has focused on mining's detrimental effects on agricultural land. This approach has helped forge alliances with the farming community and even conservative political commentators (Robertson, 2017). The organisation's popularity is symbolised today by the many bright-yellow 'Lock the Gate' signs dotted on the fences of rural landholders in the country's numerous mining regions.

A successful pushback against the extraction of coal seam gas in Australia's Northern Rivers area provides another powerful illustration of how environmentalists work to build local-level political frontiers in order to thwart the fossil fuel hegemony. In the mid-2010s, at the end of a standoff spanning several years, oil and gas company Metgasco was forced to retreat in the face of the widespread community and public opposition (Ricketts, 2020).

Yet this tendency to avoid mentioning climate change runs the risk of enforcing a politics of 'Not in my back yard' (NIMBY), as a consequence of which fossil fuel exploration may shift to areas inhabited by people with politically 'weaker' voices. For example, fracking in England has largely been pressed on more working-class and impoverished communities in the north – as opposed to the south, where much of the political and economic power is located (Nyberg et al., 2018). Opposition to coal mining in Australia has been successfully led by other industries – such as horse breeding, agriculture and winemaking – which have highlighted an array of disruptive environmental impacts on their own operations (McManus & Connor, 2013).

In the US, the fight against the Dakota Access Pipeline – intended to carry oil from North Dakota to Illinois – also illustrates efforts to build equivalence across diverse groups. Led by the Standing Rock Sioux tribe, the campaign focused on land and water rights and entailed months-long protest camps. Opposition to this fossil fuel development made worldwide headlines, in part because of the strong tactics and unusual alliances involved. With support from environmentalists, social justice advocates and veterans, the movement specifically pushed for decolonisation practices – including participants being invited onto the land – and other principles outlined by the tribe (Powell & Draper, 2020). The pipeline was ultimately constructed, but at the time of writing, it is the subject of a number of court appeals that could eventually see it shut down.

Examples such as those discussed previously show how the tactic of local environmental opposition to fossil fuel expansion can deliver results. It is important to acknowledge, though, that such efforts often fail to link to a wider strategy of limiting the growth of carbon emissions and climate change more generally.

4.4 Disruption

Perhaps the most spectacular environmental movements to emerge in recent years have been Extinction Rebellion and Fridays for Future. These have followed in the footsteps of 'direct action' groups such as the Climate Camps in Europe, Canada, Australia and New Zealand; anti-airline protesters such as Plane Stupid; the Keystone XL pipeline blockades in the US and the German anti-coal movement Ende Gelände (Malm, 2021). These earlier mobilisations sought to directly shut down fossil fuel infrastructure – including power plants, airports and coal mines – and have adopted a distinctly uncompromising view of the political change needed and the tactics required to bring it about. This, of course, has made them more controversial and open to critique – sometimes from within the broader environmental movement.

Extinction Rebellion and Fridays for Future may share these groups' more radical messages about dramatic decarbonisation, but they are arguably organisations that target a broader global audience. As such, they have brought new life to public discussions about climate change. Their campaigns have been described as 'protest cascades that have caught the popular imagination and grown so rapidly that those in power were caught off balance' (Ludlam, 2019). Importantly, both stress the need to move beyond the usual domestic political avenues and emphasise vibrant and creative responses to the crisis. They show the antagonism of people's everyday practices and demand a choice between growing affluence and genuinely responding to climate change.

Extinction Rebellion (2019) organisers argue that since the traditional models of advocacy and lobbying have not worked, the urgency of the crisis justifies their 'non-violent, disruptive civil disobedience'. This commonly includes actions such as trying to get as many protesters as possible arrested and blocking traffic in major cities at peak times (Gayle & Quinn, 2019). These actions have generated controversy and criticism, but the group has defended its tactics. To quote an Extinction Rebellion statement: 'The aim is to make these most critical and urgent issues of our time finally unignorable to decision-makers. If they want less disruption, they must act' (Extinction Rebellion, 2019).

Disruptive actions have been combined with pressuring governments to declare a climate emergency. For example, following large-scale protests that closed the centre of London over many days in April 2019, Extinction Rebellion organisers met with the Mayor of London and senior politicians, resulting in the UK parliament passing a 'climate emergency' resolution (Ludlam, 2019).

Although this has led to suggestions that Extinction Rebellion's demands invoke a potentially undemocratic securitisation discourse (Doherty et al., 2018), the group has insisted that responding to the climate emergency must be organised through the democratic processes of a Citizen's Assembly (Extinction Rebellion, 2019). One of the reasons why these more radical organisations might occasionally appear to lack cohesion is that what they ask for and how they ask for it can be largely outside the sort of political engagement previously expected of environmental and social movements.

Fridays for Future provides further evidence of how this new breed of environmental activism is defying the traditional technocratic politics of climate change. In March 2019, following the example of Greta Thunberg, the movement spread around the globe, with more than a million students walking out of their schools in the middle of the day to march for climate action (Malm, 2021). Directed towards and driven by schoolchildren, the group brought a new dynamism to climate protests – challenging previous generations, governments and companies over their selfishness and pointing out that the greed of others will mean the suffering of future generations. With the Earth overshooting its capacity on a yearly basis, protesters used slogans such as 'There is no planet B', 'This can't wait till I'm bigger' and 'If you don't act like adults, we will!' (Guardian staff, 2018) to condemn the prevalence of self-interest and short-term thinking.

Fridays for Future's 'climate strikes' aim to bring maximum disruption in order to attract more attention to the movement's cause. In September 2019, with the group calling for a general strike, businesses, trade unionists, workers and parents joined the young activists in demanding stronger climate action, with a total of 6 million people participating in a worldwide protest (Taylor et al., 2019); employees at Microsoft, Google, Amazon, Facebook and Twitter were among those to make climate-specific requests of their own companies (Singh et al., 2019).

Movements such as Extinction Rebellion and Fridays for Future challenge the everyday – and ineffective – politics of climate change. They show the paradoxical aspects of the limited societal responses to the crisis by emphasising the underlying contradiction of people's behaviour in shifting responsibilities to those least culpable for environmental catastrophe. They can be seen as reconstructing what is seen as the 'middle ground' of climate politics by developing the radical flank (Schifeling & Hoffman, 2019).

With many environmental organisations working with corporations and promoting them as the likeliest architects of a solution, there is still much to do in propelling the political frontier towards a more counter-hegemonic agenda. The paucity of meaningful climate action to date, in concert with the worsening impacts on billions around the world, seems likely to result in even more disruptive protests in the future (Malm, 2021). However, in establishing a political frontier against the fossil fuels hegemony, these movements face an increasingly sophisticated foe.

4.5 Constructing 'Shared Interests'

The public debate over climate change may have become more diverse but so has the response from the hegemonic projects of corporate capitalism. Some of the larger and more diversified corporations have made wide-ranging announcements in relation to the crisis, yet others have doubled down on their efforts to drag out policy discussions and extend the putative relevance of their activities for as long as possible.

For instance, as we noted in the previous chapter, many resource corporations have declared seemingly ambitious net-zero targets and stressed a move into the future growth of renewable technologies such as lithium batteries or 'green' hydrogen. Against this, however, other coal, oil or gas businesses, as well as the major petrostates, appear determined to continue exploiting existing resources – as witnessed, for example, when Rio Tinto announced it was exiting coal and then sold its assets to companies that were expected to work the mines 'harder' (Clarke, 2017).

The fracture of fossil-fuelled corporate capitalism can be seen both between and within industries and countries. While each business claims to invest in 'solutions' to climate change, the extent to which the various fractions represent any real systemic shift is questionable. In embracing the rhetoric of climate action, corporations try to construct a notion of shared interests with citizens. They insist they can supply cheap energy *and* manage the environmental crisis. This framing, which assists in countering dissent in the community (Nyberg et al., 2013), is often generated in collaboration with specific environmental NGOs: these are brought further into the fold, while more critical voices are labelled extremists.

Working with environmental groups has long been a means of relieving public pressure for companies to abandon their damaging practices. These strategies are supported by the managerialist practices within the NGO sector, as imposed by their funding models. It is common for funders – rather than the organisations or communities with which they are involved – to set the goals of projects (Girei, 2015), which means financing environmental groups or campaigns offers corporations a potent means of dampening or incorporating potential criticism.

Fundraising can contribute up to 30 per cent of an NGO's annual budget. As a result, competition is fierce. Many NGOs therefore turn to corporate relationships for support (Dauvergne & LeBaron, 2014). Large NGOs in particular can increasingly be run like corporations, at times even sharing board members and advisers and working in partnerships. As Klein (2014: 198) has noted, part of the legacy of the fossil fuel hegemony is the difficulty of finding financial support that is not tainted by association with the industry being critiqued.

As well as providing a veneer of credibility to implicated businesses, these relationships can affect the policies and actions of NGOs. Consider, for example, the WWF's Earth Hour event, which was launched in 2007 and involves households and businesses collectively turning off their electricity for one hour in the evening on a designated date. The promotion of Earth Hour initially centred on quantifying the event's effect as 'the equivalent of taking 48,613 cars off the road for an hour' (quoted in Pearse, 2012: 44). In due course, after it was pointed out that such an 'impact' was in fact negligible, the focus instead shifted to raising awareness. The concept was developed by celebrity advertising executives Todd Sampson and Nigel Marsh, of the Leo Burnett agency, which has also worked for Shell and Emirates National Oil Company and had helped Phillip Morris formulate responses to passive smoking.

Earth Hour has proven a major fundraiser for the WWF, which receives 'tens of millions of dollars annually in undisclosed donations' (Pearse, 2012: 49). The list of emissions-intensive companies that have provided support – including Toyota, Rio Tinto, BHP Billiton, Vale, Woodside, Origin Energy, Bluesteel, Leighton and more – might belie any assertion that climate change is truly the issue at hand. As Pearse (2012: 49) has noted: 'The genius of Earth Hour is that it allows anyone to look climate-friendly'. Much the same 'genius' can be discerned in the means by which differences between industries are nowadays increasingly highlighted. For instance, as mentioned earlier, the gas industry has continually claimed its product should be used as a so-called transition fuel in the process of shifting away from coal, which is thereby depicted as a dirtier and less desirable fossil fuel.

This argument has at times been endorsed by some of the more mainstream environmental groups. These have included the Sierra Club, the Environmental Defense Fund and the Natural Resources Defense Council in the US (Casselman, 2009). Yet it is all too apparent that such backing has not always been entirely based on the merits of the gas industry's arguments. For instance, in 2012, it was revealed the Sierra Club, one of the biggest environmental organisations in the US, had received more than US$25 million from the gas industry between 2007 and 2010 (Walsh, 2012). The funds, intended to go towards its Beyond Coal campaign, came primarily from Aubrey McClendon – CEO of Chesapeake Energy, a corporation at the forefront of the push for fracking in the US, and founder of America's Natural Gas Alliance lobbying group (Brown, 2016). McClendon and Carl Pope, the then executive director of the Sierra Club, appeared together in 2009 and, perhaps unsurprisingly, championed the benefits of using gas as a 'transition fuel' (Casselman, 2009). The Sierra Club ended the relationship amid mounting criticism of another corporate partnership – with chemical cleaning company Clorox – and after appointing a new executive director.

4.6 Resisting the Resistance

In contrast, environmental groups that maintain their critique of fossil fuels are now routinely dismissed by the corporate and political hegemony as naïve or extreme. Having constructed a frontier between the industry and more compliant environmental groups, which are depicted as rational and rooted in economic thinking, groups which challenge the status quo of the existing political frontier are portrayed as dangerous and going beyond the bounds of their allocated roles.

With executives, industry associations, politicians and conservative commentators prioritising the continuation of fossil fuel extraction and use in the face of growing environmental critique, this differentiation of the Other has become a common framing. This demonisation is then used to suggest that these groups are operating outside of the interests of the majority and to justify every increasing intervention from the state.

Even those working within the bounds of legality have been targeted in this way. For instance, environmental organisations in Australia are regularly threatened with the withdrawal of their charity status if they are seen to be engaging in politics (Slezak, 2016). The government has even intimated that campaigns and protests targeting corporations involved in fossil fuels could be made illegal. Dehumanising tactics are openly endorsed, with the leader of right-wing political party One Nation suggesting protesters should be moved along with cattle prods and one commentator on a large TV network saying they should be used as 'speed bumps' (Carey, 2019; Chung, 2019). In this context, the state-capital nexus ensures that heavy-handed action in breaking up peaceful protests is rarely disciplined – if ever.

One method of painting environmentalists with the 'criminal' brush is to take them to court. This tactic is often referred to as a SLAPP – a strategic lawsuit against public participation. With the climate movement becoming ever more effective, such action is now increasingly employed by corporations, conservative politicians and others to silence environmental groups or individuals within them. In 2016, for instance, campaigners who accused ExxonMobil of concealing its knowledge of climate risks were warned by the company that they should ensure they retained all communications on the issue (D'Angelo, 2016). The corporation was in the midst of a legal battle with a number of US state attorney generals investigating the allegation, and it suggested NGOs might also be taken to court in connection with the controversy (Sheppard, 2016).

Moreover, these labels have effects, with politicians and media buying into the language and associated myths of 'dangerous environmentalists'. For example, counter-terrorism police in the UK listed Extinction Rebellion as an 'extremist ideology' in a guide 'aimed at police officers, government organisations and teachers, who by law have to report concerns about radicalisation' (Dodd & Grierson, 2020). Such polarisation works even if one disagrees with it: after all, anyone who needs to deny being a 'terrorist' is still associated with the designation.

The efficacy of such tactics can be seen in the example of Energy Transfer, the company that built the Dakota Access Pipeline, in its lengthy battle with environmentalists and others opposing the project. The company hired TigerSwan, a private security firm, to guard the pipeline during construction. In 2017, detailing its strategy in a report to Energy Transfer, the company explained: 'Our concentrated focus is the massing of intelligence (digital and ground) to find, fix and eliminate one person from the "detachment" who will lead us to the arrest and conviction of the remainder of these terrorists' (TigerSwan, 2017).

This accusation of terrorism was reinforced in comments from Energy Transfer officials. Later in 2017, in testimony to the US House Energy and Commerce Committee Subcommittee on Energy, the company's executive vice-president, Joey Mahmoud, said: 'The protest movement induced individuals to break into and shut down pump stations on four operational pipelines. Had these actions been undertaken by foreign nationals, they could only be described *as acts of terrorism*' (Mahmoud, 2017, our emphasis). Energy Transfer also took Greenpeace to court, accusing it of committing 'acts of terrorism that violate the US Patriot Act' and branding its members 'violent eco-terrorist infiltrators' (United States District Court – District of North Dakota, 2018: 2 & 3).

The politics here is once again obvious: it is a case of demonising the Other. This type of framing clearly differentiates environmental activists from the interests of society (Potter, 2011). The references to 'foreign nationals', 'infiltrators' and patriotism infer a violation of 'good citizenship' – a categorisation that has long been used to draw boundaries around rights and exclusions. The depiction of environmentalists as working outside of the bounds of citizenship has two key impacts: one, that environmentalists have given up their democratic right to participate in public discourse and two, that their actions justify state intervention in preventing this participation (Irwin et al., 2022).

That state bodies – police, the courts, military, politicians – feature so heavily in reinforcing the power of corporations highlights an alignment between state priorities and that of the corporations. It also suggests that there are concerns that environmentalists are being effective. By bringing climate change to the forefront of public conversation, environmentalists are not only asking governments to take action on the issue; they are challenging what it means to be a citizen and attempting to give voice to what has so far, if not silenced, been obscured: the impacts of resource use.

4.7 Borders and Exclusions

By targeting environmentalists as extremists and terrorists, corporations aim to deflect attention from the damage caused by their own activities. As part of the active construction of what is legitimate and what is not, the dependence of capital on the exploitation of the environment – or 'natural resources' – has long been part of defending the nation state. Climate change, on the other hand, does not conform to such boundaries. By showing the contradiction between the construction of the nation state, economic growth, and environmental damage, environmentalists are aligning themselves with that other Other, what is, if rather unsatisfactorily, known as 'the environment'.

There are two ways in which capitalism primarily accounts for 'the environment'. The environmental damage that is not attached to an economic cost is classified as an 'externality', an unfortunate outcome of the necessary process of economic accumulation. Beyond the utility of resources, the environment is therefore excluded from consideration of the needs of society. It is only visible when there is an economic cost attached – for example, in the case of a price on carbon, or having to pay for offsets for greenhouse gas emissions – it becomes 'natural capital' (Hawken et al., 1999). Yet this, of course, transforms the environment from having any status in its own right into a commodity. In both formulations, environmental damage is to be contained.

By making visible the environmental damage wrought by climate change, environmentalists are seeking to include that which has already been excluded from the ordinary workings of capital. It is of note that the Fridays for Future protestors themselves emphasise that they are markers of the environmental damage being wrought (Nyberg et al., 2022). As Boykoff (2011) has noted, these are the very kinds of evocations that the industry and its supporters have tried to evade for so long – no one is supposed to 'speak' for the climate yet alone identify as part of the issue.

The disruption to infrastructure by grassroots activists poses a further – unacceptable – incursion into the status quo. As argued by Crosby (2021), the policing of Canadian fossil fuel infrastructure and the framing of activists as threats to it are intimately linked to the dependence of the state on unfettered economic growth. Indeed, the reliance of the state is much stronger than corporations; capital is mobile, while state power is much less so. In Crosby's study, indigenous communities blocking oil and gas projects emphasised not only the dependence of the state in controlling infrastructure but also the ways in which this control aligned with legitimising occupation of the land.

The intersections between the fossil fuel industry and state power show that the exclusion of environmentalists' critique is shaped in particular ways; if it can be incorporated, or even lowered to a level at which it is not challenging to the status quo (campaigns which utilise the systems of law, or purely promote renewables, for instance), it is part of healthy democratic debate. However, those that reveal the contradiction that is the fragilities in the ongoing growth of the economic system must be excluded, as they are operating from outside of the acceptable parameters.

4.8 Beyond the 'Win-Win'

As we have outlined in this chapter, an emphasis on some of the more spectacular actions of environmentalists is often used to suggest they are breaking the social contract of democratic engagement – while companies, by stark contrast, are depicted as good corporate citizens. This is how the hegemony erects a patent political frontier between 'us', in the form of law-abiding businesses that promote prosperity, and 'them', in the form of environmentalists and 'greenies' who threaten to destroy it all.

This, we argue, suggests that the dominant narrative that corporate capitalism can deal with climate change is coming under ever-intensifying pressure. The situation is even worse for those who specifically support fossil fuels, as evidenced by their increasingly desperate attempts to reinforce old energy solutions while at the same time advocating new yet unproven technologies.

Along with mainstream politicians, the fossil fuel industry continues to defend the status quo through appeals to the possibility of decoupling fossil fuel use and economic growth. Even so, there is little doubt that the 'win-win' outcomes promised by the proponents of ecological modernisation maintain some currency in both the environmental and broader political spheres.

This can be seen in the awarding of the Nobel Prize in Economic Sciences to William Nordhaus, who was honoured 'for integrating climate change into long-run macroeconomic analysis' (Nobel Prize, 2018). It was widely reported that recognition of his work, which illustrates the relationship between economic growth and climate change, could signal a new willingness to take climate change seriously in corporate and political circles, yet such optimism overlooked Nordhaus's own view. Nordhaus has suggested the positive relationship between growth and climate change means we should *minimise* economic impact by accepting average global warming of as much as 3.5°C – a stance significantly at odds with the IPCC's warning that anything beyond 1.5°C is likely to be catastrophic (Hickel, 2018; see also Fremstad et al., 2019 for a discussion of this). Nordhaus might not be doing humanity or the environment a favour with such an argument. However, by default, he is also underlining a message the more radical environmental movements have been fighting to get across for some time: there really is no 'win-win' scenario here because this is ultimately a question of capitalism versus the climate.

Having emerged only recently, the more radical mobilisations for climate action understand and respect this contradiction. As a consequence, one of their advantages is that – unlike many of the

established groups that preceded them – these new critics have no
incentive to succumb to the interests of corporate and industry funding.

They still have vulnerabilities, of course, as shown by Extinction
Rebellion's internal struggles. These have included questions about its
interaction with young people, claims of a race problem and disagree-
ments on how much it should look towards politics. The group has
been accused of being 'partly incoherent, naive or myopic' and participating in the 'depoliticisation' of climate politics because of its
emphasis on moral action (Slaven & Heydon, 2020: 59).

Fridays for Future and others have faced similar accusations, but this
is in many ways to be expected. By participating in the climate change
debate, these groups are *inherently* engaging in politics. In the final
reckoning, by building new communities of action, they are challenging
citizens around the world to fundamentally rethink their everyday
practices and become politically active.

PART III

The Politics of Climate Adaptation

5 | Climate Adaptation and the Maintenance of Corporate Hegemony

Insurance is a capitalist system, by and large, with for-profit companies . . . So they're always going to try to compete with each other and offer enhanced value to their higher-end customers who will pay the higher prices

US insurance industry spokesperson (quoted in Smiley, 2018).

The wildfires that swept across Northern California in late 2017 began in early October. They would come to be known by several names, including the North Bay Fires and the Wine Country Fires. As they took hold, attorney and tech entrepreneur Ronald DeKoven and his wife fled their estate to spend a night in a hotel. Their insurance company quickly organised a specialist crew to protect their property from the approaching inferno. It also paid for their evening at the Four Seasons and for a subsequent three weeks spent in San Francisco. Later, in readiness for their return, it funded an air-filtering process to remove the smell of smoke from the couple's home and spent US$50,000 on insulation replacement. DeKoven was impressed: at least on this occasion, the cost of wildfire insurance had been worthwhile. The fires ultimately killed 47 people and burnt a record-breaking 1,548,429 acres of land. Another wave of blazes the following year proved even more destructive. Such incidents have prompted the introduction of a variety of high-net-worth insurance products from companies including AIG, Chubb, Pure and Nationwide Private Client; meanwhile, for those unable to afford such extravagance, average insurance policies in vulnerable areas have skyrocketed.

While corporations are finding ever more creative ways to accumulate capital, human-induced climate disruption is wreaking havoc around the world. A perturbing procession of extreme weather events – including heatwaves, droughts, wildfires, storms and floods – now regularly features in global newsfeeds.

These incidents highlight underlying shifts in our planetary ecosystems. They represent the undeniable evidence of two centuries of rapidly increasing greenhouse gas emissions. They show it is now too late to avoid climate change, the devastating impacts of which are all too evident. They make clear that the biophysical materiality of the phenomenon should be viewed as a major counterpoint to the hegemony of corporate capitalism, fossil energy and infinite economic growth.

Climate change has already undone many of the comfortable assumptions of humanity's separation from nature. This fundamentally challenges the notion of functioning ecosystems as immutable entities that can be relied on irrespective of extraction and pollution. The multifaceted disruption of the atmosphere, the biosphere, the hydrosphere, the lithosphere and the cryosphere is now having a devastating effect on societies and communities, demanding fundamental shifts in human and social behaviour and prompting growing critique of what has come to be regarded as 'the natural order'.

However, adapting to the impacts of climate change is far from an objective, rational project of democratic deliberation. In fact, as we discuss in this chapter, it is deeply ingrained in the political process of late capitalism – in which vested interests, secure in their unparalleled wealth and power, have an outsized influence on the critical decisions societies will make about how best to address the challenges of an increasingly hot, unstable and inhospitable planet.

We begin the analysis that follows by outlining current and near-future climate impacts in a range of contexts. We explain why they pose clear dangers and explore why they threaten established ideas about social and economic progress. We then consider how the world of business engages with adaptation. We reflect on how companies and industries are exposed to different climate impacts and why adaptation exists within a short-term agenda of risk minimisation. We argue that many firm-level interventions ignore broader social and ecological contexts that are critical to business viability; we also show that some responses can provide new spaces for activity and profit-making.

We next unpack how concerns such as business and profit-making are framed as central to adaptation and how the promotion of discourses of 'resilience' and 'solutions' reinforces a continuation of business-as-usual models. We outline how, in keeping with the endless accumulation of capital as the dominant economic system, adaptation responses are driven by and directed for corporate profit.

Finally, we look to the near future and consider some of the technological responses now being championed by corporations and national governments. These include nascent attempts to geo-engineer the planet in order to perpetuate fossil energy use and economic growth. Tellingly, among the more remarkable propositions – perhaps not without a measure of perverse reason – is the prospect of one day escaping our world before it is utterly destroyed by the path corporate hegemony appears determined to maintain.

5.1 Climate Impacts and Climate Adaptation

The disturbing evidence of climate change is amassing at pace (IPCC, 2021). As the crisis continues to worsen, we are paying an ever-higher price for more than 200 years of carbon-intensive industrialisation. Heatwaves, wildfires, droughts, storms, accelerated sea-level rises and the melting of glaciers and ice shelves now routinely feature among a range of devastating impacts (IPCC, 2021). As outlined in Table 5.1, the impacts of climate change are extensive in their implications for the future of organised human civilisation and much of life on the planet over coming decades.

For example, the number of warmer-than-average or extremely hot days in both the northern and southern hemispheres is increasing (von Schuckmann et al., 2020). The Middle East suffered its hottest-ever summer in 2020, resulting in significant suffering and mass-mortality events (Vicedo-Cabrera et al., 2021). The west coast of the US and Canada sweltered under a 'heat dome' in June and July 2021, with several days of temperatures in excess of 45°C – including an unprecedented 54.4°C in Death Valley (Samenow, 2021). It has been suggested that by the end of this century large parts of the planet could be 'too hot and humid for human thermoregulation' (Matthews, 2018: 391).

Record-breaking droughts have also affected regions of North and South America, Africa, the Middle East, India, China and Australia. A graphic example of human society's vulnerability to such events was the 'Day Zero' water crisis that hit the South African city of Cape Town in early 2018, when a modern metropolis of four million people came perilously close to running out of drinkable water (Pascale et al., 2020). Researchers have warned such events are likely to increase in the

Table 5.1 *Examples of key climate change impacts*

Impacts	Implications	Examples
Increasing global temperatures	Worsening heatwaves with record daily temperatures in excess of 45°C.	Nineteen of the twenty hottest years on record have occurred since 2002 (NASA, 2021). Ten national temperature records broken or equalled in 2021, including the highest ever reliably measured on Earth (54.4°C in Death Valley, California; van der Zee, 2022).
Ocean warming and acidification	Thermal expansion of oceans is the major driver of sea-level rise. Oceans on average 30 per cent more acidic than before industrial revolution.	Oceans absorbing more than 90 per cent of excess heat generated by GHG emissions. Half of the increase in global ocean heat content since 1960 has occurred in the last twenty years (Cheng et al., 2020).
Rising sea surface temperatures	Major driver of increasingly intense hurricanes, typhoons and cyclones. Coral bleaching events increasing in frequency and severity.	Both Hurricanes Harvey (2017) and Ida (2021) fuelled by summer Gulf of Mexico water temperatures 4°C hotter than normal (Anderson, 2021). Loss of half of the coral on Great Barrier Reef as a result of 2016/2017 and 2020 bleaching events (Readfearn, 2020).
Warmer air holds more water vapour	Increasingly intense rainfall and flooding events. Disruption to supply chains and urban centres.	Extreme rainfall events now occurring four times more frequently than in 1980 (Neslen, 2018). Record-breaking floods in 2021 in the Americas, Europe, Asia and Australia.

Extra heat resulting in reduced soil moisture and drought	Prolonged hydrological drought events. Threats to food and agricultural production.	Over 90 per cent of the US southwest experiencing moderate to exceptional drought. Brazil experiencing the worst drought in ninety years (Andreoni & Londoño, 2021).
Record temperatures driving wildfires	Wildfires are becoming larger and more intense and burning hotter and longer than previously. Longer lasting fire seasons.	Record-breaking wildfires on the US west coast and throughout Europe and Russia during 2021 summer. Australian 'Black Summer' 2019/2020 largest fire event in the country's recorded history (Gutiérrez et al., 2021).
Melting snowpacks and glaciers	Growing water scarcity.	Himalayan glaciers provide water to one quarter of the world's population. Between one- and two-thirds of these glaciers are projected to melt by the end of the century (Schultz & Sharma, 2019).
Equatorial zones experiencing 'unlivable' heat, failing agricultural production and water shortages	Mass migration of populations, 'failed' states, political instability and military conflict.	Refugee crisis in Europe in 2015 following the Arab Awakening and conflict in the Middle East. Climate pressures have been argued to have exacerbated these conflicts (Femia & Werrell, 2013).
Melting Arctic and thawing permafrost	Changes to the jet stream and 'stalled' heatwaves and cold fronts. Reduced albedo effect and further warming of oceans.	Texas 'Big Freeze' in February 2021 due to shifting polar vortex, 4 million people without power (Flavelle et al., 2021). Arctic transitioning from a carbon sink to a net carbon emitter.

Table 5.1 (*cont.*)

Impacts	Implications	Examples
Greenland and West Antarctic ice sheet and glacier melt	Major contributors to accelerating sea-level rise potentially several metres this century threatening major coastal cities.	Ice shelf holding back the Thwaites Glacier in the West Antarctic (the 'Doomsday Glacier') likely to melt within decades contributing to significant sea-level rise (Voosen, 2021).
Health impacts of warming planet	Spread of infectious and insect-borne diseases to warmer and wetter geographic zones.	Increase in vector-borne diseases such as malaria, dengue fever, Nile fever and Lyme disease, schistosomiasis, leishmaniasis, Chagas disease and yellow fever as global climate warms (Campbell-Lendrum et al., 2015).

decades ahead as climate change intensifies, threatening the viability of agricultural production and human settlement in different geographies (Mukherjee et al., 2018).

Similarly, wildfires have become larger and more severe (Williams et al., 2019). During Australia's 'Black Summer' of 2019 and 2020, for instance, much of the south-east coast was caught up in huge blazes that burned 1.8 million hectares of forest, killed or injured approximately 3 billion animals and destroyed around 3,000 homes (Celermajer et al., 2021). Some researchers have posited that we now live in the so-called 'Pyrocene' – the age of fire (Pyne, 2020).

The world is also experiencing worsening storms. This is because much of the escalating heat energy is absorbed by oceans, feeding more moisture into the atmosphere and supercharging weather events of increasing scale and ferocity (Gleckler et al., 2016). These new 'super-storms' – such as Typhoon Haiyan, which devastated the Philippines in 2013 (Schiermeier, 2013), or the procession of hurricanes that have struck Caribbean nations and the southern US in recent years – have resulted not only in windborne destruction but catastrophic flooding (Trenberth et al., 2018; Marsooli et al., 2019), as illustrated by the massive property damage and loss of life seen amid floods in Europe and Asia during the summer of 2021 (Cornwall, 2021; Ni & Davidson, 2021).

Climate change is also driving more fundamental long-term shifts, such as the accelerated sea-level rise brought about by the melting of glaciers and ice shelves and the thermal expansion of oceans (Wu et al., 2016; Bamber et al., 2019). It is this last impact that is perhaps the most significant for climate adaptation, given that around 700 million people worldwide currently live in coastal areas vulnerable to rising ocean waters and more devastating storms – and that this number is estimated to reach a billion by the middle of the century (Goodell, 2017). The areas most at risk include countries such as Bangladesh; major coastal cities such as Miami, New York, Shanghai, Mumbai and Jakarta; and low-lying island nations such as the Maldives, the Seychelles and many South Pacific communities (Kulp & Strauss, 2019). Cities in more wealthy economies might be able to invest in 'hard', engineering-led responses; but such options, which are hugely expensive, are unlikely to be available to the tens of millions of people living in less affluent circumstances.

In the face of these profound impacts, there is a critical need to adapt existing ways of life in order to reduce the harm resulting from climate change (IPCC, 2014). Broadly speaking, adaptation activities fall into one of two camps: reactive measures, which respond to changes already experienced (e.g., farmers refining their irrigation methods in light of drought or warmer weather), and proactive measures, which seek to anticipate future or projected changes (e.g., constructing sea walls or implementing managed retreat from areas threatened by sea-level rise).

In practice, adaptation can involve a wide range of interventions. These might include the regeneration of mangroves, forests and other natural ecosystems; heat-proofing, fire-proofing, coastal defences and other examples of urban and infrastructure redesign; the deployment of new technologies, such as desalination plants to improve freshwater availability or the genetic engineering of drought-resistant crops; hazard mapping, disaster education and other means of enhancing community preparedness and the updating of planning and policy at local and national government levels (Berrang-Ford et al., 2011; Sovacool & Linnér, 2016).

In designing adaptation measures, researchers have emphasised how the harm from climate change can vary significantly from one community to another. This depends on a specific community's physical and social vulnerability, its adaptive capacity and its resilience. To put it another way: different communities will be exposed to different types and scales of impact, and their ability to avoid and/or recover from them will be determined by social and economic development levels (Adger et al., 2009). For instance, those with high poverty and poor governance are likely to be far more vulnerable than those with significant economic resources and good infrastructure.

However, as recent extreme weather events such as the heatwaves, fires and hurricanes affecting the US have illustrated, even the most prosperous economies sometimes struggle to respond to worsening climate impacts. This demonstrates that even substantial adaptive capacity is no guarantee of resilience. Underlying this problem is the fact that much of modern life, especially in the Global North, has been designed for a physical world that no longer exists.

A vital lesson of adaptation is therefore that pretty much *everything* will need to change. Energy sources, food and water systems, transport, the built environment, education, health, finance, considerations of national security, geopolitical dimensions, even understandings of economics and governance – nothing can stay the same. Moreover, adaptation is not simply a question of technocratic and politically neutral responses: it is a process of decision-making and action – one that reflects existing power dynamics and deeply unequal socio-economic relations (Eriksen et al., 2015; Sovacool & Linnér, 2016).

It is somewhat surprising then that, despite growing public and political awareness of the climate crisis, adaptation remains limited. It is still largely focused on responses to past events and delegated to local communities (Wise et al., 2014). For instance, a recent United Nations Environment Programme (UNEP) report found many countries are now devoting more resources to adaptation planning; but it also warned financial commitments to realise these plans, particularly in poorer countries that are least responsible for climate change, are insufficient and failing to keep pace with rapidly increasing costs (UNEP, 2021).

5.2 Business, Risk and Climate Adaptation

Corporations are key actors in how climate adaptation is framed and enacted. Research has shown how these businesses make sense of climate change principally in terms of risk and opportunity (Nyberg & Wright, 2016). Beyond the regulatory and reputational risks that exist around climate mitigation and efforts to reduce carbon emissions, businesses are also exposed to significant physical and market risks in their ability to adapt to current and future climate impacts.

For instance, energy utilities now need to plan for hotter summers, droughts and wildfires, all of which can place additional demands on peak power generation and threaten power plants and distribution networks (IEA, 2015). Tour operators have to reckon with declining snowfall, shorter seasons and other new realities (Steiger et al., 2019). Mining and resource companies have to plan for storms of intensifying ferocity and flood events that exceed previous experience (Odell et al., 2018).

Climate impacts also pose a threat to global supply chains, which, as has been shown throughout the current pandemic, are closely integrated, especially time-sensitive and notably exposed to disruption. For example, the Thailand mega-flood of 2011 – which lasted for months and shut down major industrial and distribution hubs in Bangkok – was estimated to have been one of the world's costliest natural disasters, resulting in losses of more than US$44 billion across global automotive and electronics supply chains (World Bank, 2012; Haraguchi & Lall, 2015). The Texas 'big freeze' of February 2021 halted oil and chemical production and critically damaged the US's semiconductor manufacturing, which in turn contributed to disruptions to automotive and computer industries worldwide (Flavelle et al., 2021).

Considering its business model, it is perhaps not surprising that the reinsurance industry has been paying close attention to climate change's ever-greater impacts. The likes of SwissRe and MunichRe are now heavily promoting the need for companies and governments to focus on the physical and financial risks to which global warming is increasingly giving rise (Collier et al., 2021).

One way in which corporate climate adaptation has been conceptualised is to compare it with how natural ecosystems respond to disruption: an adaptive cycle of growth, contraction, decline and reorganisation (Linnenluecke & Griffiths, 2010; Clément & Rivera, 2017). Through this lens, companies are seen as reacting to climate shocks by implementing protective measures aimed at preserving existing business models; these measures can then transition into more transformative changes – such as moving facilities to less physically vulnerable locations, diversifying operations or switching to entirely different business activities – as climate impacts worsen. Examples include winemakers relocating to cooler areas to maintain production and ski resorts reinventing themselves as seasonal tourist destinations.

Although such approaches assume a relatively unproblematic process of identification and response to climate change's effects, adaptation has not been a strategic priority for most firms. Research has highlighted senior managers' lack of awareness of potential vulnerabilities, with corporations often adjusting their operational activities only after a specific weather-related disruption has caught them by surprise (Haigh & Griffiths, 2012; Pinkse & Gasbarro, 2019).

The general assumption is that a company or an industry can somehow plough on with existing strategies. For instance, a review of corporate disclosures around climate adaptation found more than 60 per cent of reported activity focused on 'soft' measures – for example, risk planning, research and monitoring – aimed at maintaining business operations in the face of disruption (Goldstein et al., 2019). Around 30 per cent focused on 'hard' measures, including investments in new technologies and infrastructure. Examples included mining and energy companies retrofitting buildings and mines for more extreme storms and floods, agricultural producers and wineries implementing new forms of irrigation and water capture for worsening droughts and developers and architects designing more weather and fire resilient buildings. However, far less common – accounting for only around 2 per cent of reported activity – are investments in adaptation measures that extend beyond a firm to encompass broader communities and ecosystems (Nalau et al., 2018). Where they do exist, examples of this more extensive form of adaptation tend to focus on the corporate promotion of a so-called 'shared value' approach – as seen, for instance, in food company Nestlé's education programme for growers of coffee and cocoa in developing economies and investment in agroforestry (Nestlé, 2017).

As outlined in Table 5.2, much corporate attention to climate adaptation remains centred on a firm's operational orbit. Responses are often short term in outlook and usually entail relatively little interaction with external stakeholders. In addition, an emphasis on what is depicted as business resilience tends to ignore the scale of the commitments that deteriorating climate impacts necessitate. Multinational corporations may well be able to relocate to less risky parts of the world, but they consistently ignore the importance and urgency of a more fundamental transformation of economic relations. Much like the response to emissions mitigation, in adapting to climate change, corporations generally rely upon minor changes to existing business operations, push back against any significant alterations to their business models and assume that current practices can continue irrespective of external climatic shifts.

5.3 Putting Business in the Driver's Seat

Corporate adaptation to climate change has also shaped the political debate over how to respond to the world's ever-worsening environmental crisis. For instance, governments and media regularly promote companies as leaders in the race to adapt, thereby shoring up the hegemony of corporate capitalism by ensuring public discourse is replete with prevailing assumptions of the business sphere's infinite capacity for innovation, efficiency and self-regulation.

Table 5.2 *Examples of corporate climate adaptation*

Company (Industry)	Headquarters	Example
Accenture (management consulting)	Ireland	'While we lease nearly all our locations, business continuity and disaster recovery planning are critical. We know to anticipate these events our Global Asset Protection team focuses on the safety and security of our people, and recently we enhanced our technology to notify our people of risks in their vicinity … Our Business Resilience Services team proactively builds resilience into our client delivery in anticipation of disruptions'.
Allianz (insurance)	Germany	'We are using special modelling techniques for natural catastrophes which combine portfolio data (geographic location, characteristics of insured objects and their values) with simulated natural disaster scenarios to estimate the magnitude and frequency of potential losses … The results provide the basis for group-wide risk-monitoring, risk limits and subsequent business decisions'.
BHP Billiton (resources)	Australia/UK	'An example is provided by our Petroleum business, which has specifically designed severe weather mitigation systems for Floating Production and Storage Offtake vessels (FPSOs). Although the FPSOs are connected to subsea oil and gas infra-structure, they have the capability to disconnect from this infrastructure and can sail away from impending cyclonic or extreme weather events'.
Maersk (freight transport)	Denmark	'To understand and plan for protecting business value from the risks caused by the physical impacts of climate change, we conducted a hot-spot analysis in 2018, estimating the effect of five climate hazards on ports, other fixed assets and strategic commodities within a 2020–2040 timeframe. The five hazards are heat stress, floods, cyclones, water stress and sea-level rise'.

Nestlé (food)	Switzerland	'Farmer Connect is our sourcing programme for working directly with farmers to identify local farming issues … Through Farmer Connect we identify and prioritise issues through a materiality assessment. This helps to define and articulate long-term sustainability goals and outcomes; measure ongoing progress toward short- and medium-term milestones; question any assumptions we have made in defining our goals; and identify and mitigate physical and reputational risks'.
Tesco (grocery retail)	UK	'Growing public concern for the environment is expected to drive a shift in demand from animal-based to plant-based proteins. Research conducted in 2020 found that 70% of Tesco customers are actively trying to reduce their intake of meat, while 80% want supermarkets to do more to help, including offering healthier and more sustainable options. We are adapting our product portfolio accordingly'.

Source: Carbon Disclosure Project (2020), various disclosures, www.cdp.net/en; corporate websites.

As part of the broader neoliberal ideology in which governments become the handmaidens of corporations and markets, the government response to crisis invariably champions business solutions. Through the public funding of private-sector adaptation initiatives, corporations are portrayed as saviours capable of resisting climate change's ravages. In tandem, corporate environmentalism is presented as the best vehicle for boosting social and ecological resilience. This allows governments – many of which are subject to increasing public criticism over the climate crisis – to claim they are 'taking action'.

Consider, for example, the response to the unprecedented coral-bleaching events on the Great Barrier Reef. These climate-induced events during the summers of 2016 and 2017 resulted in the loss of up to half of the Reef's coral and generated widespread media attention (Wright & Nyberg, 2022). In response to growing public concern, in mid-2018 the Australian government provided a grant of AU\$440 million to a private corporate charity, the Great Barrier Reef Foundation, which had been established by the executives of some of the country's largest companies – including major carbon emitters such as BHP Billiton, Rio Tinto, Orica, Boeing and Qantas. The Foundation largely focused on hosting corporate retreats at luxury reef resorts (Ludlow, 2018) and employee-engagement programmes. It also set up a website to promote its conservation projects. As its strategy document outlined, donations could help corporations 'position [them-selves] as an employer of choice and contribute positively to reputation scoring or social licence to operate' (Smee, 2018).

Qantas's alliance with Disney offered an example of this thinking in action. Framing its efforts around hit animated movie *Finding Dory*, Australia's national airline drew on its association with the global entertainment giant to showcase its involvement in reef rehabilitation for customers (Frame, 2016). Environmentalism thus found itself justi-fied on the basis of essentially economic logic. In 2017, in a widely reported analysis commissioned by the Foundation, Deloitte estimated the 'economic, social, icon and brand value' of the Reef at AU\$56 billion. It said the Reef generated AU\$6.5 billion in revenue per annum and provided up to 64,000 jobs in tourism, fishing and associated activities (Deloitte Access Economics, 2017). The monetisa-tion of the Reef in the language of the market validated further business involvement – albeit in the form of underwater fans, coral farming and other small-scale measures that neatly skirted around the urgency of radical cuts in greenhouse gas emissions and the end of fossil fuel extraction and use.

Here, by focusing on the discourse of adaptation and resilience, the contradiction between fossil energy and climate change was avoided – and the hegemonic order was reinforced. Moreover, this by no means constitutes an isolated example: major corporations are repeatedly touted as the key suppliers of different adaptation responses, often underpinned by public financing.

The focus on building greater resilience in the world's biggest cities, for instance, has become an area of particular attention for the engineering and consultancy industries. Firms such as Arup and McKinsey & Company have partnered both with governments and with networks such as the C40 Cities Group to promote the merits of business innovation in helping cities adapt through improved risk-planning measures and hazard-specific actions to reduce the impacts of extreme weather events (Arup & C40 Cities, 2015; McKinsey Sustainability & C40 Cities, 2021). Projects in this space consistently depict property, engineering and finance corporations as key agents in the design and implementation of solutions.

However, this largely normative focus on developing 'climate resilience' ignores existing social and economic inequalities within cities. More specifically, it overlooks the ways in which those with power and resources decide which locations and communities are most vulnerable and the types of response that demand investment. Low-income areas at the mercy of extreme weather events such as flooding may be deemed not worth saving, while more prosperous locations or financial districts may be chosen for costly engineered protection. As Vale (2014: 196) has argued, the concept of resilience seems 'destined to be no more than an optimistic gloss on glaringly persistent inequalities, a "feel-good" phraseology that covers up its differential impacts and ignores its failure to help those who most need assistance'.

These corporate-friendly variants of adaptation have also resulted in a form of 'disaster capitalism', through which businesses can exploit crises as opportunities to impose profit-maximising policies that ultimately further degrade the status of vulnerable communities (Klein, 2007, 2014). Such a process could be seen in Puerto Rico in the aftermath of Hurricane Maria, a record-breaking Category 5 storm that destroyed much of the Caribbean archipelago's infrastructure and left a population of more than 3 million without power, water and communication for months. The devastation was exacerbated by delays, a paucity of coordination in reconstruction efforts and a reliance on private contractors seeking to cash in on the catastrophe. Beyond the initial death toll, an additional 3,000 people were estimated to have died in the months after the storm resulting from a lack of electricity, food, sanitation and health services. Remember, too, that Puerto Rico had already been weakened by decades of internationally forced austerity and US control. As if for good measure, the response to the disaster – both from the US and local government – doubled down on prior efforts to reduce public provision of basic services while endorsing the country as a hub for corporate tax avoidance and cryptocurrency speculators (García-López, 2018; Klein, 2018).

The promotion of business-led climate adaptation glosses over the fact that the prime objective of a corporation, despite recent patronising claims to the contrary, is to maximise shareholder value and profit. This goal goes above and beyond any social or environmental concern. The privatisation of adaptation is therefore leading to an increase in corporate control over public assets and the marginalisation of community and civic interests in decision-making, as well as growing social and economic inequality and environmental harm (Sovacool & Linnér, 2016). Meanwhile, the emphasis on resilience relentlessly and unrealistically assumes an ability to maintain or return to 'business as usual' in the face of unprecedented disruption and shocks.

5.4 Show Me the Money!

Adaptation to the prospect of environmental ruin often focuses on minimising risk. As the hoary investment adage has it, however, risk and opportunity invariably go hand in hand. It should come then as little or no surprise that businesses and industries are increasingly projecting upside opportunities in a climate-ravaged world. For instance, biotech and pharmaceutical companies such as CSL and Merck anticipate growing demand for their products as a consequence of the new disease vectors climate change will bring. Engineering contractor Downer EDI foresees a future of worsening storms and severe floods that will create new markets for disaster recovery. Water and waste business Veolia expects the market for desalination plants to expand as water supplies become more uncertain. Home Depot knows warming temperatures will boost the need for air-conditioning systems and ceiling fans (Carbon Disclosure Project, 2020).

Engineering and construction corporations perhaps have even more reason to be perversely optimistic, with a climate-challenged future offering them the possibility of large adaptation projects focused on safeguarding coastal cities from rising oceans (Sterling, 2015), or even more fanciful proposals to slowdown the relentless march of melting glaciers (Meyer, 2018). In the sphere of food production, meanwhile, a drier and hotter planet portends investments in new farmland in parts of the world once considered too cold for viable production, as well as biotechnology and genetic modification of agricultural crops (Karavolias et al., 2021).

Maybe nowhere have the business opportunities of climate change been more apparent than in the Arctic, where global warming has brought a dramatic reduction in sea ice and the ice shelves and glaciers of Greenland. For oil and gas companies, which have been significant contributors to this phenomenon, thinning ice opens up new terrain to explore and drill for massive reserves of hydrocarbon energy. As environmental campaigner Bill McKibben has noted: 'The grand irony, of course, is that, having watched the Arctic melt as global temperatures rose, Shell was first in line to drill the newly melted waters for yet more oil, which would raise the temperature some more' (McKibben et al., 2015). Supported by their respective governments, the likes of Shell, Gazprom, Novatek and Rosneft are competing for the Arctic's more accessible areas as its ice vanishes (Mower & Bradner, 2020; Farand, 2021). Other industries are also circling. Shipping companies are anticipating the opening of the once-frozen Northwest Passage, a would-be trade route that could serve as an alternative to the Panama Canal. Mining firms are planning for new mineral-extracting operations. Fishing fleets are chasing stocks north as the oceans continue to warm (Funk, 2014; Bourne, 2016).

Similarly, in Russia – one of the world's biggest petrostates – climate change is politically framed as a positive, with global warming seen as a way of opening up the former Siberian tundra to huge agricultural expansion (Lustgarten, 2020). As a spokesman for the Russian government declared: 'Global warming is not as catastrophic for us as it might be for some other countries. If anything, we'll be even better off. As the climate warms, more of Russia's territory will be freed up for agriculture and industry' (Savodnik, 2009).

Conscious of such business opportunities, the world's leading resource companies are actively promoting technology agnosticism and adaptation towards new alternative energy production. While there is recognition of the need to acknowledge growing public concern over the climate crisis and to strengthen legal and regulatory restrictions, oil and gas are still championed as key energy sources. Much as BP, more than a decade ago sought to rebrand itself as 'Beyond Petroleum' (Beder, 2002), oil and gas corporations are well aware of the need to reshape perceptions and package themselves as 'energy' companies innovating for a low-carbon future, in which new expansions are presented as necessary adaptations to a changing world. This corporate storytelling frames the fate of our environment around the centrality of capitalism, technological innovation and business growth in newly accessible parts of the world.

Beyond the PR, the sheer size and vast resources of these mega-corporations suggest an ability to acquire and diversify operations if circumstances should require. Indeed, despite the corporate rhetoric of 'shared value' and 'corporate environmentalism', the aforementioned examples suggest multinational corporations are actively anticipating an ability to avoid the physical impacts of a changing climate and seize new opportunities through their ability to transition and move operations to new locations. Such 'footloose' globalised capital underpins the way in which corporations are often separated from the spatial manifestations of a worsening climate crisis. While local communities in different parts of the world are exposed to worsening climate impacts, corporate leaders in distant headquarters scan the globe for new sources of value creation. Corporate climate adaptation is thus underpinned by the advanced mobility of capital in an increasingly uncertain and rapidly changing world. This stands in contrast to the affected communities and people who remain trapped within the 'sacrifice zones' of degraded and increasingly vulnerable environments. For the world's major companies, adapting to climate change ultimately involves a capacity for pragmatic reinvention in the drive to capture new markets and profitable opportunities. Ultimately, this is a scramble to realign interests and maintain a hegemonic position.

5.5 The Corporate Adaptation of the Planet – and Beyond

Climate adaptation perhaps finds its penultimate expression in proposals to re-engineer the atmosphere. Within a context of rapidly worsening impacts and the likelihood that attempts to reduce emissions will fail, some of the world's richest and most famous business leaders have advocated radical ideas for the redesigning of our planet. Their fundamental aim, it seems, is to accommodate the continued expansion of the global economy and corporate power. Suggestions include deliberate 'geo-engineering' interventions in the climate system to change the Earth's energy balance and reduce temperatures.

More than a decade ago, in a founding report by the Royal Society (2009), geo-engineering was separated into two distinct approaches – the first of which, carbon dioxide removal (CDR), seeks to capture CO_2 and remove it from the atmosphere. This process involves reforestation or ocean fertilisation to sequester carbon in natural cycles, as well as more technologically advanced procedures such as carbon capture and storage (CCS) at power plants through the use of filters and the sequestration of emissions in deep geological strata. Recent years have also seen the emergence of businesses promoting pilot technologies for the direct air capture (DAC) of carbon dioxide, which could then be geo-sequestered or used either in industrial processes or in the production of methane and other fuels (Hanna et al., 2021).

The second variety of geo-engineering, solar radiation management (SRM), does not focus on the rising concentration of carbon in the atmosphere: it instead bids to offset the effects of increasing greenhouse gas emissions by altering the way in which the Earth absorbs solar radiation (Royal Society, 2009). This could involve efforts to reflect radiation back into space through the injection of sulphur or calcium carbonate particles into the stratosphere – so-called stratospheric aerosol injection – or augmenting the albedo effect of clouds through cloud-brightening technology or by using white roofs, more reflective crop varieties and other means of increasing surface reflectivity.

Although geo-engineering was initially seen as a fanciful proposition, especially in the case of SRM, these techno-fixes have gained practical traction via business and government funding (Stephens & Surprise, 2020). Microsoft founder and billionaire Bill Gates even proposed in a recent book (2021) an 'all of the above' response to the climate crisis, providing significant advocacy for innovations such as SRM as part of a multifaceted approach to the issue. 'Show me a problem', wrote Gates, describing himself as a 'technophile', 'and I'll look for technology to fix it' (2021: 14). Beyond his investments in novel technologies for low-emissions cement and steel, not to mention

DAC, his philanthropic foundation is a substantial funder of the Stratospheric Controlled Perturbation Experiment (SCoPEx) – launched by Harvard University scientists to explore the feasibility of SRM (Tollefson, 2018).

It is true that many geo-engineering proposals are still in their early stages. It is also true that in some cases experimentation has been halted by public criticism and opposition from indigenous communities (Osaka, 2021). Even so, critics argue that, in addition to the feasibility of such innovations and the potentially catastrophic consequences that could result from their deployment, the promotion of geo-engineering and aligned technologies such as CCS simply deflects attention from mitigation and the urgent need to radically reduce greenhouse gas emissions (Klein, 2014; Mann, 2021).

As is evident from the previous examples, governments and corporations avoid the mitigation of emissions by promising that techno-fixes will eventually save the planet. This 'deus ex machina' approach results in predatory delay. Moreover, the move towards 'philanthrocapitalism' as the key mechanism for investments in alleged climate solutions reinforces the capitalist agenda of a self-regulated corporate sector determining social and economic outcomes; it also poses serious difficulties with regard to rising economic inequality, public accountability and democratic oversight (Bloom & Rhodes, 2018; McGoey, 2012a).

The reliance on corporate capitalism to save humanity from climate change has evolved even further in recent years, with the bizarre spectacle of the 'billionaire space race' now unfolding. The battle to commercialise the cosmos is being led by Amazon founder Jeff Bezos and Tesla CEO Elon Musk, who are also routinely engaged in the fight to be crowned the world's richest man; a third billionaire, former Virgin CEO Sir Richard Branson, is also in the running to establish a private-sector space industry.

These endeavours are not just vanity projects for the mega-wealthy. Musk's SpaceX has already secured multi-billion-dollar contracts with NASA and the US military. Maybe above all, the vision that emerges from these initiatives is of escaping the constraints of politics and the physical limits of the planet to maintain infinite economic growth and profitability.

For instance, the stated aim of SpaceX is 'to make humanity multi-planetary' and includes an acknowledgement that continued economic expansion is no longer possible within the Earth's finite physical boundaries. Similarly, asked what he hoped to achieve in the development of his space business, Bezos said: 'We're building a road to space so that future generations can build the future ... We have to keep it [the planet] safe and protect it, and the way to do that is slowly over the decades to move all heavy industry, all polluting industry, out into space' (Chow, 2021).

Ignoring the technical implausibility of such an idea, the environmental impacts of a mass expansion in fossil-fuelled rockets in a carbon-constrained world makes little sense – unless, of course, Bezos and his fellow stargazers have in truth given up on the Earth and feel further damage is therefore of negligible consequence. Regardless, the techno-fantasy of fleeing the physical limits of a finite world is immediately appealing to corporate leaders steeped in the mythology that endless growth is a non-negotiable right.

As a result, in the face of an ever-deepening climate crisis, the world's richest and most powerful individuals choose to invest their fortunes in the fundamentally flawed pursuit of abandoning the only habitable planet known to exist. This surely represents corporate-led climate adaptation in its most extreme form: a cowed retreat from a ruined Earth.

5.6 Corporate Saviour or Sacrifice?

As noted previously, it is too late to avoid climate change: the physical impacts of human-induced environmental disruption are now dramatically evident in worsening weather events around the globe. We began this chapter by setting out the different dimensions of these impacts and the ways in which communities might seek to adapt in response.

Crucially, while much research on adaptation focuses on the technical and social aspects of reacting to and anticipating climate impacts, the role of corporations is rarely considered. It has been left to a small but burgeoning literature within business scholarship to explore how companies can develop what is touted as greater climate resilience through adjustments in their operations and even major shifts in their business models. We argue that the basic corporate goal here is to reduce the physical and market risks of climate impacts on profitability.

Climate adaptation is also a deeply political process – one shaped by differences in social and economic power. Corporations hold significant sway in contemporary capitalist society, with an outsized influence on government decision-making. Business leaders and their companies regularly present themselves as central actors in responding to climate change, whether through the provision of disaster response and reconstruction, as architects of enhanced societal resilience or as pioneers in innovating technological solutions such as sequestering carbon emissions or even geo-engineering the atmosphere.

Furthermore, many businesses are already planning ways in which they can profit from the disruption climate change brings. They are eyeing new markets, products and services, as well as opportunities for more resource extraction in a warming world. This underlines how reliance on business leadership in adapting to climate impacts ignores the fact that corporations are principally defined by the maximising of shareholder value rather than by the pursuit of social or environmental wellbeing.

As the current billionaires' pivot towards space reveals, corporate leaders even appear willing to sacrifice a habitable planet in the interests of continued growth and profitability. Like so many forms of business-led adaptation, this ultimate expression of hubris is the stuff of fantasy. The reality is that the climate crisis – the supreme threat to the hegemony of corporate capitalism – is too great and too far advanced to be overcome by a far-fetched flurry of unproven techno-fixes.

6 | *Now Is Not the Time: The Social Construction of Adaptation*

To discuss the cause and effect of these storms – there's the ... place [and time] to do that ... It's not now.

Scott Pruitt, Administrator, US Environmental Protection
Agency (quoted in Sampathkumar, 2017)

In September 2017, in anticipation of an extreme weather event described by one of its scientists as unparalleled, the US's National Hurricane Center issued warnings for a trio of hurricanes. One of these, Hurricane Irma, would prove to be record-breaking in its violence, inflicting catastrophic damage in the Caribbean and the Florida Keys and directly or indirectly causing 129 deaths – most of them resulting from power outages and the exacerbation of existing medical conditions. As Florida was preparing for Irma's devastating landfall, Scott Pruitt, then Administrator of the Environmental Protection Agency (EPA), was asked about climate change's role in the unfolding disaster. He told CNN it was a question for another time. Irma, whose winds reached 180 mph, was considered the most powerful hurricane ever recorded in the open Atlantic region – until, that is, the worsening environmental crisis delivered an even more potent storm two years later. In 2019, with winds of 185 mph, Hurricane Dorian set a new and disturbing benchmark for climate-change-induced ferocity.

As corporations and politicians promote future 'win-win' solutions to climate change, communities in vulnerable regions of the world are already experiencing the effects of a devastating ecological unravelling. Increasingly intense storms, floods, hurricanes, fires and droughts are leaving myriad physical impacts – many of them in the form of loss of life and property. These 'traces' of climate change should make evident the worsening crisis and, ideally, bring about a wider realisation of the need to renegotiate current political systems.

Yet to date climate adaptation measures have been unequally applied. They have often been implemented at a local level and in an ad hoc manner. As we observed in the previous chapter, it is in large part a question of varied vulnerabilities and limited resources. While protection of property and defence of infrastructure is prioritised in prosperous communities, responses in poorer locales are frequently mustered only in the aftermath of disaster.

As illustrated by the aforementioned example, this purely reactive approach functions as a boundary: a deliberate focus on the local and the immediate serves to defer the temporal and political implications of climate change. In turn, the hegemonic legacy of the crisis is perpetuated. Even as extreme weather events are occurring, there is a reluctance to talk about severe storms, fires, floods or droughts as products of environmental collapse. Adaptation remains framed around specific impacts, referred to as resilience-building and centred on technocratic and after-the-fact solutions (Adger et al., 2009; Measham et al., 2011).

This 'enclosure' of adaptation measures is often viewed as a pragmatic reaction to the difficulties of discussing climate change within communities. It is seen as a means of avoiding the conflict that might arise from the issue. It is a strategy that some have labelled 'depoliticisation' (Kenis & Mathijs, 2014).

However, as detailed in the preceding chapter, climate adaptation is in fact deeply political (Eriksen et al., 2015; Mann & Wainwright, 2018). As with corporate responses, the preference is for technological solutions that will not disrupt the status quo or impinge on the purported exigencies of economic growth.

In examining both the unequal distribution of impacts and the inequities stemming from how they are addressed, the need for more critical engagement with adaptation becomes apparent (Webber, 2016; Meerow & Mitchell, 2017). It is important that the process is situated within an understanding of the complexities of contested social relations, where choices are made about prioritisation and exclusion. While there has been a strong focus on communicating the impacts of climate change, the existing literature remains under-theorised with regard to the 'political *mechanisms* that serve to reproduce vulnerability over time' (Eriksen et al., 2015: 525).

In this chapter we examine the politics of adaptation as the 'contestations, collaborations and negotiations through which collectives govern their everyday affairs' (Eriksen et al., 2015). In other words, having already explored the ways in which corporations engage with adaptation, we now examine the ways in which those at the forefront of climate impacts are responding. We explore the discursive framing of adaptation in both richer and poorer regions, consider how NGOs have approached the issue and reflect on how different responses are presented.

While adaptation might seem a less controversial issue than mitigation, the separation of impacts from climate change itself – along with the localised and fragmented ways in which adaptation is implemented – indicates a politics in which the connections between the traces of ecological catastrophe are broken. The so-called depoliticisation of adaptation can therefore be seen as a *political* response in which hegemonic practices are allowed not only to continue but also to escalate, further restricting our ability to imagine a society reorganised in response to climate change. We argue that attempts to depoliticise adaptation feed into denial, delay and the continuation of hegemonic, fossil fuel–dependent notions of progress.

6.1 If Not Now, Then When?

There is an entrenched unwillingness to cite the underlying role of climate change in extreme weather events. This reticence endures even as such episodes worsen. It is commonly framed as a means of focusing on immediate humanitarian impacts rather than engaging in what is known to be a polarised and frequently partisan debate (Moser, 2014).

Such a stance circumvents discussion of the climate crisis at critical moments, when the media eye and public experience of some of the worst impacts of the phenomenon are being felt. As noted by Norgaard (2011), these interpretive and implicatory denials function to create a boundary around the possibilities for transformation; concurrently, they justify ignorance of the problem.

In reference to the example highlighted at the start of this chapter, it is worth noting Pruitt's remarks when he was first appointed Administrator of the EPA: 'Science tells us that the climate is changing and that human activity in some manner impacts that change. The ability to measure with precision the degree and extent of that impact and what to do about it are subject to continuing debate and dialogue, and well it [sic] should be' (quoted in Siefter, 2017). While offering a cursory nod to science, statements such as this serve to sow doubt and delay action.

Similarly, when Australia was experiencing unprecedented bushfires in the summer of 2019 and 2020, regularly awakening to red skies and warnings to stay inside, conservative politicians pushed back against calls to discuss climate change. The message – again – was that it was not the time to talk about such matters. The deputy prime minister went even further, flatly denying any connection between global warming and the blazes and insisting such links represented 'the ravings of some pure, enlightened, woke, capital-city greenies' (quoted in Crowe, 2019).

Such comments reveal the politics at play in claims that there is a good time and a bad time to reflect on climate change. For some, it seems, there is *never* a time. The preference for feeding into popular narratives around disaster management is itself a political manoeuvre. As noted by Jolly (2020), the invocation of national resilience was also used by Australia's conservative politicians and media to silence concern about climate change in the face of the bushfires: in effect, this notion was weaponised to undermine the idea that mitigation and adaptation should be part of the response to such events.

As a result of such strategies, emphasis is placed not on dealing with climate change but on the ability of communities to withstand it. The embedding of responses within a disaster framework reorients discussion to what appear to be more manageable and contained issues. By way of further illustration, consider the prevailing narrative in Brazil, where increasingly heavy rainfall has resulted in thousands of lives being lost due to mudslides and storms.

Here, too, the link between climate change and extreme weather events has been largely ignored by the media. News coverage has instead tended to focus on the response to disasters and how to reduce future vulnerability to them (Lahsen et al., 2020). It has been argued that this simply takes account of what consumers of news wish to hear; but how can communities be expected to adapt to climate change if the issue remains unacknowledged and unspoken?

The preference for localised, reactive responses to extreme weather events draws a political boundary around which certain actions are prioritised. Through the isolation and containment of its impacts, climate change is pushed out of the discussion: because it can be neither seen nor felt, it does not have to be managed. Existing practices are thus allowed to continue, with further traces of devastation deemed preventable only in a future in which the status quo remains unchallenged.

6.2 Placing Climate Change Out of Space

As noted in the previous chapter, the failure of national governments to respond to climate change in any meaningful way means adaptation planning is often relegated to the level of local governance. It is precisely because of the complexity and localised nature of climate impacts that this option is seen as a means of overcoming political debates about climate change itself: a smaller community may be easier to bring to consensus, and impacts can be made more tangible for those familiar with a specific locality.

Yet a large body of literature has documented numerous 'barriers' to such local adaptation. These include competing interests and priorities, sense of place, a desire to protect property and a hesitancy to acknowledge climate change (Moser & Ekstrom, 2010; Barnett et al., 2013; Biesbroek et al., 2013). Despite recognition of the socially constructed nature of risk and the subjectivities of what is possible (Adger et al., 2009), this appears to have led to the development of frameworks in which 'limits to adaptation' are often reinforced rather than challenged (see, for example, the model developed in Dow et al., 2013).

Local resistance to adaptation is perhaps surprising (O'Toole & Coffey, 2013). After all, why would one *not* want to prevent the worst impacts of a disaster? However, this tendency might reflect the broader challenges of climate change as a whole.

Reviewing the literature on adaptation, Moser (2014: 344) noted how people say they are 'already perceiving changes in the environment or believe they have experienced the impacts of climate change'; but she also noted how they 'place climate change in the distant future'. This suggests the choice to respond, even when the issue is an immediate one, is superseded by the choice to defer. To put it another way: climate change might be theoretically accepted, but it is actively limited to a concept that is either incorporated into or moved outside established hierarchies of importance – rendering it little more than a 'not yet'.

Leaving adaptation measures entirely to local government authorities is another means by which the political is concealed. These efforts are extremely uneven, with a tendency to prioritise the privileged and protect wealth. The adaptation process is often caught between the existing rhetoric of social denial and the stabilisation of hegemonic power relations. Along with vested interests, an emphasis on the uncertainties of climate change comes to the fore in procedures that are routinely undermined by limited funding and dependent on individual, small-scale participation (Bowden et al., 2021).

The social and economic contradictions of adaptation are painfully clear. Research in the US and Canada has found that most plans 'fail to ... provide a detailed implementation process' and that planning in places experiencing extreme weather events does not always occur (Meerow & Mitchell, 2017). Only certain communities can afford to respond, and even then, the funding available might not be adequate. In richer nations local governments might rely on specific project funding from governments at higher levels or, in wealthier communities, a willingness to self-finance measures (Lehmann et al., 2021); in poorer nations they may be dependent on international finance, which is restricted to specific outcomes and smaller-scale projects (Keenan et al., 2019).

These differing levels of government responsibility help displace the need for sweeping political transformation in tackling the climate crisis (Serrao-Neumann et al., 2014; McClure & Baker, 2018). While local governments are commonly responsible for development and planning policy, frameworks and funding – if they exist at all – are frequently determined at a higher level of governance and therefore more prone to politicisation. A survey of sixty local government areas in the US found that, although strong perceptions of risk might assist, external policy requirements and funding were the key drivers of adaptation (Dilling et al., 2017).

One example is Boston, an acknowledged leader in climate adaptation, which is home to a broad range of projects across industries, communities and governance. The city is extremely vulnerable to sea-level rise, with areas of valuable real estate, sections of its financial district and some of its poorest neighbourhoods all at risk. Its staged planning process has developed measures within smaller, local areas (City of Boston, 2021) and has been much lauded for the outcomes it has delivered.

However, the adaptation process in Boston has given particular power to the private sector. It has supported asset management companies and real estate investors in retrofitting buildings and developing their own plans for risk management – including prioritised assistance from state services in the event of a disaster. Meanwhile, planning in East Boston and other poorer areas has been slower and dependent on philanthropic funding, which is unlikely to finance the kind of infrastructure required (Anguelovski et al., 2016). Such an overall outcome can be seen as accommodating the hegemony: as noted by Wissman-Weber and Levy (2018: 512), the primary response has 'hegemonic appeal in its apparent ability to reconcile economic growth and resilience' but 'does not reflect all stakeholder interests and viewpoints equally'.

The varied impacts of climate change mean discussions about adaptation in wealthier countries regularly focus more on, say, property than on loss of life. In line with the preferences of industry, local adaptation plans are 'dominated by infrastructure, transportation and utilities' (Ford et al., 2011: 330) and motivated by economic sensitivity to extreme weather. These measures support business growth and maintain a reliance on technology, even at the expense of preventive planning.

This is wholly in keeping with the perpetuation of the notion that environmental devastation can be managed. Such is the case even in areas where industry itself is manifestly vulnerable. Researching the attitudes of corn and soybean farmers in the American Midwest, for instance, Gardezi and Arbuckle (2018) found both a strong preference for a 'wait and see' approach and optimism about the ability of technological advances to deliver solutions.

In regions that have already suffered catastrophic weather events, as starkly illustrated by the tragic example of New Orleans, the distribution of funding and the prioritisation of planning measures bolster existing inequalities in the use of space. Historically, African-American neighbourhoods in New Orleans have been concentrated on lower-lying land; since Hurricane Katrina, which struck in 2005, this pattern has continued, with the gentrification of areas less vulnerable to flooding and 'an emphasis on increasing property values by expanding waterfront housing' (Anguelovski et al., 2016: 336–37). Hurricane Katrina was a boon for property developers, making climate adaptation a space of business opportunity.

Meanwhile, an ongoing controversy in Jakarta underlines a preference for protecting infrastructure rather than the poor. The Indonesian capital's plans for what is known as the Giant Sea Wall involve the expulsion of residents from their homes in less affluent neighbourhoods (Anguelovski et al., 2016), despite seawalls' known propensity for maladaptation – due to their flow-on effects within water systems – and their reputation as at best a temporary measure against an ever-worsening problem (Salim et al., 2019). This shows how the responses advocated with a view to 'keeping climate change out' can shore up privilege, allocating more space to those who can afford it and displacing those who cannot. That wealthier citizens are more engaged with decision-making processes merely intensifies the divide.

6.3 Who Gets to Say What Stays?

The importance of incorporating local knowledge in climate adaptation planning is regularly emphasised in the literature (O'Toole & Coffey, 2013). In part, this is precisely because of the general reluctance to recognise climate change; but it is also related to the immediacy of particular problems.

A difficulty of top-down governance approaches is that decisions might not be supported by local communities required to live with the outcomes. Moreover, these decisions are more likely to have unintended consequences in the *absence* of local knowledge (Serrao-Neumann et al., 2014). This is why deliberation has been a popular solution to local adaptation planning (Hobson & Niemeyer, 2011; Dryzek & Pickering, 2017). It is vital to recognise, though, that deliberation processes and co-learning are still subject to existing power relations, which require conscious evaluation in decision-making methodologies (Tschakert et al., 2016). They are also intensely time-consuming.

The localised nature of adaptation initiatives leaves them susceptible to a lack of resources, potential corruption, short-term preferences and other structural constraints (Keenan et al., 2019). Brought into this intersection, climate change can be deprioritised in favour of prevailing concerns – for example, clean water and healthy air (Moser, 2014) – even though it might be a major influence on those very same considerations. Environmental issues are often neglected when pitted against their economic counterparts, particularly if the principal desired outcome is the avoidance of the biggest and most immediate 'risk'. Research in Dublin, Cork and Galway, three of Ireland's coastal cities, has demonstrated as much. It found economic growth was given precedence in instances of 'double exposure' to recession and climate change, with a preference for large-scale engineering solutions 'over those that might reduce the vulnerability of the population' (Jeffers, 2013).

There is evidence of 'local knowledge' being used to push back against adaptation proposals in richer communities, where residents – especially those with time to engage and a particular interest in the issue at hand – are often more involved in the planning process. The interpretation of climate change among these individuals is subject to contestation. As Treuer (2018) has noted in the case of Miami, a city especially vulnerable to sea-level rise, a tendency to favour the past or recent events over the future and to prize certainty over uncertainty is likely to diminish the ability to visualise and plan for environmental disaster.

Our own research in Lake Macquarie, Australia, found similar dynamics (Bowden et al., 2019). Convinced that discussions about adaptation planning were reducing the value of their properties, residents of low-lying homes launched a campaign against proposed measures and claimed the information underpinning the plans was flawed. The local government ultimately opted for a 'wait and see' approach in order to appease concerns. This was another example of the urgency of a meaningful response to climate change being pushed out of an adaptation model.

Analogously, in Del Mar, a beach town in San Diego County, California, the state planning commission encountered fierce opposition to the idea of a 'planned retreat'. Around 600 properties – among the county's most expensive – were deemed at risk from sea-level rise, but their owners pressed for adaptation measures to be limited to a sand-replacement initiative. Angered by the prospect of falling values and mounting insurance premiums, residents employed lawyers, engaged in the planning process and eventually forced the exclusion of retreat from the proposals (Diehl, 2017).

The issue of privileged participation in planning processes also arises in poorer regions, as was illustrated in Santiago, Chile, when climate adaptation was undertaken in response to the impacts of drought. Following pushback from the local water regulator over attempts to augment water access among the city's 800,000 low-income households, the consultation process was specifically managed to exclude the voices of marginalised communities and civil society (Anguelovski et al., 2016: 339–40).

With adaptation implementation focusing more on infrastructure, community and resilience, difficult questions are put aside. Climate change becomes a matter for the future –allowing local governments to fall back on 'resilience' to avoid controversy and instead concentrate on immediate risks. Governance thus functions to shift responsibility between jurisdictions, subsuming adaptation within a risk-and-resilience framework and further fuelling the insistence that humans are uniquely positioned to control the environment. As a result, much of the discussion around climate adaptation planning suggests that it can be contained, sectioned off from the more complex and essential debates which are condemned to a line on some far-off and best-forgotten 'to do' list.

6.4 Climate of Ignorance

As the traces of climate change become more visible, immediate and impactful, it might be expected that recognition of the issue is close. The deferral of the impacts of actions past is, for many, no longer possible. Yet, as we note in this chapter, even in this context, climate change is sectioned off, excluded from discussions, while the repetition of hegemonic practices of 'resilience' and 'progress' are not only continued but sped up. While denial and delay have become less convincing, there remains a resistance to responding to the cause of the problem.

We argue that the sociology of ignorance can be a useful way of understanding this lack of action. Ignorance is not necessarily about a lack of knowledge – it is about *ignoring* some types of knowledge in favour of others. Following McGoey (2012b: 2–3), we see ignorance as a process, one which involves 'the mobilisation of ambiguity, the denial of unsettling facts, the realisation that knowing the least amount possible is often the most indispensable tool for managing risks and exonerating oneself from blame in the aftermath of catastrophic events'. As such, ignorance is both productive and socially produced.

Ignorance of climate change can be produced in any number of ways. It might be negotiated strategically. As we have shown elsewhere, in the process of undergoing intensive deliberation with a group of hostile landowners over climate adaptation, the local government officials made a conscious decision to stop talking about climate change, to reframe it as 'future-proofing'. This led to success in terms of consensus, but once climate change is no longer part of the framework, the role of climate science in leading the plans is diminished (if not ignored entirely; Bowden et al., 2021). Here, the production of ignorance in turn is productive of community consensus; a successful outcome to a difficult process. Yet, if the intention was to plan for climate change, how this is to be done without talking about climate science remains to be seen.

Ignorance can also be produced in the practice of politics. For corporations, politicians, and sometimes public servants, ignoring the links between climate change and its impacts avoids the difficult policy decisions – as we noted earlier; the intention may be to allow constituents to respond to more immediately tangible issues such as 'recovery' efforts. Again, this is also productive; it is likely not a coincidence that such efforts often provide better media opportunities, offering images of active involvement and empathy. Ignorance, contrary to reputation, can produce positive media images.

The bracketing of information is another way in which ignorance is constructed (Gross, 2007). For example, the focus on disaster and risk management rather than climate change is another attempt at ignoring the encompassing, interlinked impacts of climate disruption identified by scientists. This bracketing then favours one-off, reactive responses, sometimes – such as in the case of rebuilding in flood zones – in ways that completely ignore climate change. Again, this allows for governments to be seen to be acting even when they are not. Such is the case of the Great Barrier Reef in Australia, where the government has responded to the threat of an endangered listing from UNESCO with large amounts of funding focused on issues of erosion and pesticide run-off, which will have little impact on the ecosystem's ability to deal with climate change–driven coral bleaching (Butler & Readfearn, 2022).

While climate impacts are locally experienced, the consequences of the unequal and fragmented responses to adaptation reveal why the issue needs to be challenged within the space-time of climate change itself. It cannot be petitioned off; lack of funding, resources, and broader government and industry considerations mean that only those who are able to respond, do. This does not need to exclude local knowledge, democratic practices, or simply reacting to events as they occur. However, the broader framework of incorporating the science of climate change needs to be brought to the centre of these solutions. In deconstructing the dynamics within which ignorance is produced, it may be possible to articulate how the different types of information and possibilities might fit together, and to rebuild new practices that are able to respond to the actual problem itself.

6.5 The Uneven Consequences

Poorer nations often have neither the resources nor the time to concern themselves with the finer details of climate adaptation. Flooding is intensifying and becoming more frequent in countries such as Bangladesh. The populations of low-lying Pacific islands face inundation of the lands on which they live, work and rely for their livelihoods, with some already planning for forced migration (Webber, 2013). This is becoming an unwinnable race.

Yet the impacts of climate change on such nations have been known for some time. As the 2020 edition of the annual Global Climate Risk Index reported: 'Of the 10 most affected countries and territories in the period 1999 to 2018, seven were developing countries in the low-income or lower-middle-income country group, two were classified as upper-middle-income countries (Thailand and Dominica) and one was an advanced economy generating high income (Puerto Rico)' (Eckstein et al., 2019: 4).

Just as scholars have highlighted pollution and other environmental hazards' unequal distribution among those in marginalised and less affluent neighbourhoods (Bullard et al., 2002), it has been shown for many years that poorer communities – both within and between nations – are most at risk from the adverse consequences of climate change (Smith, Choy, et al., 2014). This highlights the need for an 'environmental justice' lens – one through which the breadth and depth of climate impacts compel a rethinking of resource allocation, priorities and modes of governance (Bulkeley et al., 2014; Schlosberg & Collins, 2014).

Climate adaptation in poorer nations has long been framed within the broader 'development aid' paradigm, whereby such countries depend on assistance from richer counterparts and international organisations to provide basic necessities for large sections of their populations. From the initial development of the UNFCCC in 1992, it has been accepted that poorer nations have not only contributed less to the problem of climate change but are more likely to bear its costs (Adger et al., 2003; Mann & Wainwright, 2018). The recognition of 'differential responsibilities and respective capacities' (McGinn & Isenhour, 2021: 384) sat within the formative approach of incorporating distributive justice in the UNFCCC framework and directing the agreements resulting from it; so, too, did the allocation of financial resources.

However, despite these early intentions, the voluntary nature of the commitments stemming from the Paris Agreement of 2015 indicates a shift towards a more liberal notion of justice. This threatens to further cement the position of poorer countries as the Other – helpless, largely voiceless and desperately in need of saving by wealthier, mostly Western nations – as they continue to grapple with climate impacts and the consequent need to adapt.

Civil society, particularly in the form of NGOs, has long been relied on to expose inequities and injustice and advocate for those with less power. Internationally, groups such as Greenpeace, the WWF and Ceres are among many for which climate change has become a major focus in recent years. While many NGOs were previously hesitant to discuss adaptation for fear that mitigation would be deprioritised (Pielke Jr et al., 2007), these groups have become increasingly involved in developing strategies and projects aimed at helping specific communities and regions adapt.

Yet many of these initiatives reflect the broader, inherently inequitable approach to adaptation. Ambitious, far-reaching objectives are seen as too challenging. Smaller-scale, reactive projects are preferred. This echoes wider attempts to depoliticise climate change – a stance that is arguably understandable in the NGO sector, which is often targeted for being partisan, but which nonetheless permits the replication and even the extension of hegemonic power relations.

It is left primarily to the NGOs of poorer nations to challenge hegemonic framings of environmental issues. These organisations bring to the debate a post-colonial narrative, whereby 'concerns are cast in the light of the coloniser versus the colonised; [and] the dichotomous world of affluence and poverty' (Doherty et al., 2018: 707). On average, tellingly, these groups – mostly from the Global South – make up only a quarter of the representatives at COP negotiations. While they fight for issues such as the financing of adaptation, other NGOs are more concerned with matters pertaining to technological advances and governance (Gereke & Brühl, 2019).

We have already observed how corporations and governments have targeted NGOs for critiquing existing power relations. Since they generally depend on funding from government programmes or tax relief to assist their work, they can become more focused on aid, community initiatives and disaster relief than on political campaigns – especially in poorer regions (Allan, 2018). Some may seek funds from corporate donors; others, such as Greenpeace, rely almost entirely on philanthropy.

The impacts these funding models have on NGO activity have been well documented (Dauvergne & LeBaron, 2014). Research has found the location and size of an organisation can influence its focus in terms of responding to the climate crisis. For instance, NGOs working predominantly in industrialised countries tend to concentrate on mitigation, whereas those in poorer nations emphasise adaptation (Reeve, 2008).

Activist groups, too, have tended to focus more strongly on their own audiences than on the broader issues of environmental or climate justice – as evidenced, for instance, by Extinction Rebellion's apparent embracing of the notion of societal collapse. The group has taken up the idea of 'Deep Adaptation', which originated in a self-published paper by Jem Bendell, a professor of sustainability leadership at the University of Cumbria in England (Bromwich, 2020). The paper and its associated forums and workshops explore an individual's emotional acceptance of impending disaster. Retreats around the concept – which cost between €520 and €820, according to Bendell – are centred on 'inner adaptation rather than policies for reducing the harm from societal collapse' (Bromwich, 2020).

While there is arguably nothing inherently problematic about 'personal enlightenment', this emphasis is a far cry from the kind of transformative politics that is the public face of Extinction Rebellion. In many ways, it conflicts with the fundamental basis of climate justice. By and large, the people who participate in discussions about Deep Adaptation are not those currently facing life-threatening climate impacts.

6.6 Whose Adaptation?

While these questions play out on the international stage, communities that struggle to engage at a global level are experiencing ongoing disruptions to their everyday routines and livelihoods. Mental health, income, cultural practices and knowledge are all under pressure across poorer and more vulnerable regions, with climate change – itself a product of colonisation and industrialisation – perpetuating inequitable social processes. Regimes for funding adaptation push states into competition with one another, ultimately leaving many to cope as best they can.

For instance, Webber (2013) has detailed how a delegation from Kiribati organised a UNFCCC side event to draw attention to its plight. The presentation featured a mix of scientific data, statistical information and cultural performance in a bid to highlight the country's susceptibility to sea-level rises. Like many of its fellow Pacific Island nations, Kiribati is already making plans to move its population in order to survive.

Meanwhile, Maldives is trying to use physical barriers to prevent inundation. Eighty per cent of the islands that make up the country are already only a metre above sea level, meaning they are likely to be lost by 2100 (Gilchrist, 2021). Despite the threat it faces, the country is aiming for ambitious mitigation targets in an effort to demonstrate leadership and inspire others.

Elsewhere, too, communities that have been in place for centuries find themselves confronting the unknown – as seen in the Russian village of Russkoye Ustye, where erosion from the thawing permafrost is transforming day-to-day life. Older buildings have fallen into the river. Villagers have noted changes in bird species spotted locally, as well as fewer fish and unfamiliar cycles of flowers in bloom. Even the nearby tundra is reported to have caught fire. At the same time as local knowledge is being used to observe the impacts, residents say they are losing their ability to predict what might happen next (Troianovski, 2020).

In Labrador, Canada, Inuit hunters and trappers are having to deal with some of the fastest warming in the world. This is damaging their capacity to pass on generations' worth of knowledge. Shrinking ice, sea-level rise and increases in severe weather are cutting off traditional hunting grounds, as a result of which 'more and more Inuit are relying on expensive, store-bought, processed food, because it's safer and easier than catching or shooting supper' (Mercer, 2018).

This disruption of cultural practices has brought impacts often associated with the worst effects of colonisation. Mental health problems and drug and alcohol abuse are all on the rise. The suicide rate among Canada's First Nations people – which includes both the Inuit and Métis – was three times higher than the rest of the population between 2011 and 2016 (Stober, 2019).

Saltwater intrusion due to sea-level rise in Bangladesh provides another grim illustration. It is hitting rural areas and destroying the rivers around which people live and work. As well as exacerbating a lack of drinkable water, increasing salinity has forced some rice farmers to turn to the less lucrative and more labour-intensive farming of shrimp. Large swathes of the population have been forced to move into cities, where they often live in poverty while working as 'waste-pickers, domestic workers or garment labourers' (Szczepanski et al., 2018). According to the World Bank (2015b), 'the probability that the economic status of a coastal household is in the bottom 20 percent [has risen] six-fold, from 8% to 56%'.

It is obvious even from these few examples that adapting to climate change in poorer regions involves more vulnerability, greater acquiescence to Western notions of development and a need to negotiate simply for the right to survive. The processes of colonisation and the global dominance of corporate capitalism are thus being accelerated. This is reflected both in the ways in which environmental and aid organisations have taken up the cause of adaptation and in the ways in which the impacts of ecological degradation continue to manifest themselves.

6.7 The Myth of Depoliticisation

When then President Donald Trump first signalled his intention to withdraw the US from the Paris Agreement, infamously protesting that it placed an 'unfair burden' on American businesses and taxpayers, a popular movement rose in opposition. Its constituents – including mayors, local governments, universities and companies – declared they would commit to the accord themselves (Tabuchi & Fountain, 2017). It was a feel-good moment in which the community came together, despite the poor leadership from above, to make a change for the better. The implication was that there was no need for the political machinations that had already let the process down.

In spite of claims to the contrary, climate adaptation, too, is deeply political. The idea that it could fit into existing frameworks of resilience, economic growth and development has proven too tempting for many, and the shift away from the structural responses needed to address the greatest threat to our planet and its inhabitants can neatly paper over the political failures that are horribly apparent in an array of ever-worsening impacts.

At each and every turn, climate adaptation in communities is pitched as a concern subservient to economic growth. It is depicted as a problem that can be contained within space. It is portrayed as an issue that only the maintenance (in richer nations) or speeding up (in poorer regions) of existing practices can solve. It is constantly displaced and pushed further and further into the future. It is twisted into a threat that never quite arrives. As a result, there is no need to counter the existing hegemony of fossil energy, rampant consumption and escalating carbon emissions.

We have argued that the localised ways in which adaptation occurs not only reinforce but also amplify existing divisions between the wealthy and the poor. The assumption is that the sole viable solution is to bring forward and advance the prevailing hegemonic conceit of adaptation as 'a technical problem to be addressed . . . through financial investment . . . and governance' (Mann & Wainwright, 2018: 74). While the 'right' measures are habitually seen as those most conveniently at hand, people in poorer countries and regions are already feeling the consequences of climate change – and they have little help in sight.

The divide between so-called developed and developing nations might be shrinking, but it is expanding *within* nations (United Nations, 2021a). Consequently, those practising traditional cultures and living off the land are drawn further into the colonised spaces of cities and factories. Attempts to circumvent difficult political discussions under the pretext of depoliticisation are therefore having the unexpected effect of laying bare the deep politics at play, with current approaches to adaptation endorsing and even strengthening hegemonic views of capitalism and progress.

As we elaborate in the following chapters, the sense of climate change as a distant and future problem is further ingrained through the representation of those experiencing its impacts. Seeing poorer regions endure suffering is not a new phenomenon, of course; and their wealthier counterparts, tragically, have long since perfected the means of suggesting there is only one way to respond.

PART IV

The Politics of Climate Suffering

7 | The Spectacle of Suffering

What good is it to save the planet if humanity suffers?

Rex Tillerson, CEO, ExxonMobil, 2013 (quoted in
Koening, 2013)

'Hurricane Ida Power Outages, Misery Persists 9 Days Later' is the
headline of an NBC New York online news article highlighting the
suffering of New Orleans residents in the wake of the severe weather
event that struck the city in August 2021. The piece tells of 'splintering'
properties and reveals how mismanagement led to the deaths of nursing
home residents. Mentions of the notorious, post-hurricane 'blue tarp'
conjure up images of buildings that now exist only as broken shells. It is
in many ways a powerful piece of journalism, yet reading it is not
a straightforward task. It is first necessary to negotiate an advertisement
for Dyson vacuum cleaners, which appears across the screen almost
immediately; a side-banner ad for the Star Choir Holiday Singing
Competition Television Special at Rockefeller Center pops up shortly
afterwards. Accompanying the article is a video update on storm-related
deaths. Pressing play results in yet another ad, once again for Dyson,
which lasts for 30 seconds; the news video itself, once finally accessed, is
a mere 15 seconds longer (Mcgill & Deslatte, 2021).

As climate impacts grow in severity, the suffering of people and communities becomes ever more evident. These experiences are broadcast
and consumed, becoming products in the public visualisation of environmental catastrophe. Shocking pictures of wildfires, cars floating
through flooded cities, roofless houses standing deserted in the aftermath of hurricanes and typhoons – all starkly highlight the damage that
is already occurring.

The faces shown are of desperate people who have lost their homes,
their possessions and even their friends and families. These stricken
individuals cling to loved ones and weep. As their torment cements its

position as a regular feature in media coverage of the climate crisis worldwide, the spectre of apocalypse becomes ever more familiar to us. At least in theory, such depictions should translate into meaningful action; but whether they do is another matter. These disasters clearly bring devastating human and economic costs for some, but for others they bring opportunities. For instance, for news outlets seeking drama and spectacle (Boykoff & Boykoff, 2007), such events are not only the stuff of required reporting, they are also the stuff of revenue-raising.

In Chapter 5 we described how businesses are adapting to climate change by finding new market opportunities. As Klein has argued, 'disaster capitalism' involves reshaping civic and social conventions in ways that open up space for expanded capitalist activity by 'orchestrat-[ing] raids on the public sphere in the wake of catastrophic events' (Klein, 2007: 6). Crucially, disaster capitalism also involves profiting from suffering and using it to defend the current economic system. After all, the term 'disaster' implies a singular event – one from which recovery is both possible and essential. Within this setting, to legitimise their role in society, corporations construct an equivalence with those who suffer. One means of doing this is to incorporate suffering into hegemonic projects. Fossil fuel industry representatives, for example, argue the industry itself will alleviate the inequalities embedded in climate change. This, they say, will be achieved through technological development and economic growth. They even claim that in poorer nations, because people rely on fossil energy to improve their quality of life and levels of consumption, the industry is actually *alleviating* suffering.

In richer nations, meanwhile, industry groups and those who support them portray themselves as the saviours of regions dependent on mining and industrial development. They align themselves with workers, who are depicted as being at the mercy of environmentalists' demands. Viewed from this perspective, suffering will result not from future climate impacts but from an ill-advised rejection of capitalist notions of industrial development and progress.

In this chapter we show how different forms of capitalism profit from the suffering caused by climate change. We also explore how those impacted are incorporated within a defence of hegemonic projects in order to preserve the status quo. The construction of a distant Other is employed to conceal the political by naturalising the current order – that is, that capitalism protects against the dangers of the 'natural world' and that media coverage of climate impacts can increase charitable giving and empathy. We suggest the continuous fascination with apocalyptic images, no matter what feelings they evoke, relies on those viewing a disaster being separate from it; and we explain why clear boundaries between suffering and consumption, between those who experience anguish and those who merely observe it, must therefore exist.

We do not seek to imply that corporate and political leaders revel in the misery of others. Nor do we infer that most citizens in well-off nations do not appreciate the depth of the tragedies unfolding elsewhere. We recognise that people can see through the doxa, with many cynical about excessive forms of corporate capitalism. Nonetheless, hegemonic projects that profit from climate suffering are rooted in the active and passive consent of citizens in richer nations.

7.1 Corporate Capitalism and the Other

Historically, capitalism's destruction of the natural world has often been consciously hidden from public view. So has the suffering of the people and communities closest to it. On those occasions when destruction and suffering *have* been revealed, much more often than not, they have been justified within a range of discursive claims.

For instance, a key tenet of Enlightenment thinking and the Industrial Revolution that followed was the idea that humans have a right of dominion over nature; that we can 'place ourselves above the ecosystems that support us and abuse the Earth as if it were an inanimate machine' (Klein, 2014: 177). This thinking frames nature as the Other to human progress, rendering it an endless source for resource extraction and a bottomless sink for humanity's waste. The conquest of the natural world – along with that of the indigenous peoples and communities reliant on it for their existence – has been celebrated as a kind of inevitable progress throughout the documented history of human endeavour. The violence and horror of centuries of colonial and industrial expansion have frequently been concealed; failing that, they have been neatly sanitised in heroic myths and civilising discourses of modernisation and religious conversion (Hinton, 2002; Bowden, 2009).

However, this belief system has more recently been challenged by a growing awareness of the natural world's importance and the first stirrings of an environmental consciousness in industrialising economies. In the US, for instance, the beginnings of an environmentally focused conservation movement in the early twentieth century questioned the headlong rush for the clearing of forests and industrial expansion (Nash, 2014). These pressures intensified during the 1960s, 1970s and 1980s as environmental movements emerged in the US and Europe to oppose the clearing of land, chemical pollution, nuclear testing and animal harvesting (Carson, 1962; Guha, 2000). More recently still, during the past thirty years, environmentalism has increasingly turned its attention to the existential threats of climate change and biodiversity decline – explicitly opposing not only the fossil fuel industry but also the broader assumptions of capitalist consumption and infinite economic growth (Rosewarne et al., 2013; Dietz & Garrelts, 2014). As explored in Chapters 4 and 6, this evolution of action has been linked to issues of social equity, the rights of indigenous communities and the concerns of younger generations.

As early environmentalists revealed capitalism's impact on nature and sought to protect the wild from 'extractivism', business interests started to invest in the public defence of their activities. They did so through marketing, public relations and political lobbying (Aronczyk & Espinoza, 2021). These early seeds sprouted into a multi-billion-dollar industry of corporate advertising aimed at winning over consumers, resisting regulatory action by governments, obfuscating destruction and suffering and – perhaps most extraordinarily – claiming moral worthiness (Brulle et al., 2020).

For example, in justifying and defending the industry's actions, resource and energy company advertising has stressed the quest for 'green' solutions – 'cleaner natural gas', algal biofuels and 'clean coal' among them (McKibben, 2020). It has also boasted how fossil fuels and 'cheap' energy have underpinned societal development, driven economic growth, delivered ever-rising standards of living and employment and even benefited communities and the environment itself through continued modernisation and cheap and stable energy supplies (Wright et al., 2021).

Through the promotion of corporate capitalism based on cheap energy, the concept of 'the economy' has become reified as a fundamental entity that underlies all other social and environmental concerns (Bowden, 2018). While this has been pronounced in the dominant political ideology of neoliberalism, in which corporations and markets are presented as the best guarantors of progress (Lohmann, 2016), even so-called 'ecological modernisation' theorists have declared economic growth and improved technology as the best ways to protect the natural world and associated communities (Mol & Spaargaren, 2000). Environmental or community harm might be occasionally acknowledged, but it is presented as an unfortunate but necessary cost that needs to be borne for the greater good of economic development and improved living standards for the many – which is to say others must suffer in the name of the well-being of the affluent.

Such claims are supported by national governments, which subsidise resource extraction and energy production and frame them as central to the health of their economies. Politicians are thus themselves closely linked with corporate interests (Baer, 2016; Lenferna, 2019). Physical coercion and violence by states and corporations alike have been common strategies in the defence of extractivism and continue to this day (Peluso & Watts, 2001; Downey et al., 2010), supplemented by more sophisticated PR messaging that seeks to construct an equivalence of interest or identity with the majority of citizens and thereby limit the spread of a more general environmental and social critique.

This 'brightsiding' of climate suffering is most evident in the way in which corporations, in seeking to respond to mounting criticism from NGOs and activists, have reframed themselves as forces for good. Rather than pariahs, they are saviours – busily working on 'solutions' for humanity's 'grand challenges' (Ferraro et al., 2015). The dominant emotionology in the requisite marketing and PR machinery is one of optimism and pride in continued innovation and technological advancement (Wright & Nyberg, 2012).

As we remarked in Chapter 3, corporate advertising and public relations increasingly engages with issues of 'sustainability' and the advantages of products as 'clean', environmentally sound and beneficial for the planet and future generations. There articulations invite no contradictions between the continued hyper-consumption of luxury goods and the maintenance of a habitable climate and ecosystem: both, it is claimed, can be achieved through faith in the market system.

Witness, for example, car company Nissan's award-winning TV advertisement for its Leaf electric vehicle. By way of a nod to consumers' climate concerns, a lone polar bear is shown leaving the melting Arctic, traversing the countryside and eventually arriving in a suburban neighbourhood, where it towers over the new owner of

a Leaf before embracing him in apparent gratitude for his environmentally conscious purchase. Nissan's marketing and PR wizards thus seek
to placate widespread alarm over the plight of the environment by
presenting a fanciful construction of nature's appreciation for 'green'
technology. As the tagline intones: 'Innovation for the planet.
Innovation for all' (Nissan, 2010). This type of consumer-facing
incorporation of both the environment itself and iconic – and often
endangered – animals has been further enhanced through partnerships
with corporate-friendly NGOs and the sponsoring of conservation
efforts (Dauvergne & LeBaron, 2014).

Yet nature is not alone in being enlisted in corporate communications that aim to obscure the suffering brought by the climate crisis. In
recent years, as noted earlier, coal and oil interests have projected
themselves as bringing developing nations out of 'energy poverty'
(Demetrious, 2019) or as providing a source of 'ethical oil' through
their allegiance to liberal democratic governments (Levant, 2010).

These businesses want to be seen as concerned 'corporate citizens' –
a notion epitomised in Chevron's famous 'We Agree' campaign, in
which the US oil giant responded to its critics by recognising their
grievances but insisting: 'We live on this planet, too' (Sawyer, 2010:
68). The intended implication was that Chevron, as a cohabitee of the
Earth, could not possibly be a *source* of any problems: rather, it was
fiercely determined to *address* any problems. Such appeals to the common good and claims of alleviating suffering have intensified as many
of the world's fossil fuel titans stress their commitments to carbon
neutrality and carbon pricing while at the same time projecting ongoing
expansion in extraction and processing.

These examples illustrate how corporate environmental framing
consciously seeks to incorporate various Others – including the environment itself and people in the Global South – and purportedly give
them a voice. However, this voice must be aligned with the dominant
model of business expansion and growth. Such 'woke washing', as
critics term it (Rhodes, 2022: 8), plays on consumers' environmental
and social justice concerns by emphasising how companies are working
on solutions to the climate crisis.

Take a recent Twitter commercial that sought to promote
ExxonMobil's actions to mitigate its environmental impact. The ad
centred on the story of an employee who grew up in India and was
inspired to develop lower-emission technologies to ensure 'energy

security for developing nations' (Westervelt, 2021). The strategy here was to include distant or global Others within a discourse of solidarity and social justice. However, such an approach neglects the fact, as explained in the preceding chapter, that the costs of the climate crisis are not borne equally and fall heaviest on those who have contributed the least. Despite corporate claims of a collective interest in wealth and consumption underpinned by the market and capitalism, crises tend to exacerbate inequality.

The incorporation of the environment and impoverished communities within marketing and PR also aims to further marginalise other actors, such as environmental and climate activists, who are portrayed as hypocrites or at least as naive idealists incapable of grasping the wonders of economic development and growth. Part of this framing presents those fighting for meaningful action as a cultural and economic elite disconnected from 'real' citizens (Bowden & Leahy, 2016) – a strategy that contrasts the interests of workers and communities engaged in fossil fuel extraction, energy and industrial production with the demands of mostly younger activists committed to the closure of industries that are now endangering our world (De Moor et al., 2021). This politics of difference is used to push back against climate action by depicting it as unrealistic and inequitable. Alternatively, activists are framed as violent extremists who threaten the existing social order and the sanctity of private property (Irwin et al., 2022).

These articulations also differentiate internal enemies – for example, greenies and idealists – from those suffering in other countries. This brings us to the pronouncement used to commence this chapter – the words of Rex Tillerson, then the CEO of ExxonMobil and later the US Secretary of State, at an annual shareholders' meeting in 2013. It was while defending the role of the fossil fuel industry and its contributions to developing countries that Tillerson posed his seemingly rhetorical question: 'What good is it to save the planet if humanity suffers?' (Koening, 2013). Here the Others, the victims, are those in poorer nations that will suffer if fossil energy is not extracted and consumed. The same economic hierarchy persists, but in this case the trump card is not the strengthening of national economies: rather, it is the assumption that communities value fossil fuel energy more than other concerns or values and that they could not possibly benefit from affordable renewable energy (Lamb et al., 2020).

The early industrial response to climate change stressed a political frontier between those interests supporting the economy and those wishing to avert environmental destruction. However, this relatively simple antagonism has been adapted in an era of worsening crisis and growing social concern. Today even the fossil fuel sector has moved towards a more sophisticated political strategy of playing down confrontational politics and instead promoting a public agenda that claims it is possible to support fossil energy while simultaneously taking action to address the climate crisis.

Corporate capitalism and technological innovation have thus become the solution that papers over the contradiction between expanding fossil fuel extraction and the continued ruination of our planetary systems. This is advocated as a 'win-win' discourse of relentless human progress. Antagonism is redirected to those who oppose the perpetuation of 'business as usual', with these Others articulated as a minority of radicals who must be marginalised and repressed by the state when their actions threaten capital accumulation.

As we will see next, however, corporate capitalism is not content merely with obfuscating suffering within a discourse of aligned interests around infinite economic growth. It also constructs climate change as a spectacle for consumption, so further concealing the underlying politics of the crisis.

7.2 Capitalism and the Climate Spectacle

By focusing on personal consumption, the politics of climate change shifts the debate to what type of consumption, rather than consumption itself. Consumption is naturalised as a right and corporations are merely responding to the consumers' will. However, by reifying and advertising growth and consumption as the solution, it is production that drives consumption (Stuart et al., 2020b). The necessary expansion of capitalism is upheld through linking consumption to a range of social demands in constructing an identification as a 'consumer' of an ever-increasing aspects of goods – from healthcare and education to the environment, and, as we have detailed in previous chapters, even climate change.

A consumer society organised around the production and consumption of images is what Debord (2021) describes as the spectacle: the total colonisation of social life, with an equivalence between social goods and capitalist commodities. The spectacle is reproduced and expanded by a range of means constructing a consumer with particular demands satisfied by mass consumption and mass media. For example, new technological platforms are supported by directed advertising to individual interests and searches, based on the promotion of consumption through 'influencers' and 'clickbait', designed to stir emotions and passions. Promoted by advertisement and media, 'overconsumption masks the irrationality of the capitalist system of never-ending production, consumption, and destruction' (Stuart et al., 2020b: 208). The political is forgotten under layers of glitzy celebrities and celebrations of glitz. The consumer is fed endless images for identity projects and consumption becomes the main form of expressing social demands. It is then seen as logical to address climate change through consumption, where even suffering is commodified.

The relation to climate change in countries around the world is mediated by images and stories in a diverse media-scape. In consumer societies, the connections with Others, including the environment, is a process of visual commodity fetishism. The 'climate spectacle' is not about the images of climate impacts per se, but how the relations between people and climate change are mediated by images, commodities and staged events. The 'spectacle-ized media' sit in-between the audience and the impacts of climate change (Goodman et al., 2016). The catastrophic images that now dominate the front pages of the world's news outlets are not linked to the problematics of consumption. These media corporations are not merely representing climate catastrophes, they are active in drawing attention to particular aspects of climate change – those that generate attention and, thus, profit.

Mass media in different forms – from advertising of environmentally friendly products and apocalyptic movies to celebrity promoted causes – demand intervention. Not by political actions, but by personal consumption. The spectacular media responses to climate change suffering are meant to entertain, with the climate conditions for the disasters rarely conveyed (Gunderson, 2020). The underlying contradictions driving climate change impacts are concealed and the consumers are only activated as such. The alienated consumers even use consumption of insurance and sea walls to protect properties and commodities from climate impacts (Kurmelovs, 2021).

These consumer practices uphold a particular imagery of the world that supports the hegemony. Without 'seeing' the antagonism underlying the dominant imagery of mass consumption, the politics of consumption is constrained to greening the economy, and thus incorporated. The images of floods and fires on electronic devices render the spectator passive, and the inconsequential 'likes' become substitutes for stronger political action. The spectacle mediated through these devices incorporates suffering, with the exploitation hidden behind technological optimism and stimulus. The commodified 'labour' and 'nature' are dissolved into digitally walled experiences privileging play and cynicism over collective action. The digital environments are constructed by corporate entities for commodification of data and advertising profit. The extraction of raw materials, the fossil fuel energy of computation, sweatshop manufacture and precarious work delivering services are nowhere to be seen (Faucher, 2018).

Those who suffer the consequences of climate impacts are represented in the images of disasters, but they have no agency in shaping the network relations. The equivalence is constructed among consumers, with the representation of the Other incorporated in the hegemonic regime of corporate capitalism. There is a mediated distance excluding the impacted people and environment: 'While eliminating geographical distance, this society produces a new internal distance in the form of spectacular separation' (Debord, 2021 §167: 92). This involves consumers caring at a distance, where those suffering are haunting the constructed equivalence; a potential agency and compassion yet to be realised within consumer relations.

7.3 The Politics of Pity

As any observer of the unequal distribution of global capital knows, some suffering matters more than others. Important insights in this regard can be found in the work of Boltanski (1999), who, drawing on Arendt (1963), developed the idea of the 'politics of pity'.

The concept involves constructing a 'distinction between those who suffer and those who do not' (Boltanski, 1999: 3). Crucially, it can be distinguished from compassion or demands for justice. In the context of climate change, for example, compassion would mean a caring stance towards the specific suffering of those impacted, with demands for justice constructing an equivalence with them; by contrast, pity would be mobilised towards a generalised Other – say, the poor or nature – and would represent a distanced breed of compassion in which a recognition that those who suffer are unfortunate but is unaccompanied by an equivalence in the form of a common identity or interest.

To put it another way: the politics of pity acknowledges people fleeing wildfires or wading through flooded streets do not deserve their plight, yet there is no culpability for those who are more fortunate. There is no requirement to first compare and then rectify the situation of disadvantage. It is being fortunate or *un*fortunate that creates the distinction and separation. There is no meaningful comparison of worth with the Other, which simply becomes a generalised victim.

This can be seen in the ways in which governments and humanitarian organisations respond to the suffering inflicted by climate change. Particularly in Western countries, solidarity for Others is based on solidarity at a distance. Although NGOs such as the Nature Conservancy and the WWF promote environmental sustainability and support the victims of the crisis, there is little emphasis on the political change needed to prevent *further* suffering. While a handful of environmental NGOs have worked with those affected by climate impacts, as Klein (2014: 191–229) noted in her critique of 'Big Green', many back the status quo and rely on corporate and government funding for their activities.

For example, the WWF recently announced a US$100 million donation from Amazon founder Jeff Bezos as an 'investment in community and climate'. The money has been earmarked for 'protecting and restoring mangroves', 'developing new markets for seaweed' and 'protecting forests and other ecosystems' (WWF, 2021). The donation formed part of a $10 billion pledge by one of the world's richest men, who claims that 'by coming together with the right focus and ingenuity, we can have both the benefits of our modern lives and a thriving natural world' (Moon, 2021). While laudable, such efforts fail to address the more critical need to move away from fossil energy and fund a rapid decarbonisation of the global economy. Like so much corporate greening activity, these instances of business philanthropy simply camouflage the contradiction between capitalism and environmental destruction. Providing voluntary funding for selected initiatives ignores the much larger and more pressing issue of the climate crisis and the suffering stemming from it, thereby maintaining the existing hegemony.

Moreover, within this framing, those who warn of the ruination of the planet are condemned for peddling pessimism. As Donald Trump declared in a speech at the World Economic Forum in early 2020: 'We must reject the perennial prophets of doom and their predictions of the apocalypse' (Elliott & Wearden, 2020). To mention the appalling consequences of climate change is to be accused of 'playing politics'. It is acceptable to feel pity for those who suffer – to offer 'thoughts and prayers' – but it is not acceptable to demand political action.

The politics of pity also requires that the link between those who suffer and those who do not is based not on shared experiences, not on common identities, but merely on observation. Rather than committing to action, it stresses the beholding of suffering. This creates a passive actor who looks at the 'spectacle of suffering' (Boltanski, 1999: 3). The sufferers are unfortunate; and the viewers, in the safety of their own homes, feel lucky not to be in a similar situation.

As with the images with which we opened this chapter, the victims of worsening climate impacts are not 'us'. Equally, 'we' are not 'them'. The devices through which such images are viewed provide not only a boundary but protection, which takes the form of remoteness. While consumers might be moved to give money to relief efforts, the victims cannot emerge from the screen and make demands of them. In fact, research suggests such imagery *decreases* people's sense of being able to assist (O'Neill et al., 2013).

The spectacle of suffering entails a 'chain of intermediaries between the spectator and the unfortunate' (Boltanski, 1999: 17). Key among these links are media corporations, which not only deliver news but also convey a message about distant suffering and how people ought to feel about it. As Kellner (2016) has argued, terrorism, war, conflict and disaster have become the fuel of news – and, indeed, entertainment – and leading generators of advertising and profit. Whether using mainstream or social media platforms, readers and followers are sources of revenue. 'Clicks' are counted. Elaborate algorithms are used to flag up specific content – spectacles of suffering included.

The media's reporting of climate change offers a classic demonstration of this. It plays a vital part in how citizens are encouraged to feel about this most critical of issues. While much of it has spread doubt over climate science and fomented political contestation and controversy (Boykoff, 2011; McKewon, 2012), a key theme has also been a focus on 'natural' disasters and extreme weather events as sources of spectacle and entertainment (Leyda & Negra, 2015). Indeed, climate change itself rarely features in media reporting, with a recent study finding that climate coverage made up only 0.4 per cent of total US broadcast news in 2020 (Macdonald, 2021).

As a result, media framing of the climate crisis entails a rejection of the phenomenon as a genuine concern while also framing it as something inevitable and beyond human agency. Suffering is depicted both as happening to people in faraway, vulnerable nations and as an unfortunate but unavoidable corollary of 'natural' disasters that humans are powerless to prevent. Clear, articulated boundaries are thus created in the form of, say, national borders, cultural practices or even the colour of one's skin. This framing is ultimately fatalistic: victims have made 'bad choices', and there is essentially nothing that can be done.

Such detachment – both in culpability and commitment to action – is constructed through generality (Boltanski, 1999). As remarked earlier, the Other must become a generalised entity – a 'they'. If a catastrophe is nobody in particular's fault, as this framing implies, then no responsibility for the Other's plight can be assumed – and radical change need not be an option. This kind of generality without demand is illustrated in how corporate hegemonic projects champion consumerism as the optimum response to climate change.

Let us consider again the disastrous coral-bleaching events on the Great Barrier Reef, as first discussed in Chapter 5, which prompted business-funded charities and foundations to promote corporate philanthropy and charitable giving. These endeavours aimed to encourage local responses, such as coral farming and opportunities to 'adopt a coral' (Reef Restoration Foundation, 2018). The key generality here is that 'we' are all somehow equal contributors to the climate crisis and that the answer to it must lie in more consumption. This is the same logic BP applied when it asked Twitter users to calculate their carbon footprints as part of the 'first step towards reducing your emissions' (BP, 2019). The trope that 'we are all in the same boat' ignores the suffering borne by those with the least responsibility. So does the cliché that climate change is some manner of 'great equaliser'. By developing the idea of a consensus based around the consumption of 'sustainable' products and the denial of existing miseries, the political is concealed yet again.

Reflecting this narrative, protesters are presented as 'dangerous' and extreme when they reassert antagonism and the inequality of climate suffering (Malm, 2021). For example, UK Home Secretary Priti Patel denounced Extinction Rebellion activists as 'so-called eco-crusaders turned criminals' and described them as engaged in a 'shameful attack on our way of life, our economy and the livelihoods of the hard-working majority' (Dodd, 2020). The generality at play here is there-fore contradictory, in that it constructs an equivalence or myth of common interest and concern while at the same time demonising those who expose the uncomfortable realities of the climate crisis.

This shows how the politics of pity depends on a logic of difference and a lack of equivalence. These are upheld by a failure to identify with those who suffer and by the framing served up by intermediaries such as media corporations. Spectators observe suffering from afar, with soli-darity shifted to a temporal and spatial distance.

Interestingly, the difference and lack of equivalence enforced by TV screens and political borders can turn pity into hostility as soon as climate impacts drive Others towards the West. Climate refugees are suddenly then represented no longer as sufferers but as intimidating and threatening, routinely condemned – often for political purposes – as a gathering challenge to national security and social norms (Bettini, 2013).

7.4 Climate Change as a Phantasm

Even as our newsfeeds are increasingly filled with terrible evidence of its effects, the impacts and likely consequences of climate change are almost impossible to fathom. The warnings are so stark and incompat-ible with everyday life that some sort of denial or distancing is necessary for most citizens in affluent societies. Fully considering what the crisis really means may be unconscionable (Brulle & Norgaard, 2019) – except, of course, for those already suffering from it.

Although fewer and fewer people deny the scientific reality, there remains a lack of urgency in many Western nations. Norgaard (2011) has referred to this as 'implicatory denial' – a socially organised col-lective resistance to the moral and political implications of climate change – which explains how most people can witness extreme hurri-canes, flooding and droughts that displace millions, acknowledge cli-mate change as the cause and yet still fail to accept the need for radical decarbonisation in high-consumption economies.

As we have discussed in this chapter, there are boundaries in time and space that construe suffering as a spectacle. Reflecting this, implicatory denial plays a major role in shifting recognition of the need for political and economic action to the future – thereby reducing it to a 'not yet'. As we have also discussed, suffering is seen as happening somewhere else; with ever more vivid images of destruction now a media staple, it may even become aestheticised (Chouliaraki, 2006). As a looming catastrophe irreconcilable with the normality of most people's lives, climate change is thus ultimately rendered a phantasm.

The growing popularity of apocalyptic fiction reveals how imagining the world's destruction often acts to mediate the anxiety of confronting the existential threat posed by climate change (Kaplan, 2016; Toadvine, 2018). Doomsday scenarios of environmental collapse are now also commonplace within the broader policy space, 'repeated ad nauseam by many scientists, activists, business leaders and politicians' (Swyngedouw, 2013: 9). The problem here is that envisaging ecological meltdown underplays the ongoing horror of what is already playing out.

The fiction of a climate apocalypse compresses global warming into a singular event or series of events, through which survivors endure. Missing from this vision is the awful scientific fact that climate change is a slow-motion disruption that will continue for centuries and even millennia. The viewers and readers of these fictional and media representations also escape the end of the world, which conveniently takes place somewhere remote from our present lives – providing a fanciful diversion that fails to seriously challenge or even acknowledge the cataclysmic inevitability of our current political and economic order. Again, this is climate change as a phantasm.

The irreducible difference between consumption patterns in most Western nations and their catastrophic implications creates a future that 'breaks absolutely with the constituted normality and can only be proclaimed, presented, as a sort of monstrosity' (Derrida, 1976: 5). This monstrous, proclaimed future is constructed as an apocalypse that can only be imagined and which will mark the end of civilisation. Destruction itself therefore serves to bolster the pretence of a 'common and shared world'. The phantasm here is the illusion of a mutual end, which further bolsters familiar claims that we are all in this together.

This, too, deftly overlooks that the climate catastrophe is happening *now*. As far back as 2009, for instance, the Maldives government sought to draw international attention to the destruction of its nation's islands by holding an underwater cabinet meeting in scuba gear (Ramesh, 2009). In 2014, during a visit to Australia, the Pacific Climate Warriors highlighted the plight of the residents of Vunidogoloa, Fiji, who had to be relocated after their village was lost to rising waters and violent storms (Chanel, 2014).

Media representation of such issues is often more about the audience than the needs of those left suffering. These most vulnerable communities, including the Small Island Developing States, are represented either as 'proof' of climate change, as passive victims, as refugees or even as tourist destinations (Dreher & Voyer, 2015). This has led to a growing trend of so-called bucket list or last chance tourism, where visitors – usually from developed countries – flock to see melting glaciers, bleaching coral reefs and endangered species such as elephants, tigers or polar bears 'before they are gone' (Weed, 2018). The climate crisis once more becomes a spectacle that exists elsewhere; yet even witnessing its consequences first hand does not allow their integration into the dominant value system of capitalist growth and consumption.

The phantasm of climate change achieves a spectacle of apocalypse, but this is insufficient to disrupt the existing order. It implies a common world and a shared reality, but such notions scarcely chime with the experiences of refugees from lost island nations or the suffering of Louisiana coastal communities wrecked by oil spills and hurricanes (Kang, 2018). It suggests spectacular annihilation, but it does not invite meaningful action. It portends global collapse, but it also assumes survival. Ultimately, it amounts only to a continuously shifting finitude that is forever removed from the present and perpetually devoid of an agenda for genuine sustainability.

7.5 Beyond the Spectacle of Climate Suffering?

In a highly integrated and globalised world that relies on real-time news and social media, one could be forgiven for thinking that the spectacle of worsening climate impacts might drive a fundamental change in politics; that old assumptions might at last be challenged; and that demands for meaningful climate action might become impossible to ignore. Unfortunately, such optimism assumes a commonality and solidarity sadly absent from current discussions of the climate crisis.

The evident suffering resulting from the ongoing destruction of the planet is now ever more visible in news and popular culture, yet it is routinely presented by corporate media as something that happens elsewhere. It may be portrayed as unfortunate, but it is framed as the plight of others. Rather than confronting the prevailing system of capitalism and fossil energy responsible for such misery, the dominant political framing of suffering serves up a world in which these disasters can best be alleviated through corporate innovations in 'sustainability' and new technologies – and in which those who call for more radical responses are both naive and dangerous.

Climate suffering is further presented as a space for business philanthropy and charity – thereby ignoring the underlying causes of the crisis and reinforcing the dominant role of businesses and markets in determining what, if anything, should be done. It also provides a spectacle for further media consumption, in which citizens in affluent Western nations are encouraged to view their situation as fundamentally different from that of the Others already experiencing the horrors of destruction, displacement and social upheaval: consumers can care at a distance, safe in the knowledge that what they are reading about or watching is happening to people and communities elsewhere.

Increasingly, consumers are encouraged to engage with the climate crisis not through political action or involvement but through charitable donations and the purchase of 'sustainable' products. Even the apocalyptic imaginaries of climate disaster now regularly invoked in popular culture are used to further strengthen a fantasy in which we are conveniently distanced from disaster. The underlying politics of the crisis, rather than being challenged, is reinforced at every turn.

In contrast to this dominant framing and its consequent buttressing of the hegemony of corporate capitalism, there is an urgency for promoting ways in which climate suffering might have a more profound political effect. With this in mind, we turn next to politicising suffering. In the following chapter we explore how social movements have sought to bring the fundamental inequality of climate change to the fore and so hold to account those responsible for the planet's ever-accelerating ruination.

8 | The Politics and Agency of Climate Suffering

We will remember a time when our homes stood proud and tall, for today they stand no more.

> Papua New Guinea climate activist, addressing delegates
> at COP26 (quoted in United Nations, 2021b)

As the 2021 UN Climate Change Conference moved into its second week, away from the meetings and deliberations in back rooms, space was provided for addresses from young people already coping with the destruction and chaos of a climate-challenged world. On the eighth day of the event, in the hushed Blue Room, a climate activist from Papua New Guinea read her poem about the transformation of her homeland. 'From the ocean came forth life, peace and comfort, a world not known to most but that was one with my people,' she said. 'That place is now taken by the ocean'. With tears streaming down her cheeks, she went on: 'We will never know when the tide raises and swallows our homes. Our cultures, our languages and our traditions will be taken by the ocean. When you say by 2030 to 2050 ... How can you see deadlines nine to 29 years away when my people have proved that we must act now and not waste any more time?' In the past, she said, nature had sustained her people; now, thanks to the climate crisis, it had become their 'executioner' (United Nations, 2021b).

As the physical realities of the climate crisis become ever more severe, the hegemony of corporate capitalism is having to work harder to deflect the public's gaze from an unravelling world. As recent floods, heatwaves and fires in Europe and North America have revealed, climate change is now a destructive force not only for impoverished communities in the Global South but for the affluent economies of the Global North (Mellen, 2021).

Although far better resourced to respond to its physical impacts, citizens in prosperous nations are increasingly realising the crisis is not something that can invariably be limited to distant others and

146

future generations: rather, it is now a clear and present danger to established patterns of human organisation around the planet. In relatively short order, as a result, the doubt and denial promoted by hegemonic projects supporting corporate capitalism are giving way to a growing acknowledgement that assumptions of continued economic growth and prosperity are under grave threat.

As we noted in Chapter 4, this shift in public sentiment has been evident in the emergence of a wave of climate activism. This is most apparent in popular protests by groups such as Fridays for Future and Extinction Rebellion. The counter-hegemony to continued fossil fuel dependence is growing, and it is within this burgeoning public realisation of the enormity of the crisis that the potential to go beyond the simple politics of pity is becoming a possibility.

In this chapter we explore ways in which climate suffering might have a more profound political effect. Specifically, we examine how activists, young and indigenous people and the members of the many communities impacted by environmental decline and extractivism have challenged their characterisation as powerless individuals, victims or simple consumers and so push back against prevailing framings of climate change as inevitable, necessary or unfortunate.

This required moving beyond the politics of pity and caring at a distance to embrace a more genuine form of compassion – one based on common identities and interests among global citizens facing a shared but differentiated threat. It also demands the dominant portrayal of climate change as spectacle and phantasm to be reframed by bringing the crisis into the present and making it a potential driver for democratic mobilisation.

We identify four avenues to support this mobilisation. The first is the direct use of media to provide more immediate means for scientists and those impacted by climate change to forge links with the broader public. The second comprises new representations of the crisis in art and popular culture to assist in developing more relatable narratives of climate change and what can be done in response. The third is the building of an equivalence of interests and solidarity to challenge the constructed divisions propagated by the fossil fuel hegemony. The fourth is a shifting of the political frontier by assembling a powerful narrative of the fossil fuel industry itself as the differentiated Other to future human existence.

While far from extensive or even coherent developments, these examples highlight the possibilities for a counter-hegemonic response. By making climate suffering visible and present, individuals and communities have contested portrayals of the crisis as inevitable; overturning their depiction as impotent bystanders and reclaiming agency and power by directly confronting the vested interests responsible for their woes.

8.1 Beyond the Distant Spectacle: The Climate Crisis Is Now

A major impediment to broader public engagement with climate change is the way in which the issue has been framed within media and politics as a distant spatial and temporal concern. As explained in the previous chapter, news coverage invariably presents extreme weather events and humanitarian disasters as remote developments that can be observed as spectacles in far-flung places or which might materialise in some long-off future. A key question for those advocating climate action is therefore how to go beyond this distancing and engage the public politically in recognising the urgency of the problem.

The difficulties in making climate change accessible to a mass audience are well known and can be divided into three overarching hurdles. First, the scale of the crisis is immense and hard to compartmentalise, as the reshaping of planetary systems literally 'changes everything' (Klein, 2014). Second, as also observed in the preceding chapter, focusing on the recovery from the destruction of superstorms and record-breaking wildfires leaves little room for a discussion of the causes of these disasters: they become the spectacle, and the political is ignored. Third, fossil fuel businesses have been hugely successful in casting climate change as an amorphous issue in which everyone is complicit (McKibben, 2005).

While the tendency of corporate media has been to prop up the status quo, alternative forums have been used to push back against complacency and bring climate change into the now. Often employing personal and narrative framing to bridge the gap between the audience and what is a planetary-scale biophysical phenomenon, documentaries have proven a key means of publicly highlighting the crisis.

An Inconvenient Truth (Guggenheim, 2006), which documented former US Vice-President Al Gore's efforts to communicate the urgency of global warming, was formative in this regard. It proved tremendously popular, earning more than US$50 million at the box office and winning numerous prizes – including the 2007 Academy Award for Best Documentary Feature. Offering a compelling personal narrative focused on a central character engaged in a heroic quest (Smith & Howe, 2015) – as opposed to a dry and didactic thesis – the film is credited as one of the most significant developments in shaping the public discourse on climate change. Gore was jointly awarded the Nobel Peace Prize in 2007 for his work in this sphere.

Both *Before the Flood* (Stevens, 2016), featuring movie star Leonardo DiCaprio, and *David Attenborough: A Life on Our Planet* (Fothergill et al., 2020) followed *An Inconvenient Truth* in using the narrative device of placing a famous individual's growing awareness of climate change within a broader life story. Through their renown and charisma, these central figures garnered sizeable audiences and attracted public attention to the issue while at the same time highlighting the pathos of our degraded natural world and the suffering it causes. Emotions of grief, loss and anger – as well as hope – have also been evident in films such as *Chasing Ice* (Orlowski, 2012) and *Chasing Coral* (Orlowski, 2017), which explored climate scientists' work in seeking to visually document the deterioration of glaciers and coral reefs.

While at times providing forums for denial, newer forms of media have also been used to move past the hegemonic construct of distance. Produced outside mainstream domains and sometimes termed the 'fifth estate', they are increasingly favoured by researchers and organisations campaigning to bring concerns about the crisis more directly into the public conscious. For instance, scientists such as Michael Mann launched the RealClimate.org blog to counter the large amounts of misinformation on climate change in the commercialised media. An especially interesting development has been the use of Twitter to counter climate-sceptic arguments. As Mann has remarked (in Scott, 2020): 'In the past the journalist interviewed the scientist . . . Now the scientist is much more involved in the ongoing process of dissemination . . . You no longer have the obstacles that used to exist to direct engagement in the conversation'. The intention here is to bring scientific understanding to a bigger audience and transcend the corrosive tropes that populate the mainstream narrative.

Beyond making the science of the phenomenon more relatable, new media can be used to document the impacts of climate change and bring them more clearly into view. Some studies have shown perceptions of the links between extreme weather events and global warming, as well as the stories of those who suffer, are more likely to lead to concern and action (Hamilton & Stampone, 2013; Otto, 2017). The use of social media to personalise people's experiences at least offers the potential to enhance the wider grasp of environmental disaster's impacts (Anderson, 2017).

It is right to concede that the findings of research on the efficacy of social media in motivating action on climate change are at present mixed; yet ongoing projects aimed at photographing, visualising and communicating the crisis maintain the hope of bringing the issue 'closer'. They can make it more tangible and build connections with the communities and landscapes that are being impacted. By extension, they also preserve the possibility of sparking imaginative responses yet to be realised (Newell & Dale, 2015).

For example, the growing 'solarpunk' community uses imagery, fiction and online discussion to produce 'a speculative imaginary' in which current technical, social and energy futures are configured to address not only climate change but an array of environmental challenges (Williams, 2019). Such processes of making the implications of the crisis more immediately understood, along with the forming of new connections, have the potential to evoke the far-reaching shifts necessary to break the existing hegemony.

8.2 From Spectacle to Action: Building a Radical Imagination

Since the mid-2000s, in addition to the new forms of communication discussed earlier, there has been an explosion of interest in climate change within different cultural mediums. These include art, music, performance and literature. This suggests long-standing barriers are being overcome.

Crucial here is the development of a new narrative. As we have described, the hegemony favours distance, observation and consumption. What is needed is a discourse that removes remoteness and makes the crisis something felt and understood at a deeper emotional and personal level. Climate suffering expressed through cultural modes of representation, performance and storytelling can transform how audiences relate to environmental collapse, helping muster a more meaningful challenge to the status quo. As 350.org founder Bill McKibben

(2009) has argued, artists are the 'antibodies of the cultural bloodstream': they 'bring to bear the human power for love and beauty and meaning against the worst results of carelessness and greed and stupidity'. Art and literature have the potential to play a pivotal role here by drawing upon experiences outside dominant conventions to critique the hegemony, or as Yusoff (2010: 94) put it more viscerally, '[C]limate change must force new images full of loss and rage that scream through our aesthetic orders'. Moreover, as recognised public identities, artists can share their vision to mobilise public support by constructing a relatable human concern. This highlights the importance of artists in collectivising experiences.

There is a long history of artists engaging with environmental concerns, with visual imagery playing a particularly prominent role in the evolution of conservationism in the US (Dunaway, 2005). Consider, for instance, the landscapes of the nineteenth century frontier and the romantic wilderness photography that originally inspired the conservation movement; the more political imagery that stemmed from the New Deal and the Dust Bowl during the 1930s and the overtly activist imagery – termed 'mind bombs' by contemporary Greenpeace members – used to publicise campaigns against whaling and seal hunting in the 1970s and 1980s (Mathiesen, 2015; Peter & Neville, 2011). More broadly, the political potential of photography was demonstrated by the first images of Earth from space, which have been credited with a fundamental shift in humanity's comprehension of its place in the universe and the concept of 'spaceship Earth' (Poole, 2010).

Many other mediums have been used to convey the importance and implications of climate change. Examples include Olafur Eliasson's *Ice Watch* installation, which involved the transportation of large blocks of melting glacial ice to the UN Climate Change Conference in Paris (Rea, 2018); Jill Pelto's figurative watercolours, which use illustrations of ice cores, tree rings, clownfish and burning forests to embellish graphs charting climate change's grim progression (Fessenden, 2016) and Edward Burtynsky's striking aerial photos of the industrial degradation of nature, including vast open-cut mine sites, the patterns of fields disfigured by large-scale agriculture and the surreal colours of oil spills in the Gulf of Mexico (Burtynsky et al., 2018). Beyond their aesthetic value, these works seek to provoke an emotional response and a connection to the climate crisis. Voices of grief, anger, loss and fear can provide a focus for broader citizenly activism, providing a public space for the mobilisation of more radical critiques of the world. As Eliasson (2018) has said of his art: 'Feelings of distance and disconnect hold us back, make us grow numb and passive. I hope that *Ice Watch* arouses feelings of proximity, presence and relevance – of narratives that you can identify with and that make us all engage'.

Artistic engagement with climate change has also spilled into performance, plays and literature. In the Pacific, for instance, the crisis has become a key theme for indigenous theatre groups, which use mediums such as dance to highlight the existential threat facing their homelands, societies and identities, as well as the wider politics of mobility and migration (Suliman et al., 2019). Western theatre has also begun to engage with the human and moral quandaries of the climate crisis. Plays such as *Ten Billion* (Emmott, 2013) and *2071* (Rapley & MacMillan, 2015) have adopted a lecture-like format to articulate scientists' confrontation with worsening evidence of the crisis. Narrative-based dramas, including *Earthquakes in London* (Bartlett, 2010) and *The Children* (Kirkwood, 2016), have explored climate change's influence on personal relationships and psychological catharsis (Hoydis, 2020). These dramatic interventions have extended into the use of 'street theatre' and provocative protest art such as Extinction Rebellion's 'die-ins' outside financial districts like New York's Wall Street (Keith, 2019), and the artist collective 'Liberate Tate' which has challenged oil giant BP's financial support of the Tate art galleries through 'artistic installations and performances that would maximize visual spectacle in order to attract media attention' (Motion, 2019: 736). Examples of these transgressive performances have included interventions at sponsored events recreating the devastating Deepwater Horizon oil spill complete with dead fish and birds, and troupes of naked performers smothered in an oil-like substance writhing on the floor of the museum.

In the sphere of literature, meanwhile, the genre of climate fiction – 'cli-fi' – has experienced rapid growth. Speculative climate imaginings have included Paolo Bacigalupi's *The Windup Girl* (2010), Margaret Atwood's *MaddAddam* trilogy (2003; 2009, 2013) and Kim Stanley Robinson's *Ministry for the Future* (2020); there have also been more contemporary, intergenerational and often highly personal accounts, among them Barbara Kingsolver's *Flight Behavior* (2012), James Bradley's *Clade* (2015) and Richard Powers' *The Overstory* (2018). As well as featuring climate change as an ever-present context within which characters seek to survive, these novels depict alternatives and envision how things could be different (Wright et al., 2013; De Cock et al., 2021). Cli-fi allows readers to engage with the crisis at a personal, local and emotional level and to consider possible futures that, while often dystopian and chaotic, are filled with compassion and human connection (Johns-Putra, 2016).

The final dominant cultural medium in our society, TV and film, appears to have even greater potential to raise public awareness of climate change. Climate disruption often forms part of the dystopian backdrop to the human tales of suffering central to movies such as *Children of Men* (Cuarón, 2006) and *Interstellar* (Nolan, 2014) and TV dramas such as *The Handmaid's Tale* (Miller, 2016). For instance, while criticised for its fanciful portrayal of a rapidly unfolding disaster, Hollywood blockbuster *The Day After Tomorrow* (Emmerich, 2004) has been credited with having a significant influence on the US recognition of the crisis and the voting intentions of American moviegoers (Leiserowitz, 2004). The impact of movies on popular understandings of the climate crisis has been further highlighted recently by the satirical comedy, *Don't Look Up* (McKay, 2021) which has proven a huge hit for streaming service Netflix and, given its A-star Hollywood cast and skewering of politics, popular culture and media triviality, reshaped popular discussion of the climate crisis (Kalmus, 2021). Thus, while popular culture and celebrity activism might serve to trivialise an issue (Boykoff & Goodman, 2009; Turner, 2016), the broad reach of these mediums has the power to sway public opinion on a significant scale – thereby not only breaking the interpretive denial endemic in climate politics but perhaps fostering greater awareness of, and compassion for, those communities and species already in desperate peril.

Of course, a vital question remains: to what extent can watching films, reading books or observing artworks and performances propel public understanding beyond an elementary awareness of climate change? Moreover, might these in fact be no more than additional means of consuming the spectacle? For instance, critics have pointed to the supposed hypocrisy of artists or celebrities endorsing climate action while jetting around the world or living lavish lifestyles (Smith & Howe, 2015), and there is indeed an irony that the majority of these artistic voices are from wealthier nations with a stronger capacity to respond to the vagaries of climate change. However, while there are clearly limits in their capacity to drive political action, these cultural mediums do illustrate how the suffering resulting from the crisis can take on meanings other than those promoted in the mainstream.

Here we see several possibilities. First, as noted earlier, cultural mediums such as art, literature and film often provide a personal and emotional interpretation of an issue like climate change that builds meaning and understanding beyond the abstract facts and figures of an amorphous scientific phenomenon (Wright & Nyberg, 2022). That is, they can make things which are spread across time and space, what Morton (2013) terms 'hyperobjects', into something real and relatable at an individual level that can then build connection and possibly motivation and activism.

Second, these cultural interpretations of climate change can challenge dominant social understandings and promote alternative imaginaries of how the future could be different. For instance, while the dominant social imaginary of corporate capitalism emphasises economic progress, technological optimism and endless consumption, cultural interventions can not only surface the environmental collapse and suffering that are ignored but also upset the linear progression of the present into the future (Wright et al., 2013). Art, literature, music and theatre can provide spaces to imagine the world differently and reclaim the forgotten histories and marginalised others that are ignored in the current assumptions of economic progress. This need not be some kind of naïve utopian nirvana, but rather a 'hope without optimism' that directly confronts current environmental destruction and political corruption while charting a future in fighting to alter this path (De Cock et al., 2021). As Miéville (2018: np) cuttingly notes, 'it is worth fighting even for ashes, because there are better and much, much worse ways of being too late. Because and yet. This shit is where we are. A junk heap of history and hope'.

However, this requires not only critical voices from the Global North but also more diverse narratives from those at the frontlines of the climate crisis. As Greta Thunberg declared during her speech before the UN in 2019: 'You have stolen my dreams and my childhood with your empty words. And yet I am one of the lucky ones. People are suffering. People are dying' (Thunberg, 2019a). It is to this issue of the representation of suffering from those on the frontlines of the climate crisis and how this can act as a source of political agency that we now turn.

8.3 Building Climate Solidarity: From Victims to Agents of Change

There is a fundamental inequity of suffering in the climate crisis. This has been especially palpable at the UN's annual Conference of the Parties where despite thirty years of international negotiations, any reductions in carbon emissions have failed to eventuate. However, these arenas of political dialogue have provided a critical space for the world's poorest and most vulnerable people to construct and illustrate the underlying antagonism of the climate crisis.

This has been evident in the participation of climate activists, young people and representatives of indigenous communities, as well as in the protests and other gatherings that have surrounded various COPs (Banerjee, 2012; Smith & Howe, 2015). Crucially, it has also been evident in the negotiations themselves, where the leaders of rich and carbon-intensive countries have come face to face with people from developing nations already staggering under the weight of worsening environmental impacts. As journalist Fiona Harvey has remarked:

So in the same room you will have the poorest developing countries whose lives are being shattered and destroyed by the use of fossil fuels in rich countries, and they are sitting down at the same table with the people who are making money from fossil fuels. There's nowhere else that that happens. And that is a very powerful thing, because it is the poorest and most vulnerable people who have the moral authority here (Safi & Harvey, 2021).

As illustrated at the start of this chapter, COPs are thus not only a space of international negotiation but also provide a platform for those personally affected by climate change to confront those most responsible for this crisis. In so doing, representatives from those on the frontlines of the climate crisis in the Global South can give voice to the realities of a deteriorating planet. Take the words of Maldives Environment Minister Aminath Shauna, who told the assembled national representatives at COP26 in Glasgow: 'I would like to remind us all that we have 98 months to halve global emissions. The difference between 1.5 and 2°C is a death sentence for us' (Hook, 2021). Or, consider the sentiments expressed by a young Filipino survivor of Typhoon Haiyan during a debate over proposals for rich nations to pay compensation for the 'loss and damage' arising from extreme weather events: 'They stopped counting when the death toll reached 6,000, but there are 1,600 bodies still missing … The Philippines' youth are fighting for a future that is not riddled with anxiety and fear that another Haiyan might come at any time to threaten our loved ones' lives and dreams. We do not deserve to live in fear' (United Nations, 2021b). It is through such clear, eloquent and profoundly personal articulations that the spectacle of environmental disaster gives way to the human and emotional responses to the destruction of large parts of the developing world.

These statements have a tone of sorrow, grief and loss. Offering a marked contrast to the projected role of unfortunate victims – a strategy rife in so much media reporting of climate catastrophes – they also speak of courage and mounting anger. They are pervaded by the idea of fighting for a better future and shot through with an escalating rage at the injustice of wealthy countries and corporations delaying meaningful action in order to maximise their short-term wealth. As young Pacific climate activist Brianna Fruean declared in a speech at the opening of COP26: 'We are not just victims of this crisis. We have been resilient beacons of hope. Pacific youth have rallied behind the cry "We are not drowning – we are fighting". This is our warrior cry to the world' (SPREP, 2021).

Fury at the fundamental inequities of climate suffering in the Global South is also increasingly used as a salutary warning to rich economies in the Global North. The message is that climate change is not something that can be avoided behind sea walls or in bunkers. As a UN representative of small island states said during the COP26 deliberations: 'The waters are literally lapping at our ankles in the places where we should be living. You need to look at us as the canary in the coal mine' (United Nations, 2021c).

The argument that climate inaction is not just an issue of injustice but a manifestation of abysmal self-interest was in many ways most powerfully underlined at COP26 by former Maldives President Mohamed Nasheed. His cutting remarks encapsulated the myopia of all those who are committed to the perpetuation of the fossil fuel hegemony and who insist on viewing climate change through the warped lens of others' passivity and voicelessness. Directing his comments to the world's richest nations, Nasheed warned: 'If you want to protect your way of life, your livelihood, you must change. It's no longer [a question of] we're going to lose the Maldives and these small island states. No, it's not that anymore. *You* are going to lose ... We are all going to lose' (Safi & Nasheed, 2021).

In these ways communities at the forefront of climate change impacts have brought to bear, in unavoidable ways, the injustices and the implications of the outcomes for all of the fossil fuel hegemony continues unabated. By confronting – often quite literally – those who might tend to ignore their suffering, the lens of passivity and voicelessness is turned, to instead emphasise the injustices under which many will suffer.

8.4 Flipping Hegemony: Fossil Fuels as a 'Sin Industry'

Growing awareness of climate suffering in advanced economies suggests a cultural reinterpretation of fossil energy is at last under way. An important development in this regard was the final agreement ratified at COP26, which for the first time mentioned fossil fuels by name and agreed to their 'phasing down' over time (Harvey et al., 2021).

In addition, former advocates such as the IEA, the OECD and many large financial institutions have notably changed their tune of late (IEA, 2021a; Harvey, 2021c). Their apparent acceptance that a reduction in fossil fuel use is essential to the future of the planet implies the hegemony is coming under mounting pressure, despite its ongoing structural embeddedness within the global economy.

To continue this seemingly positive direction of travel, climate activists and climate-threatened communities need to construct a broader alliance. We have already seen how the fossil fuel industry has sought to build connections with different groups in maintaining its dominance and demarcating a political frontier against its opponents; now those same opponents are attempting to reshape the frontier and shift public opinion to the idea of a 'sin industry'. The goal is to make fossil fuels the Other – a force clearly recognisable as directly at odds with human and ecological well-being.

We explained earlier how the industry, politicians and media have long framed climate change as an issue to which all citizens are contributors and for which we are all therefore equally 'guilty'. This has allowed implicated corporations to resist calls for decarbonisation and reductions in emissions and to insist they are simply meeting consumers' needs. Effectively a triumph of marketing, such a strategy has been successfully deployed for decades (Mann, 2021). In the early

2000s, for example, as part of its 'Beyond Petroleum' rebranding, BP launched one of the first personal carbon footprint calculators. The likes of ExxonMobil, Shell and Adani are still pushing the message that the fight against global warming should start with individual consumption choices (Scott, 2021; Supran & Oreskes, 2021). Conspicuously absent from this kind of demand-side framing is the issue of supply – specifically, the way in which major corporations and petrostates have carried on producing the vast bulk of the world's emissions while actively lobbying and pressuring for the relentless expansion of fossil energy (Heede, 2014; Taylor & Watts, 2019).

One of the critical ways in which environmentalists have been able to challenge this hegemonic discourse has been to recast the political frontier and invert the social legitimacy of fossil fuel capital. A powerful example of this process was the highly influential article in *Rolling Stone* magazine in 2012 by climate activist Bill McKibben, who clearly set out how the world's remaining fossil fuel reserves were five times greater than the carbon budget left if the planet was to avoid catastrophic global warming.

As McKibben (2012) noted, digging up and burning those reserves would irrevocably endanger the Earth's life-support systems. Advocating financial divestment from fossil fuel stocks, McKibben subsequently stressed the immorality of carbon-intensive energy and the politicians prepared to endorse it. 'If it's wrong to wreck the climate', he said, 'it's wrong to profit from that wreckage' (McKibben, 2013). In developing the global fossil fuel divestment movement, climate activists have increasingly stressed fossil energy is not only unethical but unjust. The fossil fuel industry 'has become a rogue industry, reckless like no other force on Earth. It is Public Enemy Number One to the survival of our planetary civilisation' (McKibben, 2012). The divestment movement has drawn attention both to those already affected and to the imperilment of the generations to come. In constructing a political frontier, they have used climate suffering as the basis for moral and ethical arguments for the financial and political marginalisation of fossil fuel capital.

There are nascent signs that these appeals are now even beginning to resonate in the highest echelons of corporate capitalism. Consider, for example, the recent revelation, as reported by the *New York Times* in the lead-up to COP26, that elite global management consultancy McKinsey & Company faced an internal rebellion from employees in light of its extensive advisory work for some of the world's largest fossil fuel companies. More than a thousand members of staff signed an open letter to McKinsey's partners, expressing outrage at the firm's continued engagement with the likes of BP, ExxonMobil, Gazprom and Saudi Aramco. Observing that the 'climate crisis is the defining issue of our generation', the signatories urged McKinsey to publicly disclose the aggregate amount of carbon pollution produced by its clients and warned: 'Our positive impact in other realms will mean nothing if we do not act as our clients alter the earth irrevocably' (Forsythe & Bogdanich, 2021).

Several of the letter's authors later resigned, citing McKinsey's ongoing involvement with fossil fuel businesses as incompatible with their own concerns. While the company's partners responded by claiming McKinsey should be seen as helping the planet transition to a net-zero future (Sternfels, 2021), critics have pointed out that much of the consultancy's work focuses on improving the efficiency of fossil fuel extraction and enhancing corporate profitability. In the words of one departing employee: 'Having looked at the actual hours billed to the world's largest polluters, it is very hard to argue today that McKinsey is the "greatest private-sector catalyst for decarbonisation" ... It may well be the exact opposite' (Forsythe & Bogdanich, 2021).

Fossil fuel capital's stranglehold on corporate and political power has also been challenged at an individual level. This has been evident in the growing number of business leaders who have embraced the need for urgent action, often following a personal epiphany of some kind (Confino, 2012; Wright et al., 2012). The story of former BP executive Tim Sanderson offers an especially compelling illustration.

Sanderson spent much of his career in the oil business, at one point even heading research into the development of offshore drilling in the Arctic. His Damascene moment came when his daughter, a climate activist, was arrested and taken to court after chaining herself to a runway at Heathrow Airport in protest at the expansion of the high-emitting aviation industry. As she faced the threat of a prison sentence, Sanderson spoke of his pride in his daughter and praised the moral stand she and her fellow activists had taken. He said her arrest had brought home to him the fundamental conflict between the political obfuscation of the climate crisis and the scientific reality. He joined other protesters outside court, where they waved placards and chanted: 'No ifs! No buts! No new runways!' 'I am appalled by the apparently

complete disconnect between what we know and what we do',
Sanderson said. 'This … is about the global environment'
(Sanderson, 2016).

With mounting evidence of the climate crisis and the manifest suffering it is causing now registering within richer economies in the Global
North, it appears even the most senior corporate figures are starting to
question the morality of working for and facilitating the fossil fuel
hegemony. This shift in sentiment has prompted the industry to go so
far as to claim it is a victim of a 'cancel culture on hydrocarbons'
(GECF, 2021). As employees and consumers alike rethink the merits
of carbon-intensive energy and the all-consuming threat it poses, climate suffering is demonstrating its political potential for ushering in
substantive and desperately needed change.

8.5 Solidarity or Borders

In this chapter, we have considered how it might be possible to move
beyond the politics of pity. We have explored means of developing
compassion and mobilising political action for those already suffering
the impacts of climate change and those apparently doomed to suffer
them in the future. Perhaps optimistically, we have shown how this is
occurring in four key ways: direct connections through alternative
media; new representations in art and popular culture; the building of
greater solidarity through the political agency of people and communities and the inversion of the existing hegemony through the realisation
of fossil fuel capital as the true Other to future human well-being.

It remains to be seen how long the growing suffering and injustice of the
climate crisis can be contained within the comfortable fantasy that nothing significant can or will change. The fallacy that a rapidly worsening
climate crisis, which now threatens large parts of the world's population,
can be accommodated by vague pledges to reduce emissions and embrace
more 'sustainable' business practices is increasingly apparent. Just as the
tone is shifting in the discourse of climate activists and those directly
threatened by climate change, it is becoming harder for richer economies
and the Global North to deny the unfolding of the crisis. It is becoming
ever more difficult to maintain the delusion of a distant spectacle. What is
happening can now increasingly be seen, smelt, felt and feared.

It must be acknowledged, of course, that these counter-hegemonic
developments we have explored are far from universal or coherent.

While climate mobilisation has grown significantly in recent years, reshaping political debates around the world, there still stands against them a vast network of corporations, industry associations, financiers, lobbyists, politicians, advisers and PR professionals advocating the continuation of 'business as usual' and the perpetuation of suffering as a strictly remote concern. Moreover, many states show signs of further intensifying their coercive approaches – including broadening definitions of extremist activity, amplifying the discourse of so-called 'eco-terrorism' and stepping up the criminalisation of environmental protest (Irwin et al., 2022). This is often backed by an increasingly aggressive nationalism, rejection of international responsibilities and reassertion of resource extraction as essential to economic development. Climate mobilisation may have grown significantly in recent years, reshaping political debates around the world; but so, alas, has the reactive politics supporting a continuation of fossil fuel–driven capitalist growth and the further destruction of the planet's life-support systems. In response to climate change, history might suggest that the more likely responses are harder borders, new walls and geopolitical competitions.

In the battle for public legitimacy, as we have noted, the hegemony of fossil fuel capital is now fighting for its life. This gives rise to the question of how desperate the fight might now become? There remains the danger that differences, divisions and inequalities will only worsen; that governments will become more authoritarian and autocratic; that citizens will become more enraged and more fiercely determined in seeking change and that societies will break apart in a grim spiral of 'barbarisation' (Gallopín & Raskin, 1998; Urry, 2008). As we noted earlier in this chapter, this is one possible future imaginary; however, there are others which offer the possibility of greater solidarity and persistence in the face of catastrophe.

PART V

The Politics of Climate Futures

9 | Decarbonisation, Degrowth and Democracy

They weren't radicals. They were elderly people, well-respected seniors from the Bentley area, farmers.

> Michael Daley, Australian Labor Party politician, discussing
> the blockade of Metgasco's planned gasfield
> in Bentley, New South Wales (ABC News, 2014)

The Bentley Blockade rose to prominence in 2014, becoming one of Australia's most successful community-led campaigns against fossil fuel extraction. Driven by concerns over the encroachment of the gas industry, proposals for fracking and climate change in general, it took the form of a round-the-clock protest that brought together a wide cross-section of stakeholders – ranging from Aboriginal elders to 'knitting nanas'. The blockade was supported by local businesses. In a rare show of agreement, representatives from across the political spectrum – from the conservative National Party to the environmentally conscious Australian Greens – also gave their backing. As the campaign grew, attracting individuals from neighbouring communities, protester numbers topped 10,000 – eventually prompting the New South Wales Government to plan Operation Stapler, a multi-million-dollar response that would see riot squads and around 800 police officers descend on the site to dismantle the camp. Yet the raid never happened. Instead, just days before the operation was due to take place, the NSW Government announced it was suspending Metgasco's licence on the basis that the company had not conducted appropriate community consultation. The victory ultimately paved the way for the same government's 2021 decision to cut the amount of land eligible for gas exploration by 77 per cent (NSW Government, 2021).

The responses needed to avoid utterly devastating future impacts arising from climate change are relatively clear. Leave fossil fuels in the ground; radically decarbonise economic activity around the globe; and draw down CO_2 in the atmosphere through the fostering and regeneration of forests and other carbon sinks. Despite the characterisation of a 'wicked' problem (Grundmann, 2016), the science is settled; moreover, there are recognised responses that are being developed and which simply await the political will to be implemented.

The challenge of climate change is therefore political – which is to say this is a question of addressing 'the political' by constructing a new foundation for societies. This foundation must *not* be built on the notion of fossil energy as the basis for perpetual growth and endless consumer capitalism: rather, it must be built on stronger democratic organisation and on institutions that sustain life on this planet. Victories such as that achieved by the Bentley Blockade are few in number, but they show how to construct a logic of equivalence among a diverse set of groups in developing the necessary counter-hegemony.

In this chapter we set out a path for a more climate-friendly politics. We discuss the required decarbonisation of the economic system; we consider the eventual degrowth needed not only to address the existing crisis but also to avoid the creation of another; and we explore the strengthening of democracy essential to breaking the fossil fuel hegemony that still dominates global market relations. Such ideas are often accused of being naive, unrealistic and contrary to so-called 'common sense', but responding to climate change demands an epochal rethink of what should be seen as 'sensible' – not least since this conceit is currently associated with destroying the life-support systems humanity depends on for survival.

This chapter is directed towards Western capitalist democracies, principally because the Global North is by far the foremost source of greenhouse gases. Historically, it has been responsible for the vast majority – 92 per cent, to be exact – of emissions beyond the safe planetary boundary of 350ppm atmospheric CO_2 concentration (Hickel, 2020b). This inequality in carbon profligacy continues today, with annual emissions per capita in the US – to take an obvious example – of 15.2 tonnes, compared to only 2.2 tonnes in Indonesia (Climate Watch, 2021). In addition, Western countries have the resources and wealth to bring about the necessary political shift both within their own nations and in the Global South – which, as remarked in the previous chapter, disproportionately suffers the most significant impacts of the climate catastrophe.

The solutions we propose, then, are guided not only by the ecological limits dictated by the Earth's climate system but also by the fundamental notion of a response whose burden is justly distributed. However, it is important to stress that our intention is not to replace the contingent *capitalist* foundation of society with a simple *ecological* foundation; we want to avoid the reification that occurs when discussing 'nature' or 'Mother Earth'.

We instead argue that the current breed of capitalism is a relatively new form of human organising (Wallerstein, 2004) and that it is this particular system, with its steely focus on the ceaseless accumulation of capital, that leads to the contradictions underpinning ecological destruction. The idea of conquering the natural realm through technology provides a classic illustration of the dualistic thinking that supposes a split between society and nature. Rejecting the idea that society stops where nature starts is perhaps the most important step in finding solutions to the current crisis. Caring for the planet means supporting the societies that inhabit it – and vice versa.

9.1 Decarbonisation

As detailed in earlier chapters, growing social concerns over the climate crisis have prompted the fossil fuel industry to embrace – at least apparently – the concept of net-zero emissions. Many businesses have made public commitments to net-zero targets, as well as proposing technological 'solutions' such as carbon capture and storage and geo-engineering. Beyond such posturing, though, the basic message is that the extraction, production and consumption of fossil fuels can continue and that very little – if anything – should actually change.

Notwithstanding twenty-six annual UN Climate Change Conferences, greenhouse gas emissions are still increasing. Even if technological innovations were to slow their growth, their accumulation throughout hundreds of years of carbon-intensive industrialisation is set to produce an unhabitable planet. Many will linger in the atmosphere for centuries (IPCC, 2021). Climate science clearly shows the only viable solutions involve rapid and unprecedented decarbonisation, which entails an exit from fossil energy as quickly as possible; but the lack of progress in this regard is only too evident.

It is equally clear that current responses from the fossil fuel hegemony ultimately constitute a concerted attempt to hide the conflict between corporate capitalism and the sustainability of functioning ecosystems. By papering over this contradiction, debates over how to react to the worsening crisis are limited to what is possible within the existing business system – as a result of which they stay at the level of politics, with industries and nations competing over faux 'solutions' by constructing an equivalence between their own interests and societal demands. What is needed is a more fundamental discussion of how societies can be rebuilt to exist within planetary boundaries in both the present and the future.

Alternatives to a fossil fuel–based economy are not only technologically possible: they are already being implemented – albeit in a belated and partial fashion. Such innovations focus on the key industrial sectors that produce the bulk of carbon emissions – for example, energy, manufacturing, transport, agriculture and food production (Harvey et al., 2018). Most notable are the moves across many economies towards large-scale adoption of renewable energy as a path towards decarbonisation.

It is now feasible to move the current 'combustion-based' energy system to '100 per cent clean, renewable wind, water and solar (WWS) electricity and heat' (Jacobson, 2020: xiii). This would involve replacing the dominant model of extracting and combusting coal, oil and gas with renewables such as onshore and offshore wind turbines, solar farms, rooftop photovoltaic (PV) systems, hydroelectric power and geothermal and wave energy. Led by fossil fuel businesses and their political allies, critics have argued for years that such technologies cannot satisfy the energy needs of a growing global population; yet a recent quantitative analysis across twenty-four regions claims that not only can renewables meet projected demand but they can do so in ways that limit spatial footprints and land use (Jacobson, 2020).

As outlined in Chapter 3, worldwide investment in renewable energy has accelerated dramatically during the past decade and now dwarfs new investment in fossil energy sources. Estimates indicate well over half of all electricity production is likely to be derived from renewables by 2050 (BloombergNEF, 2019). Evidence of this shift can be seen in advances in battery storage technology, which are enabling far wider application of renewable electrification across economies (Katz, 2020); proposals to export solar-generated electricity to neighbouring countries via high-voltage direct current (HVDC) transmission lines (Vorrath, 2021) and the production through electrolysis of 'green' hydrogen for use in key industrial processes, shipping and heavy transport (Oliveira et al., 2021).

Fewer sectors now remain technologically difficult to decarbonise. An obvious example, given its reliance on hydrocarbon jet fuel, is aviation (Chiaramonti, 2019). A compelling illustration of what could be achieved elsewhere can be found in agriculture and food production, where new technologies offer enormous scope to reduce methane emissions from livestock, cut the amount of land needed for crop production and limit the destruction of valuable carbon sinks (Smith, Bustamante, et al., 2014).

However, there is a marked difference between what is technologically viable in creating a decarbonised world and the realpolitik of attempting to shift away from a global economy that depends on fossil energy and continuous economic growth. It is here that the political economy of corporate capitalism exhibits such a powerful grip.

For instance, a key policy driver for the widespread adoption of renewable energy is the regulation and taxation of carbon pollution (Metcalf & Weisbach, 2009). Unfortunately, any attempts by governments to implement tax regimes on emissions have faced vehement opposition for many decades from the historical bloc comprised of fossil fuel companies, business associations, media, conservative politicians and affected workforces (Copland, 2020). The hegemony has been highly successful in limiting any efforts even to *reduce* emissions, let alone to tax them and thereby somehow promote rival technologies.

Other proposals to shift the policy dial towards decarbonisation have included more supply-side levers, such as removing fossil fuel subsidies, imposing quotas and moratoriums on extraction and production, providing low-carbon infrastructure and offering renewable energy subsidies and feed-in incentives (Green & Denniss, 2018). Again, though, these viable options almost invariably run up against dominant interests that are fiercely opposed to any scaling back of fossil energy and which, given their place at the centre of political power, are ideally positioned to perpetuate their established ascendency.

As a result, the desperately needed decarbonisation of economies and societies faces repeated and massive political hostility. This is starkly illustrated by the fact that, even in light of a dramatic increase in renewables investment and the rapidly expanding application of solar and wind power, fossil fuels still account for 83 per cent of the world's energy consumption (BP, 2021). Richer nations may have been able to cut their greenhouse gases by outsourcing manufacturing to their so-called developing counterparts, but global emissions continue to increase (IEA, 2021b).

While richer nations, and many businesses, rely on carbon offsets to fulfil their net-zero commitments, this concept fails to address the fundamental problem of rising emissions. It is rather like paying someone else not to eat so you can enjoy an extra meal: the 'net' result may be thought of as zero, but the fact is that two meals have still been consumed. While the corporate and political machinations of climate policy and carbon accounting serve to obfuscate blame and mitigate criticism, the unfortunate physical evidence is that the planet reacts solely to the aggregate atmospheric concentrations of greenhouse gases.

The implementation of renewable energy alongside existing industrial models raises further environmental and social concerns – and not just because extant infrastructure can constrain the location of new installations (Clark, 2021). Novel technologies are generally less impactful on landscapes and ecosystems, but they can still cause environmental damage and negatively affect the quality of life in poorer and indigenous communities. Witness, for instance, the rush to construct hydroelectric dams in Asia, Africa and South America (Moran et al., 2018), and mounting allegations of 'renewable energy colonialism' (Batel, 2021).

The successful deployment of renewable energy projects demands several conditions to be met. From a corporate perspective, these might include profitability and shareholder returns; from a broader perspective, they include extensive local community consultation and what we might think of as the democratisation of energy. At present, as has almost invariably been the case, the requirements of the corporate sphere appear more likely to be met than those of communities – or even those of the environment.

We believe it is insufficient merely to construct an equivalence around the social demands for renewable energy and to then differentiate these from the fossil fuel hegemony on the other side of the political frontier. This represents only a first step because the arguments to date have almost always neglected to address the contingent and antagonistic foundation of society through which the notion of exponential, fossil-fuelled growth is maintained.

To put it another way: simply implementing renewable energy on a large scale does not necessarily break the links between environmental damage and the constructed foundations on which capitalism rests. It is essential that the unsustainability of exponential growth is also revealed and that the inherent failings of capitalism are laid bare and recognised. This is where the degrowth movement enters the picture.

9.2 Degrowth

The global economy is already breaching a range of critical planetary boundaries (Rockström et al., 2009). As a result, even if greenhouse gas emissions stabilise or decline, the Earth faces an array of environmental disruptions that endanger the functioning of basic biological and physiological systems.

As we have argued, the endless accumulation of capital is the defining objective of modern capitalism. The underpinning idea is that expansion creates further profit and that compound growth can proceed ad infinitum. The escalating environmental disasters arising from this ethos – and in particular from the consumption practices of the Global North – extend far beyond climate change.

For instance, overfishing has decimated fish stocks. As well as posing a serious problem to the billion-plus people worldwide who rely on fish for survival, this threatens marine food chains and complex ecosystems such as coral reefs (Sumaila & Tai, 2020). Similarly, commercial farming practices – which have relied on large-scale deforestation and the widespread use of fertilisers and pesticides – have eroded the quality of topsoil, making it more difficult to produce the food needed to sustain a growing global population (Schiffman, 2017).

Generally speaking, continued economic growth serves to ride roughshod over planetary boundaries in areas such as climate disruption, biodiversity decline, ocean acidification, soil degradation, stratospheric ozone depletion, the disruption of phosphorous and nitrogen cycles and freshwater availability (Steffen, Richardson, et al., 2015). This far-reaching deterioration gives rise to an alarming assortment of existential threats, the responses to which involve two broad possibilities: decoupling or degrowth.

Let us first consider the former, which has become a common argument in policy circles. It is essentially rooted in the idea that economic growth can be separated from its material impacts – which is to say capitalism can go on thriving without producing detrimental environmental effects so long as novel technologies are developed and greenhouse gases and other 'externalities' are incorporated within a market framework (Stern, 2007).

This is how social critique is subsumed into political debate (Boltanski & Chiapello, 2005). Corporate capitalism is criticised for the inequalities or environmental destruction it causes, but compromising logics are used to overcome the conflict and justify a further expansion of existing political and economic relations (Nyberg & Wright, 2013). Issues such as carbon emissions or biodiversity decline are priced and thus internalised with the market (Farber et al., 2002), becoming commodities that can be exchanged like any other (Newell & Paterson, 2010). There is no need for heavy-handed state regulation, taxation or any other measures that might upset the prevailing system. The business sphere will thrive on good relations with its stakeholders and the planet and will eventually deal with any difficulties to the satisfaction of all concerned – a classic 'win-win' scenario.

This, in a nutshell, is the logic of decoupling. Environmental protection becomes an opportunity for further economic expansion, with negative material impacts seen as disconnected from the growth imperative. Proposals for so-called 'green growth' fall into this category of wishful thinking, with faith in capitalism overriding all else (Jackson & Victor, 2019). Many countries in the Global North are in thrall to the accompanying discourse of 'sustainable development'; so are key international organisations such as the European Commission, the OECD and the UN (Farber et al., 2002). The notion relies heavily on wealthier nations and major corporations outsourcing environmentally destructive practices or industries to poorer countries, geographically remote locations and upstream links in supply chains (Somerville & Burton, 2019).

The 'big picture', of course, is that there is no decoupling per se. There is really only relocation. This is obvious on a planetary scale, with no historical evidence or theoretical modelling suggesting absolute decoupling can be achieved – even under optimistic or best-case scenarios (Hickel & Kallis, 2019; Hickel, 2021). Indeed, as outlined in Figure 9.1, the only times in history where global carbon emissions have ceased their remorseless increase have been in periods of dramatic economic recession and contraction, with the outbreak of the COVID pandemic in 2019 being the most recent example.

Politically, decoupling proposals and policies provide extra support for the growth-dependent economic system that has dominated

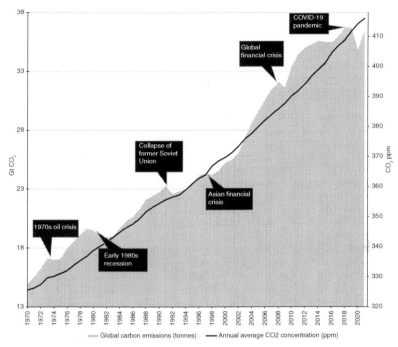

Figure 9.1 Global carbon emissions, atmospheric CO_2 concentrations and economic crisis, 1970–2021
Source: Global Carbon Project. (2021); NOAA. (2021).

for so long. Intended to rectify so-called 'market failures', they further obfuscate the contradiction between capitalism and climate change. Ultimately, they legitimise and prop up the existing hegemony.

Degrowth offers a markedly different solution. Crucially, it recognises incessant capital expansion is not an inevitable phenomenon: instead, considering ecological limits and the prospect of our planet's destruction, it is the very opposite that should be regarded as ineluctable – whether it is managed, as would be wise, or forced on us by environmental collapse, as could yet happen if we stay on our present path (Kallis et al., 2012). Degrowth is less a question of desirability and more one of necessarily ensuring equitable, lasting quality of life for the global population (Nyberg & Wright, 2022).

Unlike decoupling, degrowth highlights the contradiction between capitalism and climate change. It therefore opens up the political. It involves a planned contraction of energy and resource throughput in a way that enhances human well-being and ecological conditions both locally and globally (Hickel, 2021). It aims not only to reduce environmental impacts but also to redistribute income and wealth – both within and between nations – and to strengthen democratic participation.

This all sounds decidedly utopian, to say the least, which is why the main criticism directed towards the degrowth agenda is that it is unrealistic (Pollin, 2018). However, such an accusation stems from hegemonic assumptions of economic growth as somehow natural and immutable. Articulated both as a means of avoiding unnecessary waste and consumption and as a vehicle for working less and enjoying better health, degrowth becomes a nodal point to minimalist living and other societal goods.

In response to claims that the concept could lead to economic turmoil and further suffering, especially for people in poorer countries (Pollin, 2018), degrowth scholars have proposed numerous key policies that differentiate the idea from accidental or unplanned recession (Hickel, 2021). These include carbon-trading systems with a rapidly lowering cap; limits on fossil fuel extraction; employee autonomy and shorter working hours; and job guarantees and living wages. Such policies rest on tax reforms to constrain resource use and reduce carbon emissions while promoting work-sharing and limiting production and consumption (Kallis, 2018).

What is beyond dispute is that degrowth calls for an altogether different kind of economy (Hickel, 2020a) – one in which wealthy societies must restructure to reduce their ecological impacts. This means shifting to renewables *and* cutting energy use. In practice, such a transformation would entail many of the supply-side initiatives mentioned earlier – for example, abolishing subsidies for fossil fuels and divesting from related industries – as well as a switch to community-based, renewable energy (Stuart et al., 2020a).

For instance, in 2011 the Scottish government set a target of 500MW (megawatts) of community-owned renewable energy by 2020. Having been achieved in just four years, this goal was subsequently doubled (Grillanda & Khanal, 2020). In tandem, Community Energy Scotland has stressed its determination 'to strengthen and empower local communities by helping you to own, control and benefit from your local renewable energy resources – reducing your energy costs, regenerating your communities and playing your part in the low-carbon transition' (Community Energy Scotland, 2021). Such a shift to local ownership is at the core of a politics of transition and speaks directly to the 'localisation' of solutions that move away from corporate profits and the pursuit of ever-increasing yields; it also addresses the growth dependence of the private ownership of energy production (Walker & Devine-Wright, 2008).

This means degrowth is discriminatory in reining in harmful industries – among them fossil fuels, meat production and private transport. By extension, it is also discriminatory in promoting socially important sectors – among them renewable energy, health and education (Hickel, 2021). Its emphasis on reducing energy and material throughput aims to curb capitalist interdependence, which would otherwise lead to further expansion. The key is to identify a *sufficient* and more *equal* level of production and consumption within planetary means, so allowing the Global South to catch up in terms of throughput and encouraging a move to a more sustainable economy worldwide. The possibilities are supported by research showing economic growth has a much stronger connection to environmental degradation than to human wellbeing (Mikkelson, 2021).

Degrowth requires alternative forms of economic exchange, many of which already exist beneath the surface of dominant capitalist relations. There are alternative market types, such as local trading systems and barter; there are non-market transactions, such as indigenous exchanges and household flows; there are alternative kinds of labour relations, such as cooperatives and reciprocal labour; there is unpaid work, such as housework and volunteering; and there are communal, independent and other non-capitalist organisations (Nyberg & Wright, 2022). All these provide a conceptual path towards reorganising society to stay within planetary boundaries, with their proponents capable of constructing a collective position that clearly depicts endless capitalist accumulation as the Other.

It is notable that, as a discourse, degrowth is much harder for the existing hegemony to incorporate. This is because it is directed not towards specific corporate practices but towards the prevailing economic system as a whole. It includes different forms of ownership. It encompasses the dynamics within organisations and the communities in which they operate. It is about realigning and de-commodifying human relationships.

For many decades now mainstream policies have nudged responsibility and blame towards individual citizens. Ideas around personal entrepreneurship and competition have further tightened the grip that capitalism exerts over liberal democracies. Acting collectively might appear strange after so long, but it is through greater participation in decision-making and shared deliberation (Kallis et al., 2012) that degrowth seeks to develop more active, democratic citizenship.

While still a marginal movement, degrowth is finding support among a growing number of activists and natural scientists who recognise incremental changes to the current economic system are not sufficient. Going forward, it needs to develop more alliances in order to spur the transition away from growth. Considering the emphasis on worker autonomy and ownership, there is certainly potential to build equivalence with labour movements (Chertkovskaya & Paulsson, 2021). This is a matter of differentiation from the increasingly authoritarian politics and rank inequality that have come to dominate the global political economy, with capitalism's simultaneous ruination of the environment and dismantling of democracy offering both the impetus and the opportunity to establish an alternative political frontier.

9.3 Democracy

While decarbonisation and degrowth can go some way towards providing a meaningful response, the climate crisis – as we observed at the start of this chapter – is ultimately a political problem. In our view, this means that successfully addressing climate change depends on strengthening democracy.

There is clear evidence that the current perpetuation of the fossil fuel hegemony relies on the capture of political processes in the service of capitalism. As noted in Chapter 3, fossil energy's close relationship with governmental decision-making has ensured a massive public underwriting of the viability of carbon-intensive activities around the globe. A recent IMF report calculated industries linked to fossil fuels worldwide benefited from public subsidies in the order of US$11 million every minute, amounting to a total of US$5.9 trillion, in 2020 (Parry et al., 2021). With renewable energy now price-competitive, the configurations supporting the hegemony are to this day upheld by the construction of an equivalence of interest with governments at different levels.

This equivalence is routinely promoted through financial contributions. For example, in 2018 fossil fuel companies were responsible for more than US$84 million in contributions to US Congressional candidates during the midterm elections (Goldberg et al., 2020). Money brings political access that citizens do not have, undermining democratic processes by encouraging decision-makers to accommodate fossil fuel interests instead of representing the people and communities they are meant to serve. Consider Peoples' (2010: 670) study of campaign contributions in the US, which showed so-called 'political action committees' (PACs) that pool campaign contributions 'almost always lead lawmakers to vote more similarly'. The research found a causal relationship between PAC contributions and voting in seven out of eight US Houses of Representatives seats between 1991 and 2006.

Either acting alone or through associations such as business roundtables or chambers of commerce, corporations also devote substantial resources to lobbying (Baumgartner et al., 2009). Private interests spent approximately US$12.5 million per member of US Congress in 2012 (Teachout, 2014: 246), with the majority of lobbying conducted by fewer than 300 firms (Kerr et al., 2014), while lobbying in the UK is reckoned to be a £2 billion industry (Cave & Rowell, 2014). By providing them with information and incentives to adopt a particular position, corporations expect politicians to sustain a favourable legislative environment (Funk & Hirschman, 2017). Lobbyist Ian Greer infamously explained such activities to Mohamad Al-Fayed, then owner of London's Harrods department store: 'You need to rent an MP, just like you rent a London taxi' (Hencke, 2014).

The hegemony is further strengthened by 'revolving door' appointments between the economic and political spheres. These operate in both directions, with fossil fuel executives often ushered into senior political and bureaucratic positions and politicians frequently moving on to careers in consultancy, industry association roles or appointments to the boards of major corporations. For example, having retired from the Australian parliament, Martin Ferguson, a former Minister for Resources and Energy, was named Chairman of APPEA, the Australian Petroleum Production and Exploration Association (APPEA, 2013). His successor, Ian MacFarlane, went on to head the Queensland Resources Council (Chan, 2016). Movers the other way have included former ExxonMobil CEO Rex Tillerson, who served as

US Secretary of State in the Trump administration in spite of having no diplomatic or public-sector experience (Borger, 2016).

This co-dependency extends throughout the arms of government and bureaucracy, affecting a broad range of decisions regarding energy and climate policy. One study of corporate influence in Australian politics found the fossil fuel sector had 'constructed a covert network of lobbyists and revolving-door appointments, which has ensured that industry interests continue to dominate Australia's energy policy and that its emissions from fossil fuel use continue to rise' (Lucas, 2021: 1). The money and people flowing in both directions can be seen as central to maintaining the equivalence that has shaped current politics (Nyberg, 2021).

This explains the use of terms such as 'post-democracy' (Crouch, 2004) and 'corporate society' (Barley, 2007: 201) in describing how companies have come to exercise inordinate influence in moulding public policies to suit their own needs. As Streeck (2016) has argued, democracy has been replaced by capitalism. Yet it is vital to note that these two models of governance are far from compatible: whereas the former should promote equality of entitlement and collective choices, the latter is based on *in*equality of property ownership and the dominance of competitive market forces.

This is why attempts to address climate change demand a strengthening of democracy and the consequent shattering of existing hegemonic configurations. The necessary counter-hegemonic project requires a broader alliance of different forms of democratic struggles, from environmentalists and anti-racists to feminists and LGBTIQ+ advocates. What these movements have in common are existing antagonisms and democratic demands. They may be based on numerous *forms* of antagonism, but in the final reckoning they are all committed to the extension of democratic practices and the inclusion of excluded or marginalised groups.

However, attempts to establish this political frontier have been hampered by the traditional capital-labour alliance against any kind of green transition that might threaten economic growth (Azmanova, 2020). Polluting industries and consumer capitalism have constructed an equivalence of interests with the labour movement, as well as with the general population in Western democracies, by promoting a discourse of both economic growth and job creation. Challenging this discourse becomes even more problematic in a context of decades of neoliberal rationalisation, a trajectory that has resulted in greater corporate power, waves of government-imposed austerity, the decimation of the organised labour movement and the expansion of precarious work – much of which has in turn brought further economic insecurity, thereby reinforcing citizens' dependence on corporate capitalism (Streeck, 2011). The key fault line for mobilisation, then, is not between capitalism and climate change or even between capitalism and labour: it is between capitalism and democracy.

Democratic processes need to be separated from the expansionist practices of capitalism if climate change is to be addressed. This means constructing an equivalence around the demands of collective ownership and the climate crisis. The only way to prevent governments from giving corporations licences to extract fossil fuels, thereby preserving the destructive conceit of endless growth, is to combine green mobilisation with the social question by uprooting the continued articulations of free markets, private property and entrepreneurial individualism (Mouffe, 2018).

After all, these sedimented articulations are by no means natural and can be organised in different ways. Radicalising democracy for climate change involves 'renovating and making "critical" an already existing activity' (Gramsci, 1971: 330). By showing how these practices lack foundation, it is possible to democratise previously competitive activities such as energy production and labour relations.

For instance, 'energy democracy' is one alternative championed by a burgeoning array of social movements (Burke & Stephens, 2017). A way of linking decarbonisation with shifts in who controls the means of energy production and distribution (Van Veelen, 2018), it is based on communities' direct involvement in energy governance and their increased participation in decisions on production and consumption. In essence, it is a process of reshaping social relations towards an energy system that functions for the collective good: as such, it represents a move away from competitive and individualistic responses to climate change within the framing of corporate capitalism and an embracing of a shared focus on sufficient needs.

Several studies have identified a growing number of community projects based on renewable energy across Europe (Kunze & Becker, 2014) and the US (Burke & Stephens, 2017). Drawing on these experiences, it is possible to identify three broad objectives: (i) resisting the dominant energy agenda and keeping fossil fuels in the ground; (ii) reclaiming the energy sector from private corporations and democratising it for the public interest; and (iii) refocusing the sector away from the profit motive and towards governance of energy as a commons.

However, shifting energy questions towards shared decisions can be fraught with personal ambitions and local power plays, with research suggesting participation is often tilted towards higher socioeconomic groups (Grossmann & Creamer, 2017). There is not necessarily a common interest as a basis for deliberation, and to assume there is might even stifle democratic processes. Energy democracy can be constructed and maintained through 'agonistic pluralism', which legitimises contestations and debates about democratic governance (Mouffe, 2018). On balance, however, the notion of democratising energy at least has the potential to support decarbonisation and degrowth.

A further arena in which to develop a more democratic response to the climate crisis is encouraging greater labour movement involvement in reducing working hours. Several studies have confirmed shorter hours can be linked with lower carbon emissions and smaller ecological footprints (see e.g., Knight et al., 2013; Fitzgerald et al., 2018; Mallinson & Cheng, 2021), with longer hours instead leading to greater production and consumption. Trials of reduced working hours in Japan and across Europe have shown the scope for degrowth and radically restructuring the economy without hugely increasing unemployment (Mallinson & Cheng, 2021). In tandem, it can be argued that economic inequality further exacerbates emissions by fostering a detrimental desire for ever more consumption.

The influence of longer working hours and inequality on emissions supports the development of greater economic democracy to address climate change. Organisational models such as worker-owned cooperatives are not based on the assumption of capital's incessant accumulation: they can target insufficiency rather than remorseless expansion and are therefore more likely to pursue environmental goals (Stuart et al., 2020a). Collective control and ownership positively impact pay dispersion (Connelly et al., 2016), as well as potentially equipping employees and communities alike with a more meaningful purpose beyond paid labour. Not least with the climate crisis in mind, the many social and economic benefits of renewing the labour movement should not be ignored.

9.4 Rethinking the Political

The current political focus on technology, financial instruments and individual responsibility as purported remedies for climate change represents an attempt to depoliticise the greatest existential threat confronting our planet. It suggests that citizens need not worry about societal solutions; that they should instead simply consume more 'climate-friendly' products and services and that any shifts intended to address the crisis can be achieved within existing institutions and 'greener' business models.

This existing hegemony is based on linking consumerist demands with wealth as a reference point for desire and success. As Gramsci (1971) argued, hegemony over society cannot be separated from hegemony over nature: the same political formations are commodifying labour and climate change into the logic of a dominant economic system – one in which even carbon emissions can be privatised and traded within a market. Capitalism is in effect naturalised as the foundation of the world – the political.

In this chapter we have outlined decarbonisation, degrowth and democracy as possible means of challenging the hegemony that supports fossil fuel energy and corporate capitalism. An obvious first step in responding to the worsening climate crisis is to reduce the world's dependence on fossil energy as quickly as possible, but decarbonisation is far from a complete solution: as we have explained, there is also a need to undo assumptions of infinite economic growth and plutocratic control.

10 | *After the Interregnum*

Yes, the planet got destroyed. But for a beautiful moment in time we created a lot of value for shareholders.

New Yorker cartoon caption (Toro, 2012)

During the early stages of the COVID-19 crisis, if only briefly, the pandemic could be seen as providing a fork in the road. Fleetingly, amid the worldwide uncertainty brought by a life-threatening and highly communicable disease, an alternative way of organising societies appeared genuinely possible. Governments provided hundreds of billions of dollars' worth of support packages to prop up their economies in the face of lockdowns and shutdowns. Public spending as a proportion of GDP increased markedly as policymakers bailed out failing businesses, subsidised wages and funded the development and distribution of new vaccines in record time. Such a degree of direct intervention in social and economic life defied prevailing political mantras of necessary austerity and harked back to a kind of state intervention not witnessed since World War II. The vast majority of people recognised the need for dramatic upheaval as an unfamiliar reality swiftly came to be accepted. Working from home and social distancing were among the many new normals established in short order. While there were massive inequities – including the sacrifices borne by frontline workers and the varied levels of vaccine access globally – this showed how a critical threat could spur previously inconceivable political and economic disruption and unite communities against a common foe. However, an even greater threat – climate change – has somehow failed to inspire an even remotely comparable response.

While COVID-19 has demonstrated how societies can undertake rapid transformation in extremis, the climate crisis demonstrates a road not taken. As Malm (2020) has argued, the contrast between the response to the pandemic and the response to the prospect of environmental collapse could not be starker. One has bordered on revolution; the other remains mired in inertia.

In an especially bitter irony, governments have now used the spectre of COVID-19 to promote the need to restart economic growth through established industries – that is, through the continued expansion of fossil fuel production and consumption. This has occurred because of the embedded political influence of fossil fuel companies and their industry associations. Even the pandemic has been appropriated as an opportunity to push back against the groundswell of global climate activism that had finally been gaining momentum in recent years.

In maintaining the hegemonic formations of corporate capitalism, the fossil fuel industry and its political allies have incorporated growing social concern over climate change within conventional business models. This has been achieved through fanciful commitments to net-zero goals, carbon offsets and novel technologies that allow a continuation of fossil energy; it has also been achieved by selling the spectacle of climate change and shifting the responsibility for still-mounting emissions to those who have produced the least. As a result, despite increasingly bleak scientific projections, the insanity of fossil fuel expansion and endless consumption continues to be justified – and the need for urgent, radical action continues to be ignored.

As we have detailed throughout this book, the hegemonic formations of corporate capitalism have actively hindered the necessary transformation of society by concealing the contradiction between the interminable accumulation of capital and the preservation of the planet's life-support systems. While the worsening climate crisis has become ever more evident through extreme weather events around the globe, the fossil fuel industry and its supporters have been working feverishly to ensure nothing significant changes. As we argued in Chapter 1, there is much 'busyness' and activity in climate negotiations and corporate sustainability reporting; but this simply serves to further promote the prevailing economic order as something that is inherently natural and which can be taken for granted.

This narrative is not only misleading but wholly unfounded, because even a cursory survey of history reveals corporate capitalism to be a relatively recent and unusual form of social organisation. There is nothing natural about it, and there is no reason whatsoever why it should be taken for granted. As the climate crisis reveals, humanity needs a new set of contingent foundations if it is to have any sort of viable future.

In Chapter 9 we highlighted three thematic responses to climate change: decarbonisation, degrowth and democracy. Each is intended to bring meaning to efforts to address the crisis, and each is designed to break up the existing hegemonic order that supports planetary suicide. Such solutions might appear far-fetched, but this is because the construction of a 'common sense' of corporate capitalism and consumption as the unwavering underpinnings of society has long since rendered any alternatives all but unthinkable.

The evidence of this tragic reality is overwhelming. Any alternative that challenges the existing hegemony and exposes the awful contradiction underlying the economic order is not only fiercely resisted but persistently undermined through active and deliberate politics. Established institutions and private interests engage in politics to hide the political – sidelining the potential for the radical changes required.

The growth of the global climate movement as a political force – as embodied in groups such as Fridays for Future, Extinction Rebellion and other activist organisations – has also led to more explicit and coercive state intervention in support of the fossil fuel hegemony. The construction of equivalence has become more and more dependent on a demonised Other and a polarisation between those who favour the status quo and those who dare oppose it. In countries around the world, fossil fuel expansion has increasingly relied on the backing of the judiciary, the military and the police in limiting protests and stifling criticism. The forces of the right hand of the state – in contrast to the left hand, which is associated with education and welfare – are now routinely employed to coerce the Other into submission to the dominant regime (Bourdieu, 2002).

Though fundamentally contemptible, this development might actually be viewed as something of a positive. Strengthening the right hand of the state could indicate the hegemonic regimes are losing or have already lost the political consensus – which is to say they are 'no longer "leading" but only "dominant"' (Gramsci, 1971: 275–6).

Reflecting this idea, scholars have suggested Western liberal democracies have entered a post-capitalist interregnum (Bauman, 2012; Streeck, 2016; Mouffe, 2018). Similarly, Gramsci (1971: 276) articulated the grim period of suspended order during the 1930s as follows: 'The old is dying, and the new cannot be born; in this interregnum, a great variety of morbid symptoms appear'. Notable symptoms today include the mass extinction of species; the building of walls to keep out those who are least responsible for climate change yet who are none-theless condemned to flee its impacts; and the commercialisation of space travel, complete with long-term aspirations of colonising other planets rather than ensuring an inhabitable Earth. These signs of climate change are truly 'morbid' in the Gramscian sense, in as much as they show the prevailing hegemonic formations of corporate capitalism are unlikely to be able to deal with the crisis.

Gramsci's historical analysis of the civil and political unrest during the nineteenth and early twentieth centuries, when growing disquiet eventually gave way to communist revolution and the subsequent spread of fascism, helps us explore today's interregnum. Later in the text, drawing on his thinking, we endeavour to identify existing social processes in Western capitalist democracies in response to climate change.

We suggest three particular processes – trasformismo, Caesarism and scission – are observable as we write. As we explain in the following pages, they suggest different trajectories for reframing and dealing with the climate crisis. Crucially, the interregnum offers a historical moment for the reconstruction of the political.

10.1 Trasformismo

Many European countries have witnessed a convergence of mainstream left and right political programmes in relation to climate change. Parties might differ in their levels of commitment and action, but they all support a perpetuation of the conventional political economy – albeit framed as somewhat 'greener' and more 'sustainable'.

This discourse, which has unfolded in recent decades, is basically a continuation of third-way politics (Curran, 2001) – what has been called an extreme centre (Ali, 2015). Along with key national indus-tries, political parties are flexible enough to accommodate the general critique of a worsening climate crisis by promoting renewable energy, encouraging green consumption and making pledges to accomplish carbon neutrality. While being careful not to alienate each country's core industries, national politicians support an incremental net-zero transition based on the idea of eventually decoupling GDP growth from its material environmental impacts.

Gramsci referred to this type of response to crisis as 'trasformismo'. It occurs when the population is incorporated into the hegemonic regime. Allegiance to the dominant political order, at least in most Western nations, is rooted in constructing an equivalence between a more 'sustainable' growth economy and individual consumption.

Thus, faced with the horrors of climate change, the population is assured that no radical transformation is needed and that piecemeal reforms will suffice. In reacting to criticism of mounting social and economic inequality, a government does not champion a commitment to redistribution: rather, it promotes the unquestionable need for further economic expansion. 'Growth and jobs' is the political mantra of the age.

This is arguably the dominant trajectory of the Global North, and it fits within the vision of a linear history of continuous progress. Hegemonic regimes benefit from the perpetuation of the status quo and, as we have outlined, resist the need for any radical disruption of the prevailing political economy. Responses to climate change are sold through the discourses of 'clean coal' or gas as a 'bridge fuel', despite the obvious fact that all fossil fuels – gas included – should now stay in the ground.

For instance, Szabo (2022) employs the concept of trasformismo to describe how natural gas advocates within the EU have 'sold' gas as a climate-friendly, transition-centric energy source that should be viewed as preferable to other fossil fuels. This has allowed the industry to increase production and expand – a faux response to the climate crisis. It is through such acts of assimilation and subjugation that hegemonic formations try to avoid confrontation in holding on to their dominance.

As we have noted, this unswerving determination to maintain the trajectory of carbon emissions poses an existential threat not only to organised human societies but also to much of life on the planet. The cascading effects of a rapidly warming Earth, with temperatures several degrees above the pre-industrial norm, translates into a hellish future in which extreme weather events, failing ecosystems and rising seas threaten a sizeable proportion of the global population. These are not fanciful projections from a dystopian fiction: they are the best estimates of thousands of climate scientists who have documented the unprecedented ecological harm that industrial society has already visited on the planet (Steffen et al., 2018; IPCC, 2021).

10.2 Caesarism

Crisis can also result in what Gramsci (1971) referred to as 'Caesarism' – 'the emergence of a "great personality" who presents themselves as the solution to the uncertainty of the moment or even sometimes as the saviour or redeemer of the nation' (Hoare & Sperber, 2016: 69). An interregnum or a period of doubt is represented as perilous in these instances, with societies compelled to turn to 'men of destiny' (Gramsci, 1971: 210) – and, yes, they *are* generally men.

Gramsci used the term 'Caesarism' mockingly. He employed it in reference to Mussolini and the fascists' analogy between Il Duce and Julius Caesar (Hoare & Sperber, 2016). Today, a century later, similar grandiosity can be witnessed in relation to an array of would-be men of destiny across different continents.

Consider, for example, Donald Trump in the US, Xi Jinping in China, Vladimir Putin in Russia, Rodrigo Duterte in the Philippines and Jair Bolsonaro in Brazil. Each is an authoritarian figure who is hailed by his supporters as the solution to democracy's shortcomings. Each is viewed as a beacon of hope, with the traditional political parties of the left and right derided as incapable of genuinely representing the interests of 'the people'. The logic of equivalence here is not based on constructing social demands across diverse groups or individuals: it is instead based on constructing identification. This is a totalitarian inclination, in that the aim is to unify a population by eliminating difference. In a form of nationalist populism, the authoritarian figure is constructed as representing or even embodying, the 'real people'.

In tandem, a logic of difference may be constructed against an 'elite' that is portrayed as preventing the people from obtaining their will. This 'enemy from the inside' might be 'the establishment' – that is, those who hold leading positions within national politics. The elite is generally seen as corrupt, as in the 'Washington swamp', or ideological, as in 'cultural Marxists'. This allows the authoritarian figure to build a political frontier in fighting for the people. Alternatively, a logic of difference may be constructed against a foreigner. This 'enemy from the outside' will differ in light of a country's geopolitical position, but it is usually someone who is perceived as 'threatening our way of life' and who might even be branded a 'terrorist'. For those in the Global North, increasingly, it might include those fleeing the effects of climate change in the Global South.

Distrustful of experts, today's Caesarisms have determinedly spread doubt about climate change. They articulate it as an invention of the enemy – be that environmentalists who want to remove people's freedoms, international agencies plotting to take over the world or foreign countries bent on undermining national security. The real threat is not 'climate change' but those who speak of it – greens, vegans, scientists and anyone else accused of 'threatening our way of life'.

This warped view has repeatedly been espoused by leaders in the US, Australia, Canada and other countries traditionally opposed to moving away from fossil fuels. For them the problem is not the fossil fuel industry, which must not be challenged in any meaningful way. The problem is the people who engage in environmental protests and boycotts: these are the despised, supremely dangerous enemies of the authoritarian figure and his supporters.

Spreading denial of climate change has led to a stagnation of international political responses. It has also emboldened local support for further environmental destruction. Former US President Trump exemplified the impacts of such a stance when he declared climate change a hoax, dismantled his government's policies on the issue and torpedoed numerous environmental regulations (Bomberg, 2021).

Given the territorial and divisional politics involved in addressing climate change, such an exercise of sovereign power is particularly problematic. Measures such as those taken by Trump significantly dent the likelihood of the crisis being dealt with as a global concern in the present. The men of destiny strive to protect national interests of competitiveness, jobs and economic growth through the radical winding back of decades of environmental legislation and the pursuit of aggressive foreign policy – and in doing so they prove themselves especially detrimental to hopes of advancing worldwide climate action.

While corporate leaders have generally been careful in their public endorsement of such populist leaders, the fact is that many traditional industries have benefited greatly from the diminishing of environmental protections and the rejection of any form of emissions mitigation. Political dismissal of climate change has ensured further delays in tangible regulatory control, and improved corporate profitability has added to the global fossil fuel lock-in. With their absurdist views providing a 'radical flank' for the more extreme expressions of climate change denial and fossil fuel addiction, populist political figures are in many senses the 'useful idiots' in the relentless reproduction of hegemony.

A shift towards Caesarism in reacting to crises also underpins a movement towards increasingly authoritarian and draconian responses to social dissent. The same undemocratic forces that have so far hindered action on climate change can just as easily be called upon to address the inevitable social upheavals that result from the phenomenon.

For instance, the policies of right-wing parties in Europe often frame responses to climate change in terms of national energy security and the preservation of 'the homeland' (Selk & Kemmerzell, 2021). At a global scale, in detailing how one-party regimes could seek to regulate the problem in a command-and-control manner, Wainwright and Mann (2018) termed this scenario 'Climate Mao'. Perhaps the most obvious example is China's capitalist strain of state socialism, in which reducing emissions or investing in renewable energy is the stuff of executive decree, all-consuming surveillance and the power of a single-party state. Given the failings to date of any sort of coherent action by nominally democratic governments, there is already speculation that surrendering democracy – at least temporarily – might be necessary (Lovelock, 2009).

Finally, as we saw in Chapter 5, the narrative of Caesarism often couples the idea of men of destiny with a desire to master nature through technology. The growing interest in geo-engineering follows this arc, and it may be unsurprising that tech billionaires such as Bill Gates are investing so heavily in expectation of being able to manipulate ecosystems on the grandest scale. Witness, too, the current phallogocentrism of the 'billionaire space race', with the likes of Elon Musk, Jeff Bezos and Richard Branson competing to escape the Earth in order to colonise the next frontier for capitalist expansion.

10.3 Scission

In contrast to the parochial nationalism underpinning many countries' promotion of fossil fuel expansion, the climate movement has embraced a global perspective that stresses compassion and demands solidarity and engagement with those already confronting the destruction of their lands, homes and identities. A growing number of movements emphasise the need to rupture dominant regimes. This schism – or scission – is genuinely counter-hegemonic, in that it aims to disrupt the practices and policies of the institutional order. While still at the margins of most societies, those demanding radical action against the established hegemony have highlighted ways in which new constructions of equivalence can be built across interests and priorities to challenge the status quo.

Like past groups such as Occupy, present-day movements such as Black Lives Matter, Me Too and Extinction Rebellion have brought into public view an evocative critique of existing hegemonic regimes. They have done so by making everyday oppressions explicit and by revealing the extent to which issues such as unequal wealth distribution, racial and sexual violence and the impacts of carbon emissions maintain systems of power that are against the interests of the vast majority – the '99%' or the 'future'. Notwithstanding questions around their efficacy, such campaigns at least articulate the reconfigurations of social and political relations needed to address the climate crisis.

Central to their demands is a fundamental reordering of priorities to develop a more inclusionary democracy – one that recognises the full diversity of interests and identities. This is among the many areas in which capitalism fails. As we argued in Chapters 7 and 8, while it is important not to romanticise or underestimate the suffering wrought in the name of capitalism, the current climate trajectory suggests a further revelation of the basic contradictions of the hegemony is imminent.

As we have outlined, to avoid incorporation into capitalism, the construction of a political frontier is necessary (Mouffe, 2018). This must separate the endless accumulation of capital from the needs of democracy. Without recognition of social division and political antagonism, there is always the danger that democratic demands could fall into forms of Caesarism. Ideally, new ways of political organising and the building of shared interests can offer the possibility of democracy's renewal.

The previous chapter outlined the policy basis for an alternative hegemony. What can be termed 'climate democracy' depends on cooperative economic systems and principles of climate justice. There are indications that the new climate movements are attempting to make these necessary links. For instance, while environmental action has long been accused of recreating ethnic inequalities, Greta Thunberg has worked to bring forward the voices of campaigners from Kenya, Uganda and South Africa to counter the prominence of white activism in the Fridays for Future movement (BBC News, 2020). Meanwhile, in light of the disproportionate impacts its tactics of provoking mass arrest have had on people of colour, Extinction Rebellion has reconsidered its claim to be 'beyond politics' (Hakimi Zapata, 2020). Lessons have also been learnt in grassroots movements, with environmentalists not only seeking to include indigenous peoples but securing permission to be on their lands and follow their leadership in relation to appropriate practices (Klein, 2014; Ricketts, 2020). While incomplete, processes such as these demonstrate a willingness to work towards creating truly counter-hegemonic spaces.

There are also lessons to be learnt from the experiences of left-wing governments in Kerala, India, and Podemos, Spain, and the Left-Green Movement in Iceland (Foran, 2020). These regional entities seek to connect climate policies with democratic struggles and aim to interlink on a global level to cooperatively negotiate and create climate democracy. Of course, there is still much work to be done in drawing connections between climate change and issues such as worker exploitation.

We should make clear that it is not our intention to suggest the environmental movement alone must 'save' the planet from the worst impacts of climate change. We recognise everyone has a part to play. Our point here is that, while there may be a hesitancy to take on their arguments at full scale, it is possible to view these groups as examples and to at least identify glimpses of ways to break out of the present impasse. The technical answers are there; but the organisational and political answers are still waiting to be built.

10.4 Hope without Optimism

Having presented three possible scenarios, it remains to be seen which will dominate. As each of the preceding chapters should make clear, it is our view that scission is the only sufficient response to the climate crisis; trasformiso simply supports the existing corporate hegemony and Caesarism offers the danger of authoritarianism. The question then becomes, how can the scission be supported and developed? It is not enough to criticise the current inadequacies of the climate response. If the claim is that the answers exist, they need to be brought into being.

However, in doing so, it is important to move beyond a naïve hope that things will get better. There are, understandably, passionate debates within the climate movement about the issue of hope. Given

daily news reports of soaring temperatures, melting icecaps, unprecedented fires, and largely inadequate government responses, the question as to how long is left to prevent the worst impacts is asked
regularly. Indeed, you can see a literal answer at the website of climate-
clock.net.

For some, hope is seen as a replacement for taking action – as Derrick
Jensen argues 'when you give up on hope … you [cease] relying on
someone or something else to solve your problems' (2006). Others,
such as Rebecca Solnit (2021), worry that a loss of hope leads to
inaction. While recognising that such discussions are important, especially for those involved in social movements which require vast
amounts of emotional labour, we suggest that it is possible to act in
either situation; what is important is to break the linear expectations of
time, to disrupt the present in order to build a future (De Cock et al.,
2021).

The first and perhaps most important break for this to occur is in the
imagination. We are hardly alone or new in suggesting this. For
instance, Khasnabish and Haiven (2014) argue that we need
a 'radical imagination' in order to overcome the multiple ecological
and social challenges wrought by capitalism. This, they argue, needs to
be critical, reflexive and innovative – however they also suggest that the
radical imagination is 'an aspirational term, largely hollow of any
concrete content or meaning' (2014: 2–3). Yet there are some hints as
to how a 'radical imagination' might be constructed. Activists have
found the role of building community and alternative systems of care to
be one such method (Scurr & Bowden, 2021). As we noted in
Chapter 8, there are multiple inputs from art, fiction, and performance
which seek to challenge the assumptions of hegemony, and provide
insight into alternatives.

Secondly, such insights need to be translated into praxis. This process – of using theoretical insight to engage in social change – is often
used by activists in resistance to, for instance, the hegemony of market
economics by instead using barter systems, or in building communities
of care which are outside of the nuclear family norms. As we have noted
elsewhere, the power of theory is realised when it becomes performative (Bowden et al., 2021).

In Chapter 2 we noted the reliance of hegemony on the repetition of
practice in space. This repetition maintains the hegemony by implying
the future is simply a natural progression of the past; it is accepted as

inevitable because of the assumption of linearity and in doing so the political is hidden. The traces of climate change, however, reveal such assumptions. They haunt the present, showing the result of decisions past, and inevitably revealing that these decisions could have been otherwise. Examples can be seen, for instance, in the dying corals, burnt forests, rising waters and refugees; often the living result of choices by government and corporations to maintain and develop an economic system which is destroying life on this planet.

Reminding others that decisions now have consequences later has been much of the focus of the climate movements we have explored in this book. Often for this, they are criticised as being ideological or naïve – or, at worst, as we noted in Chapter 4, dangerous. Readers will not be surprised that we do not share such accusations. Rather, we argue that they are engaging in what is needed; they are creating the scission. It is a messy, sometimes difficult to comprehend process. But it is surely better than following the current trajectory.

10.5 A Last Word

We began conceiving and writing this book at the beginning of 2020, just as the COVID-19 pandemic first appeared on global news screens and following the catastrophic Australian 'Black Summer' bushfires. It was a time when it appeared the politics of climate change around the world might finally be shifting, with businesses and governments accepting growing public concern over the crisis.

In terms of the organisation of climate change as a political and economic issue, in the face of extreme weather events and mass protests, outright denial shifted to acknowledgement and a steady uptake in public commitments to reducing emissions. It looked like a turning point had at last been reached. Unfortunately, as we have documented in the intervening two years, the prevailing hegemony of fossil-fuelled corporate capitalism has largely proven as resilient as ever.

Despite hopes that the pandemic would act as a break from the past and usher in a new and lower-carbon future, global consumption of fossil fuels has reached new highs – jumping nine per cent in 2021 on the back of renewed economic growth. As IEA Executive Director Fatih Birol noted: 'This year's historically high level of coal power generation is a worrying sign of how far off track the world is in its efforts to put emissions into decline toward net zero' (Gillespie, 2021). The hegemony has once again incorporated public critique while ensuring nothing significant tangibly alters.

And so, the world stays locked within an economic system that endangers the future of societies, ecosystems and the vast diversity of life on this planet. While there are clear paths that can be taken to lessen the harm and destruction a worsening climate crisis will bring, it remains to be seen whether the current dominant political and economic configurations can ever reorganise sufficiently to avoid catastrophe.

Ultimately, the conceit of the prevailing hegemony is that corporate capitalism will somehow continue independently of the Earth's life-support systems. The decades to come appear likely to put such magical thinking to the most serious test.

References

ABC News. (2014). NSW government attacked over rumours 800 police will be sent to break up Bentley anti-gas protest. *ABC News*, 8 May. https://mobile.abc.net.au/news/2014-05-08/bentley-police/5440154

Adger, W. N., Dessai, S., Goulden, M. et al. (2009). Are there social limits to adaptation to climate change? *Climatic Change*, 93(3), 335–54.

Adger, W. N., Huq, S., Brown, K., Conway, D. & Hulme, M. (2003). Adaptation to climate change in the developing world. *Progress in Development Studies*, 3(3), 179–95.

AEA. (2015). 10 reasons to oppose a carbon tax. *American Energy Alliance*, 11 April. www.americanenergyalliance.org/2015/11/10-reasons-to-oppose-a-carbon-tax/

Ali, T. (2015). *The extreme centre*. London: Verso.

Allan, J. I. (2018). Seeking entry: Discursive hooks and NGOs in global climate politics. *Global Policy*, 9(4), 560–69.

Alova, G. (2020). A global analysis of the progress and failure of electric utilities to adapt their portfolios of power-generation assets to the energy transition. *Nature Energy*, 5, 920–27. https://doi.org/10.1038/s41560-020-00686-5

Anderson, A. A. (2017). Effects of social media use on climate change opinion, knowledge, and behavior. In *Oxford research encyclopedia of climate science*. Oxford: Oxford University Press. https://oxfordre.com/climatescience/view/10.1093/acrefore/9780190228620.001.0001/acrefore-9780190228620-e-369

Anderson, B. (2021). Increase in ocean heat is adding fuel to hurricanes like Ida. *Accuweather*, 31 August. www.accuweather.com/en/weather-blogs/climatechange/increase-in-ocean-heat-is-adding-fuel-to-hurricanes-like-ida/1009173

Andreoni, M. & Londoño, E. (2021). Brazil beseiged by Covid now faces a severe drought. *New York Times*, 19 June. www.nytimes.com/2021/06/19/world/americas/brazil-drought.html

Anguelovski, I., Shi, L., Chu, E. et al. (2016). Equity impacts of urban land use planning for climate adaptation: Critical perspectives from the Global North and South. *Journal of Planning Education and Research*, 36(3), 333–48.

Antonio, R. J. & Brulle, R. J. (2011). The unbearable lightness of politics: Climate change denial and political polarization. *Sociological Quarterly*, 52(2), 195–202.

AP News. (2021). Germany pledges to adjust climate law after court verdict. *AP News*, 30 April. https://apnews.com/article/germany-europe-climate-climate-change-environment-and-nature-191b8ffca5ba6994ebd402b04432e6c8

APPEA. (2013). Martin Ferguson appointed chair of APPEA advisory board. *APPEA Media Release*, 1 October. www.appea.com.au/all_news/martin-ferguson-appointed-chair-of-appea-advisory-board/

APPEA. (2020). Industry action on emissions reduction. Canberra: Australian Petroleum Production & Exploration Association. www.appea.com.au/wp-content/uploads/2020/08/Industry-Action-on-Emissions-Reduction-1.pdf

Apple. (2020). Apple commits to be 100 percent carbon neutral for its supply chain and products by 2030. *Apple Newsroom*, 21 July. www.apple.com/newsroom/2020/07/apple-commits-to-be-100-percent-carbon-neutral-for-its-supply-chain-and-products-by-2030

Arendt, H. (1963). *On revolution*. London: Faber.

Aronczyk, M. & Espinoza, M. I. (2021). *A strategic nature: Public relations and the politics of American environmentalism*. New York: Oxford University Press.

Arup & C40 Cities. (2015). *Climate action in megacities 3.0*. London: C40.

Atwood, M. (2003). *Oryx and crake*. London: Bloomsbury.

Atwood, M. (2009). *The year of the flood*. London: Bloomsbury.

Atwood, M. (2013). *Maddaddam*. London: Bloomsbury.

Azmanova, A. (2020). *Capitalism on edge: How fighting precarity can achieve radical change without crisis or utopia*. New York: Columbia University Press.

Bacigalupi, P. (2010). *The windup girl*. San Francisco, CA: Night Shade Books.

Bäckstrand, K. & Lövbrand, E. (2007). Climate governance beyond 2012: Competing discourses of green governmentality, ecological modernisation and civic environmentalism. In M. Pettenger (ed.), *The social construction of climate change*. Burlington, VT: Ashgate, pp. 123–47.

Baer, H. A. (2016). The nexus of the coal industry and the state in Australia: Historical dimensions and contemporary challenges. *Energy Policy*, 99, 194–202.

Bakan, J. (2004). *The corporation: The pathological pursuit of profit and power*. London: Constable.

Bamber, J. L., Oppenheimer, M., Kopp, R. E., Aspinall, W. P. & Cooke, R. M. (2019). Ice sheet contributions to future sea-level rise from structured expert judgment. *Proceedings of the National Academy of Sciences*, 116(23), 11195–200.

Banerjee, S. B. (2012). A climate for change? Critical reflections on the Durban United Nations climate change conference. *Organization Studies*, 33(12), 1761–86.

Barlai, M., Fähnrich, B., Griessler, C. & Rhomberg, M. (eds.). (2017). *The migrant crisis: European perspectives and national discourses*. Berlin: LIT Verlag.

Barley, S. R. (2007). Corporations, democracy, and the public good. *Journal of Management Inquiry*, 16(3), 201–15.

Barnett, J., Waters, E., Pendergast, S. & Puleston, A. (2013). *Barriers to adaptation to sea-level rise: The legal, institutional and cultural barriers to adaptation to sea-level rise in Australia*. Gold Coast: National Climate Change Adaptation Research Facility.

Bartlett, M. (2010). *Earthquakes in London*. London: Methuen Drama.

Batel, S. (2021). A brief excursion into the many scales and voices of renewable energy colonialism. In A. M. Feldpausch-Parker, D. Endres, T. R. Peterson & S. L. Gomez (eds.), *Routledge handbook of energy democracy*. London: Routledge, pp. 119–32.

Bauman, Z. (2012). Times of interregnum. *Ethics & Global Politics*, 5(1), 49–56.

Baumgartner, F. R., Berry, J. M., Hojnacki, M., Leech, B. L. & Kimball, D. C. (2009). *Lobbying and policy change: Who wins, who loses, and why*. Chicago, IL: University of Chicago Press.

BBC News. (2020). Greta Thunberg seeks Africa climate change action. *BBC News*, 31 January. www.bbc.com/news/world-africa-51324958

Beauregard, C., Carlson, D. A., Robinson, S.-A., Cobb, C. & Patton, M. (2021). Climate justice and rights-based litigation in a post-Paris world. *Climate Policy*, 21(5), 652–65.

Beder, S. (2002). BP: Beyond petroleum? In E. Lubbers (ed.), *Battling big business: Countering greenwash, infiltration and other forms of corporate bullying*. Totnes: Green Books, pp. 26–32.

Bell, S. E., Fitzgerald, J. & York, R. (2019). Protecting the power to pollute: Identity co-optation, gender, and the public relations strategies of fossil fuel industries in the United States. *Environmental Sociology*, 5(3), 323–38.

Berchin, I. I., Valduga, I. B., Garcia, J. & de Andrade Guerra, J. B. (2017). Climate change and forced migrations: An effort towards recognizing climate refugees. *Geoforum*, 84, 147–50.

Bereiter, B., Eggleston, S., Schmitt, J. et al. (2015). Revision of the EPICA Dome C CO2 record from 800 to 600 kyr before present. *Geophysical Research Letters*, 42(2), 542–49.

Berrang-Ford, L., Ford, J. D. & Paterson, J. (2011). Are we adapting to climate change? *Global Environmental Change*, 21(1), 25–33.

Bettini, G. (2013). Climate barbarians at the gate? A critique of apocalyptic narratives on 'climate refugees'. *Geoforum*, 45, 63–72.

BHP Billiton. (2015). *Climate change: Portfolio analysis*. Melbourne: BHP Billiton. www.bhp.com/-/media/bhp/documents/investors/reports/2015/b hpbillitonclimatechangeporfolioanalysis2015.pdf?

Biesbroek, G. R., Klostermann, J., Termeer, C. & Kabat, P. (2013). On the nature of barriers to climate change adaptation. *Regional Environmental Change*, 13(5), 1119–29.

Biesheuvel, T. (2020). Big coal escapes Blackrock's new climate plan. *Bloomberg Green*, 14 January. www.bloomberg.com/news/articles/2020 -01-14/blackrock-s-tough-on-coal-plan-skirts-around-the-biggest-miners

Black, R., Cullen, K., Fay, B. et al. (2021). *Taking stock: A global assessment of net zero targets: Scrutinising countries, states and regions, cities and companies*. Oxford: Energy & Climate Intelligence Unit. https://ca1-eci.edcdn.com/reports/ECIU-Oxford_Taking_Stock.pdf

Bloom, P. & Rhodes, C. (2018). *CEO society: The corporate takeover of everyday life*. London: Zed Books.

Bloomberg, R. (2019). Pipelines add room on 'unrelenting' demand for Canada's oil. *The Star*, 2 August. www.thestar.com/business/2019/08/02 /pipelines-add-room-on-unrelenting-demand-for-canadas-oil.html

BloombergNEF. (2019). *New energy outlook 2019*. London: BloombergNEF.

BloombergNEF. (2021). *Climate policy factbook: Three priority areas for climate action*. New York: BloombergNEF.

Böhm, S., Misoczky, M. C. & Moog, S. (2012). Greening capitalism? A Marxist critique of carbon markets. *Organization Studies*, 33(11), 1617–38.

Boltanski, L. (1999). *Distant suffering: Morality, media and politics*. Cambridge: Cambridge University Press.

Boltanski, L. & Chiapello, E. (2005). *The new spirit of capitalism*. London: Verso.

Bomberg, E. (2017). Shale we drill? Discourse dynamics in UK fracking debates. *Journal of Environmental Policy & Planning*, 19(1), 72–88.

Bomberg, E. (2021). The environmental legacy of President Trump. *Policy Studies*, 42(5–6), 628–45.

Borger, J. (2016). Rex Tillerson: An appointment that confirms Putin's US election win. *The Guardian*, 13 December. www.theguardian.com/us-news/2016/dec/11/rex-tillerson-secretary-of-state-trump-russia-putin

Bothello, J. & Salles-Djelic, M.-L. (2018). Evolving conceptualizations of organizational environmentalism: A path generation account. *Organization Studies*, 39(1), 93–119.

Bourdieu, P. (2002). *Counterfire: Against the tyranny of the market*. London: Verso.

Bourne, J. (2016). The cold rush. *National Geographic*, 229, 57–81.

Bowden, B. (2009). *The empire of civilization: The evolution of an imperial idea*. Chicago, IL: University of Chicago Press.

Bowden, V. (2018). 'Life. Brought to you by' … coal? Business responses to climate change in the Hunter Valley, NSW, Australia. *Environmental Sociology*, 4(2), 275–85.

Bowden, V., Gond, J.-P., Nyberg, D. & Wright, C. (2021). Turning back the rising sea: Theory performativity in the shift from climate science to popular authority. *Organization Studies*, 42(12), 1909–31.

Bowden, V. & Leahy, T. (2016). Don't shoot the messenger: How business leaders get their bearings on a matter of science. *Journal of Sociology*, 52(2), 219–34.

Bowden, V., Nyberg, D. & Wright, C. (2019). Planning for the past: Local temporality and the construction of denial in climate change adaptation. *Global Environmental Change*, 57, 101939.

Boykoff, M. T. (2011). *Who speaks for the climate? Making sense of media reporting on climate change*. Cambridge: Cambridge University Press.

Boykoff, M. T. & Boykoff, J. M. (2007). Climate change and journalistic norms: A case-study of US mass-media coverage. *Geoforum*, 38(6), 1190–204.

Boykoff, M. T. & Goodman, M. K. (2009). Conspicuous redemption? Reflections on the promises and perils of the 'celebritization' of climate change. *Geoforum*, 40(3), 395–406.

BP. (2019). The first step to reducing your emissions is to know where you stand. Find out your #carbonfootprint with our new calculator & share your pledge today! [Tweet]. 23 October, Twitter. https://twitter.com/bp_plc/status/1186645440621531136

BP. (2020a). BP statement in response to Greenpeace protest at head office in London. *BP*, 5 February. www.bp.com/en/global/corporate/news-and-insights/press-releases/bp-response-5-feb-2020.html

BP. (2020b). *Statistical review of world energy*. London: BP. www.bp.com/content/dam/bp/business-sites/en/global/corporate/pdfs/energy-economics/statistical-review/bp-stats-review-2020-full-report.pdf

BP. (2021). *Statistical review of world energy*, 70th ed. London: BP. www.bp.com/content/dam/bp/business-sites/en/global/corporate/pdfs/energy-economics/statistical-review/bp-stats-review-2021-full-report.pdf

Bradley, J. (2015). *Clade*. Melbourne: Hamish Hamilton.

Bromwich, J. E. (2020). The darkest timeline. *New York Times*, 26 December. www.nytimes.com/2020/12/26/style/climate-change-deep-adaptation.html

Brown, A. (2016). The noxious legacy of fracking king Aubrey McClendon. *The Intercept*, 8 March. https://theintercept.com/2016/03/07/the-noxious-legacy-of-fracking-king-aubrey-mcclendon/

Brulle, R. J. (2014). Institutionalizing delay: Foundation funding and the creation of us climate change counter-movement organizations. *Climatic Change*, 122(4), 681–94.

Brulle, R. J. (2018). The climate lobby: A sectoral analysis of lobbying spending on climate change in the USA, 2000 to 2016. *Climatic Change*, 149(3), 289–303.

Brulle, R. J., Aronczyk, M. & Carmichael, J. (2020). Corporate promotion and climate change: An analysis of key variables affecting advertising spending by major oil corporations, 1986–2015. *Climatic Change*, 159 (1), 87–101.

Brulle, R. J. & Norgaard, K. M. (2019). Avoiding cultural trauma: Climate change and social inertia. *Environmental Politics*, 28(5), 886–908.

Bulkeley, H., Edwards, G. & Fuller, S. (2014). Contesting climate justice in the city: Examining politics and practice in urban climate change experiments. *Global Environmental Change*, 25, 31–40.

Bullard, R. D., Agyeman, J. & Evans, B. (2002). *Just sustainabilities: Development in an unequal world*. London: Taylor & Francis.

Burke, M. J. & Stephens, J. C. (2017). Energy democracy: Goals and policy instruments for sociotechnical transitions. *Energy Research & Social Science*, 33, 35–48.

Burtynsky, E., Baichwal, J. & de Pencier, N. (2018). *Anthropocene*. Göttingen: Steidl.

Butler, J. & Readfearn, G. (2022). Morrison government announces $1bn pledge for Great Barrier Reef over the next decade. *The Guardian*, 28 January. www.theguardian.com/environment/2022/jan/28/morrison-government-announces-1bn-pledge-for-great-barrier-reef-over-the-next-decade

Campbell-Lendrum, D., Manga, L., Bagayoko, M. & Sommerfeld, J. (2015). Climate change and vector-borne diseases: What are the implications for public health research and policy? *Philosophical Transactions of the Royal Society of London. Series B: Biological Sciences*, 370(1665), 20130552.

Carattini, S., Carvalho, M. & Fankhauser, S. (2018). Overcoming public resistance to carbon taxes. *WIREs Climate Change*, 9(5), e531.

Carbon Disclosure Project. (2020). Climate change corporate disclosures. *CDP*. www.cdp.net/en/climate

Carbon Tracker Initiative. (2021). *Do not revive coal: Planned Asia coal plants a danger to Paris*. London: CTI. https://carbontracker.org/reports/do-not-revive-coal/

Carey, A. (2019). Pauline Hanson suggests police should use cattle prods on climate protesters. *News.com.au*, 22 August. www.news.com.au/finance/work/leaders/pauline-hanson-suggests-police-should-use-cattle-prods-on-climate-protesters/news-story/5c30f34969af0af84a794e9c68e0531d

Carney, M. (2015). Breaking the tragedy of the horizon – climate change and financial stability. *Bank of England*, 29 September. www.bankofeng land.co.uk/-/media/boe/files/speech/2015/breaking-the-tragedy-of-the-horizon-climate-change-and-financial-stability.pdf

Carson, R. (1962). *Silent spring*. Boston, MA: Houghton Mifflin.

Casselman, B. (2009). Sierra Club's pro-gas dilemma: National group's stance angers on-the-ground environmentalists in several states. *Wall Street Journal*, 22 December. www.wsj.com/articles/SB126135534799299475

Cave, T. & Rowell, A. (2014). *A quiet word: Lobbying, crony capitalism and broken politics in Britain*. London: Bodley Head.

Celermajer, D., Lyster, R., Wardle, G. M., Walmsley, R. & Couzens, E. (2021). The Australian bushfire disaster: How to avoid repeating this catastrophe for biodiversity. *WIREs Climate Change*, 12(3), e704.

Ceres. (2019). CEOs of major companies call on US Congress to set a national price on carbon. *Ceres*, 22 May. www.ceres.org/index.php/ne ws-center/press-releases/LEAD-on-carbon-pricing

Chan, G. (2016). Former minister Ian Macfarlane takes job with mining industry lobby group. *The Guardian*, 26 September. www.theguardian .com/australia-news/2016/sep/26/former-minister-ian-macfarlane-takes-job-with-mining-industry-lobby-group

Chancel, L. & Piketty, T. (2015). *Carbon and inequality: From Kyoto to Paris*. Paris: Paris School of Economics.

Chanel, A. (2014). Pacific Warriors refuse to drown, take a stand on climate change. *Future Challenges*, 18 June. https://blog.futurechallenges.org/loc al/pacific-warriors-refuse-to-drown-take-a-stand-on-climate-change/

Cheng, L., Abraham, J., Zhu, J. et al. (2020). Record-setting ocean warmth continued in 2019. *Advances in Atmospheric Sciences*, 37, 137–42.

Chertkovskaya, E. & Paulsson, A. (2021). Countering corporate violence: Degrowth, ecosocialism and organising beyond the destructive forces of capitalism. *Organization*, 28(3), 405–25.

Chiaramonti, D. (2019). Sustainable aviation fuels: The challenge of decarbonization. *Energy Procedia*, 158, 1202–07.

Chivers, D. & Worth, J. (2015). Paris deal: Epic fail on a planetary scale. *New Internationalist*, 6 August. https://newint.org/features/web-exclusive /2015/12/12/cop21-paris-deal-epi-fail-on-planetary-scale

Chouliaraki, L. (2006). *The spectatorship of suffering*. London: Sage.

Chow, D. (2021). Jeff Bezos says spaceflight reinforced his commitment to solving climate change. *NBC News*, 21 July. www.nbcnews.com/science/ science-news/jeff-bezos-says-spaceflight-reinforced-commitment-solving-climate-chan-rcna1467

Chung, F. (2019). 'Use them as a speed bump': Kerri-Anne Kennerley suggests running over climate change protesters. *News.com.au*, 11 October. www

.news.com.au/technology/environment/climate-change/use-them-as-a-spee d-bump-kerrianne-kennerley-suggests-running-over-climate-change-protesters/news-story/6dcec4f260d9df8f2cf3f6f4542e8614

CIC. (2019). Thousands of fossil fuel 'observers' attended climate negotiations – UNFCCC data 2005–2018 COP1–COP24. *Climate Investigations Center*, 21 June. https://climateinvestigations.org/thousands-of-fossil-fuel-observers-attended-climate-negotiations-unfccc-data-2005-2018-cop1-cop24/

City of Boston. (2021). *Preparing for climate change.* www.boston.gov/dep artments/environment/preparing-climate-change

Clark, M. (2021). The wind farms angering renewable energy fans. *ABC News*, 12 December. www.abc.net.au/news/2021-12-12/queensland-wind-farms-clearing-bushland/100683198

Clarke, C. (2017). Rio Tinto's NSW coal mines taken over by China-backed Yancoal. *ABC News*, 29 June. www.abc.net.au/news/2017-06-29/rio-tinto-nsw-coal-mines-taken-over-by-china-backed-company/8664914

Clément, V. & Rivera, J. (2017). From adaptation to transformation: An extended research agenda for organizational resilience to adversity in the natural environment. *Organization & Environment*, 30(4), 346–65.

Climate Action Tracker. (2021). Glasgow's 2030 credibility gap: Net zero's lip service to climate action. *Climate Action Tracker*, 9 November. https:// climateactiontracker.org/publications/glasgows-2030-credibility-gap-net-zeros-lip-service-to-climate-action/

Climate Watch. (2021). Historical GHG emissions. Washington, DC: World Resources Institute. www.climatewatchdata.org/ghg-emissions

CNA Military Advisory Board. (2014). *National security and the accelerating risks of climate change.* Alexandria, VA: CNA Corporation.

Coady, D., Parry, I., Sears, L. & Shang, B. (2017). How large are global fossil fuel subsidies? *World Development*, 91, 11–27.

Coll, S. (2012). *Private empire: ExxonMobil and American power.* New York: Penguin.

Collier, S. J., Elliott, R. & Lehtonen, T.-K. (2021). Climate change and insurance. *Economy and Society*, 50(2), 158–72.

Collins, L. (2019). Are these the real reasons why big oil wants a carbon tax? *Recharge*, 31 October. www.rechargenews.com/transition/are-these-the-real-reasons-why-big-oil-wants-a-carbon-tax-/2-1-695383

Community Energy Scotland. (2021). *Empowering communities.* https://co mmunityenergyscotland.org.uk/

Confino, J. (2012). Moments of revelation trigger the biggest transformations. *The Guardian*, 9 November. www.theguardian.com/sus tainable-business/epiphany-transform-corporate-sustainability

Connelly, B. L., Haynes, K. T., Tihanyi, L., Gamache, D. L. & Devers, C. E. (2016). Minding the gap: Antecedents and consequences of top management-to-worker pay dispersion. *Journal of Management*, 42(4), 862–85.

Copland, S. (2020). Anti-politics and global climate inaction: The case of the Australian carbon tax. *Critical Sociology*, 46(4–5), 623–41.

Cornwall, W. (2021). Europe's deadly floods leave scientists stunned. *Science*, 20 July. www.sciencemag.org/news/2021/07/europe-s-deadly-floods-leave-scientists-stunned

Crosby, A. (2021). The racialized logics of settler colonial policing: Indigenous 'communities of concern' and critical infrastructure in Canada. *Settler Colonial Studies*. https://doi.org/10.1080/2201473X.2021.1884426

Crouch, C. (2004). *Post-democracy*. Cambridge: Polity.

Crowe, D. (2019). Deputy PM slams people raising climate change in relation to NSW bushfires. *Sydney Morning Herald*, 11 November. www.smh.com.au/politics/federal/raving-inner-city-lunatics-michael-mccormack-dismisses-link-between-climate-change-and-bushfires-20191111-p539ap.html

Crowley, K. (2017). Up and down with climate politics 2013–2016: The repeal of carbon pricing in Australia. *Wiley Interdisciplinary Reviews: Climate Change*, 8(3), e458.

Cuarón, A. (2006). *Children of men*. Universal Pictures.

Curran, G. (2001). The third way and ecological modernization. *Contemporary Politics*, 7(1), 41–55.

D'Angelo, C. (2016). Exxon goes after climate NGOs, warns them not to destroy communications. *Huffington Post*, 4 November. www.huffpost.com/entry/exxon-letter-to-climate-groups_n_581bb87be4b0d9ce6fbae7ab

Daly, M. (2017). Pipeline exec compares Dakota protesters to terrorists. *AP News*, 16 February. https://apnews.com/article/8dfd252ea2f74db7a4a5c4fef15b57f4

Dauvergne, P. & LeBaron, G. (2014). *Protest Inc.: The corporatization of activism*. Cambridge: Polity Press.

Dauvergne, P. & Lister, J. (2013). *Eco-business: A big-brand takeover of sustainability*. Cambridge, MA: MIT Press.

Davenport, C. (2015). Nations approve landmark climate deal. *New York Times*, 13 December. www.nytimes.com/2015/12/13/world/europe/climate-change-accord-paris.html

De Cock, C., Nyberg, D. & Wright, C. (2021). Disrupting climate change futures: Conceptual tools for lost histories. *Organization*, 28(3), 468–82.

De Moor, J., De Vydt, M., Uba, K. & Wahlström, M. (2021). New kids on the block: Taking stock of the recent cycle of climate activism. *Social Movement Studies*, 20(5), 619–25.

Debord, G. (2021). *The society of the spectacle*. Glasgow: Good Press.

Delina, L. L. & Diesendorf, M. (2013). Is wartime mobilisation a suitable policy model for rapid national climate mitigation? *Energy Policy*, 58, 371–80.

Deloitte Access Economics. (2017). *At what price? The economic, social and icon value of the Great Barrier Reef*. Brisbane: Deloitte Touche Tohmatsu.

Demetrious, K. (2019). 'Energy wars': Global PR and public debate in the 21st century. *Public Relations Inquiry*, 8(1), 7–22.

Dempsey, H. (2019). Gas is 'not a low-carbon fuel', UK watchdog rules. *Financial Times*, 16 September. www.ft.com/content/788005cc-d3e9-11 e9-8367-807ebd53ab77

Derrida, J. (1976). *Of grammatology*. Baltimore, MD: Johns Hopkins Press.

Derrida, J. (1982). *Margins of philosophy*. Chicago, IL: University of Chicago Press.

Diehl, P. (2017). No 'retreat' from rising sea levels for homes in Del Mar. *The San Diego Union-Tribune*, 4 December. www.sandiegouniontribune.com /communities/north-county/sd-no-sea-level-20171129-story.html

Dietz, M. & Garrelts, H. (eds.). (2014). *Routledge handbook of the climate change movement*. Abingdon: Routledge.

Diffenbaugh, N. S. & Burke, M. (2019). Global warming has increased global economic inequality. *Proceedings of the National Academy of Sciences of the United States of America*, 116(20), 9808–13.

Dilling, L., Pizzi, E., Berggren, J., Ravikumar, A. & Andersson, K. (2017). Drivers of adaptation: Responses to weather- and climate-related hazards in 60 local governments in the intermountain western US. *Environment and Planning A: Economy and Space*, 49(11), 2628–48.

Dimitrov, R. S. (2016). The Paris agreement on climate change: Behind closed doors. *Global Environmental Politics*, 16(3), 1–11.

DiMuzio, T. (2012). Capitalizing a future unsustainable: Finance, energy and the fate of market civilization. *Review of International Political Economy*, 19(3), 363–88.

Dochuk, D. (2019). Oil-patch evangelicals: How Christianity and crude fueled the rise of the American right. *Washington Post*, 15 July. www .washingtonpost.com/outlook/2019/07/15/oil-patch-evangelicals-how-christianity-crude-fueled-rise-american-right/

Dodd, V. (2020). Extinction Rebellion 'criminals' threaten UK way of life, says Priti Patel. *The Guardian*, 9 September. www.theguardian.com/environment/ 2020/sep/08/extinction-rebellion-criminals-threaten-uks-way-of-life-says-prit i-patel

Dodd, V. & Grierson, J. (2020). Terrorism police list Extinction Rebellion as extremist ideology. *The Guardian*, 11 January. www.theguardian.com/u k-news/2020/jan/10/xr-extinction-rebellion-listed-extremist-ideology-police-prevent-scheme-guidance

Doherty, B., de Moor, J. & Hayes, G. (2018). The 'new' climate politics of Extinction Rebellion? *OpenDemocracy*, 27 November. www.open democracy.net/en/new-climate-politics-of-extinction-rebellion/

Dow, K., Berkhout, F. & Preston, B. L. (2013). Limits to adaptation to climate change: A risk approach. *Current Opinion in Environmental Sustainability*, 5(3), 384–91.

Downey, L., Bonds, E. & Clark, K. (2010). Natural resource extraction, armed violence, and environmental degradation. *Organization & Environment*, 23(4), 417–45.

Downie, C. (2019). *Business battles in the US energy sector: Lessons for a clean energy transition*. Abingdon: Routledge.

Dreher, T. & Voyer, M. (2015). Climate refugees or migrants? Contesting media frames on climate justice in the Pacific. *Environmental Communication*, 9(1), 58–76.

Dryzek, J. S. & Pickering, J. (2017). Deliberation as a catalyst for reflexive environmental governance. *Ecological Economics*, 131, 353–60.

Dunaway, F. (2005). *Natural visions: The power of images in American environmental reform*. Chicago, IL: University of Chicago Press.

Dunlap, R. E. & McCright, A. M. (2011). Organized climate change denial. In J. S. Dryzek, R. B. Norgaard & D. Schlosberg (eds.), *The Oxford handbook of climate change and society*. Oxford: Oxford University Press, pp. 144–60.

Dyer, G. (2010). *Climate wars: The fight for survival as the world overheats*. Oxford: Oneworld.

Eckstein, D., Künzel, V., Schäfer, L. & Winges, M. (2019). *Global climate risk index 2020*. Bonn: Germanwatch.

Egan, M. (2021). Undercover Exxon video reveals an anti-climate campaign. *CNN Business*, 1 July. https://edition.cnn.com/2021/07/01/business/exxon-tape-video-keith-mccoy/index.html

Eliasson, O. (2018). *Icewatch*. https://icewatchlondon.com/

Elliott, L. & Wearden, G. (2020). Trump blasts 'prophets of doom' in attack on climate activism. *The Guardian*, 22 January. www.theguardian.com/business/2020/jan/21/trump-climate-1tn-trees-davos

Emmerich, R. (2004). *The day after tomorrow*. 20th Century Fox.

Emmott, S. (2013). *Ten billion*. New York: Vintage Books.

Eriksen, S. H., Nightingale, A. J. & Eakin, H. (2015). Reframing adaptation: The political nature of climate change adaptation. *Global Environmental Change*, 35, 523–33.

Extinction Rebellion. (2019). *This is not a drill: An Extinction Rebellion handbook*. London: Penguin.

ExxonMobil. (2013). Energy lives here. *ExxonMobil*, 28 November. www.ispot.tv/ad/76n7/exxon-mobil-energy-lives-here

ExxonMobil. (2022). *Advancing climate solutions: 2022 progress report*. Irving, TX: ExxonMobil. https://corporate.exxonmobil.com/-/media/Global/Files/Advancing-Climate-Solutions-Progress-Report/2022/ExxonMobil-Advancing-Climate-Solutions-2022-Progress-Report.pdf

Farand, C. (2021). Mega oil project in Russia's far north threatens Arctic indigenous communities. *Climate Home News*, 25 June. www.climate changenews.com/2021/06/25/mega-oil-project-russias-far-north-threatens-arctic-indigenous-communities/

Farber, S. C., Costanza, R. & Wilson, M. A. (2002). Economic and ecological concepts for valuing ecosystem services. *Ecological Economics*, 41(3), 375–92.

Faucher, K. X. (2018). *Social capital online*. London: University of Westminster Press.

Femia, F. & Werrell, C. (2013). Climate change before and after the Arab awakening: The cases of Syria and Libya. In C. Werrell & F. Femia (eds.), *The Arab spring and climate change*. Washington, DC: Center for American Progress, pp. 23–32.

Ferraro, F., Etzion, D. & Gehman, J. (2015). Tackling grand challenges pragmatically: Robust action revisited. *Organization Studies*, 36(3), 363–90.

Fessenden, M. (2016). These watercolor paintings actually include climate change data. *Smithsonian Magazine*, 11 March. www.smithsonianmag .com/arts-culture/these-watercolor-paintings-actually-include-climate-change-data-180958374/

Fitzgerald, J. B., Schor, J. B. & Jorgenson, A. K. (2018). Working hours and carbon dioxide emissions in the United States, 2007–2013. *Social Forces*, 96 (4), 1851–74.

Flavelle, C., Plumer, B. & Tabuchi, H. (2021). Texas crisis exposes a nation's vulnerability to climate change. *New York Times*, 20 February. www.ny times.com/2021/02/20/climate/united-states-infrastructure-storms.html

Foran, J. (2020). What is climate x? An essay on Joel Wainwright and Geoff Mann's *Climate leviathan: A political theory of our planetary future*. *Rethinking Marxism*, 32(4), 417–24.

Ford, J. D., Berrang-Ford, L. & Paterson, J. (2011). A systematic review of observed climate change adaptation in developed nations. *Climatic Change*, 106(2), 327–36.

Forsythe, M. & Bogdanich, W. (2021). McKinsey employees outraged by work with many of biggest polluters. *New York Times*, 28 October. www .nytimes.com/2021/10/27/business/mckinsey-climate-change.html

Fothergill, A., Hughes, J. & Scholey, K. (2020). *David Attenborough: A life on our planet*. Netflix.

Frame, C. (2016). How Qantas is using *Finding Dory* to save the Great Barrier Reef. *IAB Australia*, 4 August. www.iabaustralia.com.au/iab-blog/blog-art icles/entry/how-qantas-is-using-finding-dory-to-save-the-great-barrier-reef

Fremstad, A., Petach, L. & Tavani, D. (2019). Climate change, innovation, and economic growth: The contributions of William Nordhaus and Paul Romer. *Review of Political Economy*, 31(3), 336–55.

Funk, M. (2014). *Windfall: The booming business of global warming.* New York: Penguin.

Funk, R. & Hirschman, D. (2017). Beyond nonmarket strategy: Market actions as corporate political activity. *Academy of Management Review*, 42(1), 32–52.

Gallopín, G. C. & Raskin, P. (1998). Windows on the future: Global scenarios & sustainability. *Environment: Science and Policy for Sustainable Development*, 40(3), 6–11.

Garcia-Freites, S. & Jones, C. (2020). *A review of the role of fossil fuel based carbon capture and storage in the energy system.* Manchester: Tyndall Centre for Climate Change Research. https://foe.scot/wp-content/uploads/2021/01/CCS_REPORT_FINAL.pdf

García-López, G. A. (2018). The multiple layers of environmental injustice in contexts of (un)natural disasters: The case of Puerto Rico post-Hurricane Maria. *Environmental Justice*, 11(3), 101–08.

Gardezi, M. & Arbuckle, J. G. (2018). Techno-optimism and farmers' attitudes toward climate change adaptation. *Environment and Behavior*, 52(1), 82–105.

Garnaut, R. (2008). *The Garnaut climate change review: Final report.* Melbourne: Cambridge University Press.

Gates, B. (2021). *How to avoid a climate disaster: The solutions we have and the breakthroughs we need.* New York: Alfred A. Knopf.

Gayle, D. & Quinn, B. (2019). Extinction rebellion rush-hour protest sparks clash on London underground. *The Guardian*, 18 October. www.theguardian.com/environment/2019/oct/17/extinction-rebellion-activists-london-underground

GECF. (2021). *Gas exporting countries forum statement at COP26.* Doha: GECF Secretariat. https://unfccc.int/sites/default/files/resource/GECF__cop26cmp16cma3_HLS.pdf.pdf

Gereke, M. & Brühl, T. (2019). Unpacking the unequal representation of northern and southern NGOs in international climate change politics. *Third World Quarterly*, 40(5), 870–89.

Gilchrist, K. (2021). 'There's no higher ground for us': Maldives' environment minister says country risks disappearing. *CNBC*, 18 May. www.cnbc.com/2021/05/19/maldives-calls-for-urgent-action-to-end-climate-change-sea-level-rise.html

Gillespie, T. (2021). The world is burning the most coal ever to keep the lights on. *Bloomberg Green*, 17 December. www.bloomberg.com/news/articles/2021-12-17/global-coal-use-at-record-level-despite-pledges-to-cut-emissions

Girei, E. (2015). NGOs, management and development: Harnessing counter-hegemonic possibilities. *Organization Studies*, 37(2), 193–212.

Gleckler, P. J., Durack, P. J., Stouffer, R. J., Johnson, G. C. & Forest, C. E. (2016). Industrial-era global ocean heat uptake doubles in recent decades. *Nature Climate Change*, 6(4), 394–98.

Global Carbon Project. (2021). *Supplemental data of global carbon budget 2021 (Version 1.0) [Data set]*. https://doi.org/10.18160/gcp-2021

Global Divestment Commitments Database. (2021). *Invest/divest 2021*. https:// divestmentdatabase.org/wp-content/uploads/2021/10/DivestInvestRepor t2021.pdf

Gold, R. (2014). *The boom: How fracking ignited the American energy revolution and changed the world*. New York: Simon & Schuster.

Goldberg, M. H., Marlon, J. R., Wang, X., van der Linden, S. & Leiserowitz, A. (2020). Oil and gas companies invest in legislators that vote against the environment. *Proceedings of the National Academy of Sciences*, 117(10), 5111–12.

Goldenberg, S. (2015). The truth behind Peabody's campaign to rebrand coal as a poverty cure. *The Guardian*, 19 May. www.theguardian.com/environ ment/2015/may/19/the-truth-behind-peabodys-campaign-to-rebrand-coal-as-a-poverty-cure

Goldstein, A., Turner, W. R., Gladstone, J. & Hole, D. G. (2019). The private sector's climate change risk and adaptation blind spots. *Nature Climate Change*, 9(1), 18–25.

Goodell, J. (2017). *The water will come: Rising seas, sinking cities, and the remaking of the civilized world*. New York: Little Brown.

Goodman, M. K., Littler, J., Brockington, D. & Boykoff, M. (2016). Spectacular environmentalisms: Media, knowledge and the framing of ecological politics. *Environmental Communication*, 10(6), 677–88.

Gramsci, A. (1971). *Selections from the prison notebooks*. New York: International Publishers.

Green, F. & Denniss, R. (2018). Cutting with both arms of the scissors: The economic and political case for restrictive supply-side climate policies. *Climatic Change*, 150(1–2), 73–87.

Green, J., Hadden, J., Hale, T. & Mahdavi, P. (2021). Transition, hedge, or resist? Understanding political and economic behavior toward decarbonization in the oil and gas industry. *Review of International Political Economy*. https://doi.org/10.1080/09692290.2021.1946708

Grillanda, A. & Khanal, P. (2020). *Community and locally owned renewable energy in Scotland at June 2019: A report by the energy saving trust for the Scottish government*. Edinburgh: Energy Saving Trust.

Gross, M. (2007). The unknown in process: Dynamic connections of ignorance, non-knowledge and related concepts. *Current Sociology*, 55 (5), 742–59.

Grossmann, M. & Creamer, E. (2017). Assessing diversity and inclusivity within the transition movement: An urban case study. *Environmental Politics*, 26(1), 161–82.

Grundmann, R. (2016). Climate change as a wicked social problem. *Nature Geoscience*, 9(8), 562–63.

Guardian Staff. (2018). Schools climate strike: The best protest banners and posters. *The Guardian*, 30 November. www.theguardian.com/environ ment/2018/nov/30/schools-climate-strike-the-best-protest-banners-and-posters

Guggenheim, D. (2006). *An inconvenient truth*. Paramount Classics.

Guha, R. (2000). *Environmentalism: A global history*. New York: Longman.

Gunderson, R. (2020). Spectacular reassurance strategies: How to reduce environmental concern while accelerating environmental harm. *Environmental Politics*, 29(2), 257–77.

Gunderson, R. & Fyock, C. (2021). The political economy of climate change litigation: Is there a point to suing fossil fuel companies? *New Political Economy*, 27(3), 451–4.

Gutiérrez, P., Kirk, A., Watts, J. & Hulley-Jones, F. (2021). How fires have spread to previously untouched parts of the world. *The Guardian*, 19 February. www.theguardian.com/environment/ng-interactive/2021/feb/19/how-fires-have-spread-to-previously-untouched-parts-of-the-world

Haigh, N. & Griffiths, A. (2012). Surprise as a catalyst for including climatic change in the strategic environment. *Business & Society*, 51(1), 89–120.

Hakimi Zapata, N. (2020). Extinction Rebellion's long overdue reckoning with race. *The Nation*, 5 October. www.thenation.com/article/politics/ex tinction-rebellion-climate-race/

Hamilton, L. C. & Stampone, M. D. (2013). Blowin' in the wind: Short-term weather and belief in anthropogenic climate change. *Weather, Climate, and Society*, 5(2), 112–19.

Hanna, R., Abdulla, A., Xu, Y. & Victor, D. G. (2021). Emergency deployment of direct air capture as a response to the climate crisis. *Nature Communications*, 12(1), 368.

Hanoteau, J. (2014). Lobbying for carbon permits in Europe. *Recherches économiques de Louvain*, 80(1), 61–87.

Hansen, J., Sato, M., Hearty, P. et al. (2016). Ice melt, sea level rise and superstorms: Evidence from paleoclimate data, climate modeling, and modern observations that 2°C global warming could be dangerous. *Atmospheric Chemistry and Physics Discussions*, 16, 3761–812.

Haraguchi, M. & Lall, U. (2015). Flood risks and impacts: A case study of Thailand's floods in 2011 and research questions for supply chain decision making. *International Journal of Disaster Risk Reduction*, 14, 256–72.

Harvey, F. (2021a). COP26 draft text annotated: What it says and what it means. *The Guardian*, 11 November. www.theguardian.com/environ ment/ng-interactive/2021/nov/10/cop26-draft-text-annotated-what-it-says-and-what-it-means

Harvey, F. (2021b). Major climate changes inevitable and irreversible – IPCC's starkest warning yet. *The Guardian*, 9 August. www.theguardian.com/sci ence/2021/aug/09/humans-have-caused-unprecedented-and-irreversible-ch ange-to-climate-scientists-warn

Harvey, F. (2021c). 'Put a big fat price on carbon': OECD chief bows out with climate rally cry. *The Guardian*, 18 February. www.theguardian.com/busi ness/2021/feb/17/oecd-chief-angel-gurria-environment-covid-price-carbon

Harvey, F., Carrington, D. & Brooks, L. (2021). COP26 ends in climate agreement despite India watering down coal resolution. *The Guardian*, 14 November. www.theguardian.com/environment/2021/nov/13/cop26-countries-agree-to-accept-imperfect-climate-agreement

Harvey, H., Orvis, R. & Rissman, J. (2018). *Designing climate solutions: A policy guide for low-carbon energy*. Washington, DC: Island Press.

Hawken, P., Lovins, A. & Lovins, L. H. (1999). *Natural capitalism: Creating the next industrial revolution*. Boston, MA: Little Brown.

Healy, N. & Barry, J. (2017). Politicizing energy justice and energy system transitions: Fossil fuel divestment and a 'just transition'. *Energy Policy*, 108, 451–59.

Heede, R. (2014). Tracing anthropogenic carbon dioxide and methane emissions to fossil fuel and cement producers, 1854–2010. *Climatic Change*, 122(1–2), 229–41.

Helmore, E. (2020). Activists cheer Blackrock's landmark climate move but call for vigilance. *The Guardian*, 15 January. www.theguardian.com/envir onment/2020/jan/15/blackrock-climate-change-environment-divestment-coal

Hencke, D. (2014). Tory MPs were paid to plant questions says Harrods chief. *The Guardian*, 20 October. www.theguardian.com/politics/1994/o ct/20/conservatives.uk

Henn, J. (2017). A fossil fuel scandal at the climate talks in Lima. *Huffington Post*, 12 May. www.huffpost.com/entry/a-fossil-fuel-scandal-at-_b_6278018

Hestres, L. E. & Hopke, J. E. (2020). Fossil fuel divestment: Theories of change, goals, and strategies of a growing climate movement. *Environmental Politics*, 29(3), 371–89.

Hickel, J. (2018). The Nobel prize for climate catastrophe. *Foreign Policy*, 6 December. https://foreignpolicy.com/2018/12/06/the-nobel-prize-for-climate-catastrophe/

Hickel, J. (2020a). *Less is more: How degrowth will save the world*. London: William Heinemann.

Hickel, J. (2020b). Quantifying national responsibility for climate breakdown: An equality-based attribution approach for carbon dioxide emissions in excess of the planetary boundary. *The Lancet Planetary Health*, 4(9), e399–e404.

Hickel, J. (2021). What does degrowth mean? A few points of clarification. *Globalizations*, 18(7), 1105–11.

Hickel, J. & Kallis, G. (2019). Is green growth possible? *New Political Economy*, 25(4), 469–86.

Hinton, A. L. (2002). The dark side of modernity: Toward an anthropology of genocide. In A. L. Hinton (ed.), *Annihilating difference: The anthropology of genocide*. Berkeley, CA: University of California Press, pp. 1–40.

Hoare, G. & Sperber, N. (2016). *An introduction to Antonio Gramsci: His life, thought and legacy*. London: Bloomsbury.

Hobson, K. & Niemeyer, S. (2011). Public responses to climate change: The role of deliberation in building capacity for adaptive action. *Global Environmental Change*, 21(3), 957–71.

Hoffman, A. J. (2005). Climate change strategy: The business logic behind voluntary greenhouse gas reductions. *California Management Review*, 47(3), 21–46.

Holmes à Court, S. (2018). It is no wonder the world has gone cold on so-called clean coal. *The Australian*, 9 February. www.theaustralian.com.au/commentary/opinion/it-is-no-wonder-the-world-has-gone-cold-on-socalled-clean-coal/news-story/ed014de70d08ea8b43aa5d7752f11ede

Holter, M. & Sleire, S. (2019). Norway's $1 trillion fund wins go-ahead for oil stock divestment. *Bloomberg*, 12 June. www.bloomberg.com/news/articles/2019-06-11/norway-s-1-trillion-fund-set-to-win-go-ahead-for-oil-divestment

Hook, L. (2021). COP26 deal offers relief for rich nations but vulnerable fear 'death sentence'. *Financial Times*, 15 November. www.ft.com/content/cdee515a-40d7-4605-a25c-c49401327264

Howarth, D. (2015). Gramsci, hegemony and post-Marxism. In M. McNally (ed.), *Antonio Gramsci*. Basingstoke: Palgrave Macmillan, pp. 195–213.

Howarth, D. R. (2013). *Poststructuralism and after: Structure, subjectivity and power*. London: Palgrave Macmillan.

Howarth, R. W., Santoro, R. & Ingraffea, A. (2011). Methane and the greenhouse-gas footprint of natural gas from shale formations. *Climatic Change*, 106(4), 679–90.

Hoydis, J. (2020). (In)attention to global drama: Climate change plays. In D. C. Holmes & L. M. Richardson (eds.), *Research handbook on communicating climate change*. Cheltenham: Edward Elgar, pp. 340–48.

Hudson, M. (2017). Ultra, super, clean coal power? We've heard it before. *The Conversation*, 20 January. https://theconversation.com/ultra-super-clean-coal-power-weve-heard-it-before-71468

IEA. (2015). *Making the energy sector more resilient to climate change.* Paris: International Energy Agency. www.iea.org/reports/making-the-energy-sector-more-resilient-to-climate-change

IEA. (2021a). *Net zero by 2050: A roadmap for the global energy sector.* Paris: International Energy Agency. www.iea.org/reports/net-zero-by-2050

IEA. (2021b). *World energy outlook 2021.* Paris: International Energy Agency. https://iea.blob.core.windows.net/assets/ed3b983c-e2c9-401c-8633-749c3fefb375/WorldEnergyOutlook2021.pdf

InfluenceMap. (2019). Big oil's real agenda on climate change. *InfluenceMap*, 1 October. https://influencemap.org/report/How-Big-Oil-Continues-to-Oppose-the-Paris-Agreement-38212275958aa21196dae3b76220bddc

IPCC. (2014). *Climate change 2014: Impacts, adaptation and vulnerability. Part a: Global and sectoral aspects. Contribution of working group II to the fifth assessment report of the intergovernmental panel on climate change.* Cambridge: Cambridge University Press.

IPCC. (2018). *Global warming of 1.5°C: An IPCC special report on the impacts of global warming of 1.5°C above pre-industrial levels and related global greenhouse gas emission pathways.* Geneva: Intergovernmental Panel on Climate Change.

IPCC. (2019). *Climate change and land: An IPCC special report on climate change, desertification, land degradation, sustainable land management, food security, and greenhouse gas fluxes in terrestrial ecosystems.* Geneva: Intergovernmental Panel on Climate Change.

IPCC. (2021). *Climate change 2021: The physical science basis. Contribution of working group I to the sixth assessment report of the intergovernmental panel on climate change.* Cambridge: Cambridge University Press.

Irwin, R., Bowden, V., Nyberg, D. & Wright, C. (2022). Making green extreme: Defending fossil fuel hegemony through citizen exclusion. *Citizenship Studies*, 26(1), 73–89.

Jackson, T. & Victor, P. A. (2019). Unraveling the claims for (and against) green growth. *Science*, 366(6468), 950–51.

Jacobson, M. Z. (2020). *100% clean, renewable energy and storage for everything.* Cambridge: Cambridge University Press.

Jeffers, J. M. (2013). Double exposures and decision making: Adaptation policy and planning in Ireland's coastal cities during a boom-bust cycle. *Environment and Planning A: Economy and Space*, 45(6), 1436–54.

Jensen, D. (2006). Beyond hope. *Orion*, May/June. https://orionmagazine .org/article/beyond-hope/

Jermier, J. M., Forbes, L. C., Benn, S. & Orsato, R. J. (2006). The new corporate environmentalism and green politics. In S. R. Clegg, C. Hardy, T. B. Lawrence & W. R. Nord (eds.), *The Sage handbook of organization studies*. London: Sage, pp. 618–50.

Johns-Putra, A. (2016). Climate change in literature and literary studies: From cli-fi, climate change theater and ecopoetry to ecocriticism and climate change criticism. *WIREs Climate Change*, 7(2), 266–82.

Jolly, M. (2020). Bushfires, supercyclones and 'resilience': Is it being weaponised to deflect blame in our climate crisis? *Scottish Geographical Journal*, 136(1–4), 81–90.

Jones, S. (2006). *Antonio Gramsci*. Oxford: Routledge.

Kallis, G. (2018). *Degrowth*. Newcastle upon Tyne: Agenda.

Kallis, G., Kerschner, C. & Martinez-Alier, J. (2012). The economics of degrowth. *Ecological Economics*, 84, 172–80.

Kalmus, P. (2021). I'm a climate scientist. *Don't Look Up* captures the madness I see every day. *The Guardian*, 30 December. www.theguardian.com/com mentisfree/2021/dec/29/climate-scientist-dont-look-up-madness

Kang, S. (2018). States of emergence/y: Coastal restoration and the future of Louisiana's Vietnamese/American commercial fisherfolk. *Open Rivers*, 26 May. https://editions.lib.umn.edu/openrivers/article/states-of-emergence-y/

Kaplan, A. E. (2016). *Climate trauma: Foreseeing the future in dystopian film and fiction*. New Brunswick, NJ: Rutgers University Press.

Karavolias, N. G., Horner, W., Abugu, M. N. & Evanega, S. N. (2021). Application of gene editing for climate change in agriculture. *Frontiers in Sustainable Food Systems*, 7 September. www.frontiersin.org/article/10 .3389/fsufs.2021.685801

Katz, C. (2020). In boost for renewables, grid-scale battery storage is on the rise. *Yale Environment 360*, 15 December. https://e360.yale.edu/features/ in-boost-for-renewables-grid-scale-battery-storage-is-on-the-rise

Keenan, J. M., Chu, E. & Peterson, J. (2019). From funding to financing: Perspectives shaping a research agenda for investment in urban climate adaptation. *International Journal of Urban Sustainable Development*, 11 (3), 297–308.

Keith, S. (2019). Climate change protests: With fake blood, Extinction Rebellion hits NY. *New York Times*, 7 October. www.nytimes.com/201 9/10/07/nyregion/extinction-rebellion-nyc-protest.html

Kellner, D. (2016). *Media spectacle and the crisis of democracy: Terrorism, war, and election battles*. Abingdon: Routledge.

Kenis, A. & Mathijs, E. (2014). Climate change and post-politics: Repoliticizing the present by imagining the future? *Geoforum*, 52, 148–56.

Kerr, R. A. (2009). Amid worrisome signs of warming, 'climate fatigue' sets in. *Science*, 326(5955), 926–28.

Kerr, W. R., Lincoln, W. F. & Mishra, P. (2014). The dynamics of firm lobbying. *American Economic Journal: Economic Policy*, 6(4), 343–79.

Khasnabish, D. A. & Haiven, M. (2014). *The radical imagination: Social movement research in the age of austerity*. London: Bloomsbury.

Khurana, R. (2007). *From higher aims to hired hands: The social transformation of American business schools and the unfulfilled promise of management as a profession*. Princeton, NJ: Princeton University Press.

Kilvert, N. (2019). Australia is the world's third-largest exporter of CO_2 in fossil fuels, report finds. *ABC News*, 19 August. www.abc.net.au/news/s cience/2019-08-19/australia-co2-exports-third-highest-worldwide /11420654

Kingsolver, B. (2012). *Flight behavior: A novel*. New York: Harper Collins.

Kirkwood, L. (2016). *The children*. London: Nick Hern.

Klein, N. (2007). *The shock doctrine: The rise of disaster capitalism*. New York: Picador.

Klein, N. (2014). *This changes everything: Capitalism vs. The climate*. New York: Simon & Schuster.

Klein, N. (2018). *The battle for paradise: Puerto Rico takes on the disaster capitalists*. Chicago, IL: Haymarket Books.

Knight, K. W., Rosa, E. A. & Schor, J. B. (2013). Could working less reduce pressures on the environment? A cross-national panel analysis of OECD countries, 1970–2007. *Global Environmental Change*, 23(4), 691–700.

Knox-Hayes, J. & Levy, D. L. (2011). The politics of carbon disclosure as climate governance. *Strategic Organization*, 9(1), 91–99.

Koening, D. (2013). Exxon holders to vote on gay discrimination ban. *USA Today*, 29 May. www.usatoday.com/story/money/business/2013/05/29/e xxon-shareholders-gay-discrimination-ban/2369109/

Kolbert, E. (2006). *Field notes from a catastrophe: Man, nature, and climate change*. New York: Bloomsbury.

Kolbert, E. (2014). *The sixth extinction: An unnatural history*. New York: Henry Holt.

Kraushaar-Friesen, N. & Busch, H. (2020). Of pipe dreams and fossil fools: Advancing Canadian fossil fuel hegemony through the Trans Mountain pipeline. *Energy Research & Social Science*, 69, 101695.

Kulp, S. A. & Strauss, B. H. (2019). New elevation data triple estimates of global vulnerability to sea-level rise and coastal flooding. *Nature Communications*, 10(1), 4844.

Kunze, C. & Becker, S. (2014). *Energy democracy in Europe: A survey and outlook*. Brussels: Rosa Luxemburg Foundation.

Kurmelovs, R. (2021). A 7m wall has gone up on a Sydney beach: Are we destroying public space to save private property? *The Guardian*, 24 October. www.theguardian.com/environment/2021/oct/24/a-7m-wall-has-gone-up-o n-a-sydney-beach-are-we-destroying-public-space-to-save-private-property

Laclau, E. (1990). *New reflections on the revolution of our time*. London: Verso.

Laclau, E. (2005). *On populist reason*. London: Verso.

Laclau, E. & Mouffe, C. (1985). *Hegemony and socialist strategy: Towards a radical democratic politics*. London: Verso.

Lahsen, M., Couto, G. D. A. & Lorenzoni, I. (2020). When climate change is not blamed: The politics of disaster attribution in international perspective. *Climatic Change*, 158(2), 213–33.

Lamb, W. F., Mattioli, G., Levi, S. et al. (2020). Discourses of climate delay. *Global Sustainability*, 3, e17.

Lammi, M., Repo, P. & Timonen, P. (2012). Consumerism and citizenship in the context of climate change. In M. Rask, R. Worthington & M. Lammi (eds.), *Citizen participation in global environmental governance*. New York: Earthscan, pp. 123–35.

Lash, J. & Wellington, F. (2007). Competitive advantage on a warming planet. *Harvard Business Review*, 85(3), 94–102.

Laurie, R. (2019). Still ethical oil: Framing the Alberta oil sands. In H. Graves & D. Beard (eds.), *The rhetoric of oil in the twenty-first century: Government, corporate, and activist discourses*. New York: Routledge, pp. 169–88.

Le Quéré, C., Jackson, R. B., Jones, M. W. et al. (2020). Temporary reduction in daily global CO_2 emissions during the COVID-19 forced confinement. *Nature Climate Change*, 10(7), 647–53.

Le Quéré, C., Peters, G. P., Friedlingstein, P. et al. (2021). Fossil CO_2 emissions in the post-COVID-19 era. *Nature Climate Change*, 11(3), 197–99.

Leahy, S. (2019). Most countries aren't hitting 2030 climate goals, and everyone will pay the price. *National Geographic*, 5 November. www .nationalgeographic.com/science/2019/11/nations-miss-paris-targets-climate-driven-weather-events-cost-billions/

Lehmann, M., Major, D. C., Fitton, J., Doust, K. & O'Donoghue, S. (2021). The way forward: Supporting climate adaptation in coastal towns and small cities. *Ocean & Coastal Management*, 212, 105785.

Leiserowitz, A. A. (2004). Before and after *The Day after Tomorrow*: A US study of climate change risk perception. *Environment: Science and Policy for Sustainable Development*, 46(9), 22–39.

Lenferna, A. (2019). Fossil fuel welfare versus the climate. In G. Wood & G. Baker (eds.), *Palgrave handbook on managing fossil fuels and energy transitions*. London: Palgrave Macmillan, pp. 551–67.

LeQuesne, T. (2019). Petro-hegemony and the matrix of resistance: What can Standing Rock's water protectors teach us about organizing for climate justice in the United States? *Environmental Sociology*, 5(2), 188–206.

Levant, E. (2010). *Ethical oil: The case for Canada's oil sands*. Toronto: McClelland & Stewart.

Levy, D. L. & Egan, D. (1998). Capital contests: National and transnational channels of corporate influence on the climate change negotiations. *Politics and Society*, 26(3), 337–61.

Levy, D. L. & Egan, D. (2003). A neo-Gramscian approach to corporate political strategy: Conflict and accommodation in the climate change negotiations. *Journal of Management Studies*, 40(4), 803–29.

Levy, D. L. & Spicer, A. (2013). Contested imaginaries and the cultural political economy of climate change. *Organization*, 20(5), 659–78.

Leyda, J. & Negra, D. (eds.). (2015). *Extreme weather and global media*. New York: Routledge.

Linnenluecke, M. K. & Griffiths, A. (2010). Beyond adaptation: Resilience for business in light of climate change and weather extremes. *Business & Society*, 49(3), 477–511.

Lohmann, L. (2016). Neoliberalism's climate. In S. Springer, K. Birch & J. MacLeavy (eds.), *Handbook of neoliberalism*. New York: Routledge, pp. 480–92.

Lovelock, J. (2009). *The vanishing face of Gaia: A final warning*. New York: Basic Books.

Lucas, A. (2021). Investigating networks of corporate influence on government decision-making: The case of Australia's climate change and energy policies. *Energy Research & Social Science*, 81, 102271.

Luciani, G. (2013). Corporations vs. states in the shaping of global oil regimes. In R. Dannreuther & W. Ostrowski (eds.), *Global resources: Conflict and cooperation*. Houndmills: Palgrave Macmillan, pp. 119–39.

Ludlam, S. (2019). The extinction rebels. *The Monthly*, July. www.themonthly.com.au/issue/2019/july/1561989600/scott-ludlam/extinction-rebels#mtr

Ludlow, M. (2018). Great Barrier Reef Foundation chairman's panel getaway about opening wallets. *Australian Financial Review*, 17 August. www.afr.com/news/politics/great-barrier-reef-foundation-chairmans-panel-getaway-about-opening-wallets-20180817-h143i5

Lustgarten, A. (2020). How Russia wins the climate crisis. *New York Times*, 16 December. www.nytimes.com/interactive/2020/12/16/magazine/russia-climate-migration-crisis.html

Macdonald, H. (2019). Delayed government figures show greenhouse gas emissions up for fourth year in a row. *ABC News*, 7 June, www.abc.net.au

/radionational/programs/breakfast/figures-show-emissions-have-risen-for
-fourth-consecutive-year/11188756.

Macdonald, T. (2021). How broadcast TV networks covered climate change
in 2020. *Media Matters for America*, 10 March. www.mediamatters.org/b
roadcast-networks/how-broadcast-tv-networks-covered-climate-change
-2020

Mahmoud, J. (2017). Modernizing energy and electricity delivery systems. *U.S.
House Energy and Commerce Committee Subcommittee on Energy*,
15 February. https://energycommerce.house.gov/sites/democrats.energycom
merce.house.gov/files/Testimony-Mahmoud-EP-Hrg-Energy-Infrastructure-
2017-02-15.pdf

Mallinson, D. J. & Cheng, K. J. G. (2021). The relationship between state-level
carbon emissions and average working hours in the United States:
A replication study. *Environmental Sociology*, 8(1), 88–93.

Malm, A. (2016). *Fossil capital: The rise of steam power and the roots of
global warming*. London: Verso.

Malm, A. (2020). *Corona, climate, chronic emergency: War communism in
the twenty-first century*. London: Verso.

Malm, A. (2021). *How to blow up a pipeline: Learning to fight in a world on
fire*. London: Verso.

Mann, G. & Wainwright, J. (2018). *Climate leviathan: A political theory of
our planetary future*. London: Verso.

Mann, M. (2021). *The new climate war: The fight to take back our planet*.
New York: PublicAffairs.

Mann, T. & Puko, T. (2021). Oil trade group is poised to endorse carbon
pricing. *Wall Street Journal*, 1 March. www.wsj.com/articles/oil-trade-
group-considers-endorsing-carbon-pricing-11614640681

Marchart, O. (2018). *Thinking antagonism: Political ontology after Laclau*.
Edinburgh: Edinburgh University Press.

Marsooli, R., Lin, N., Emanuel, K. & Feng, K. (2019). Climate change
exacerbates hurricane flood hazards along US Atlantic and Gulf coasts in
spatially varying patterns. *Nature Communications*, 10(1), 3785.

Mathiesen, K. (2015). How to change the world: Greenpeace and the power
of the mindbomb. *The Guardian*, 11 June. www.theguardian.com/envir
onment/2015/jun/11/how-to-change-the-world-greenpeace-power-
mindbomb

Matthews, T. (2018). Humid heat and climate change. *Progress in Physical
Geography: Earth and Environment*, 42(3), 391–405.

McClure, L. & Baker, D. (2018). How do planners deal with barriers to
climate change adaptation? A case study in Queensland, Australia.
Landscape and Urban Planning, 173, 81–88.

Mcgill, K. & Deslatte, M. (2021). Hurricane Ida power outages, misery persist 9 days later. *NBC New York*, 8 September. www.nbcnewyork.com/news/nati onal-international/hurricane-ida-power-outages-misery-persist-9-days-later /3260038/

McGinn, A. & Isenhour, C. (2021). Negotiating the future of the adaptation fund: On the politics of defining and defending justice in the post-Paris agreement period. *Climate Policy*, 21(3), 383–95.

McGoey, L. (2012a). Philanthrocapitalism and its critics. *Poetics*, 40(2), 185–99.

McGoey, L. (2012b). Strategic unknowns: Towards a sociology of ignorance. *Economy and Society*, 41(1), 1–16.

McGrath, M. (2021a). Climate change: Courts set for rise in compensation cases. *BBC News*, 28 June. www.bbc.com/news/science-environment-57641167

McGrath, M. (2021b). COP26: Fossil fuel industry has largest delegation at climate summit. *BBC News*, 9 November. www.bbc.com/news/science-environment-59199484

McKay, A. (2021). *Don't look up*. Netflix.

McKewon, E. (2012). The use of neoliberal think tank fantasy themes to delegitimise scientific knowledge of climate change in Australian newspapers. *Journalism Studies*, 13(2), 277–97.

McKibben, B. (2005). What the warming world needs now is art, sweet art. *Grist*, 22 April. https://grist.org/article/mckibben-imagine/

McKibben, B. (2009). Four years after my pleading essay, climate art is hot. *Grist*, 6 August. https://grist.org/article/2009-08-05-essay-climate-art-update-bill-mckibben/

McKibben, B. (2012). Global warming's terrifying new math. *Rolling Stone*, 19 July. www.rollingstone.com/politics/news/global-warmings-terrifying-new-math-20120719

McKibben, B. (2013). The case for fossil-fuel divestment. *Rolling Stone*, 22 February. www.rollingstone.com/politics/news/the-case-for-fossil-fuel -divestment-20130222

McKibben, B. (2020). When 'creatives' turn destructive: Image-makers and the climate crisis. *The New Yorker*, 21 November. www.newyorker.com /news/daily-comment/when-creatives-turn-destructive-image-makers-and -the-climate-crisis

McKibben, B., Klein, N. & Leonard, A. (2015). Shell's Arctic drilling is the real threat to the world, not kayaktivists. *The Guardian*, 9 June. www .theguardian.com/environment/2015/jun/09/shell-oil-greed-undeterred-by-science-climate-change-bill-mckibben-naomi-klein-annie-leonard

McKinsey Sustainability & C40 Cities. (2021). *Focused adaptation: A strategic approach to climate adaptation in cities*. New York: McKinsey.

McManus, P. & Connor, L. H. (2013). What's mine is mine(d): Contests over marginalisation of rural life in the upper hunter, NSW. *Rural Society*, 22(2), 166–83.

Measham, T. G., Preston, B. L., Smith, T. F. et al. (2011). Adapting to climate change through local municipal planning: Barriers and challenges. *Mitigation and Adaptation Strategies for Global Change*, 16(8), 889–909.

Meerow, S. & Mitchell, C. L. (2017). Weathering the storm: The politics of urban climate change adaptation planning. *Environment and Planning A: Economy and Space*, 49(11), 2619–27.

Mellen, R. (2021). Floods, flames and heat: Images of this year's extreme weather offer a stark backdrop for COP26 climate summit. *Washington Post*, 26 October. www.washingtonpost.com/world/interactive/2021/cop26-extreme-weather-climate-change-action/

Mercer, G. (2018). 'Sea, ice, snow … it's all changing': Inuit struggle with warming world. *The Guardian*, 30 May. www.theguardian.com/world/2018/may/30/canada-inuits-climate-change-impact-global-warming-melting-ice

Metcalf, G. E. & Weisbach, D. (2009). The design of a carbon tax. *Harvard Environmental Law Review*, 33(2), 499–556.

Met Office Hadley Centre. (2021). *Median Temperature Anomaly from 1961–1990 average*. www.metoffice.gov.uk/hadobs/hadcrut4/index.html

Meyer, R. (2018). A radical new scheme to prevent catastrophic sea-level rise. *The Atlantic*, 11 January. www.theatlantic.com/science/archive/2018/01/a-new-geo-engineering-proposal-to-stop-sea-level-rise/550214/

Miéville, C. (2018). A strategy for ruination. *Boston Review: A Political and Literary Forum*, January. http://bostonreview.net/literature-culture-china-mieville-strategy-ruination

Mikkelson, G. M. (2021). Invisible hand or ecological footprint? Comparing social versus environmental impacts of recent economic growth. *Organization & Environment*, 34(2), 287–97.

Miller, B. (2016). *The handmaid's tale*. MGM Television.

Millman, O. (2018). New York city plans to divest $5bn from fossil fuels and sue oil companies. *The Guardian*, 10 January. www.theguardian.com/us-news/2018/jan/10/new-york-city-plans-to-divest-5bn-from-fossil-fuels-and-sue-oil-companies

Mitchell, T. (2013). *Carbon democracy: Political power in the age of oil*. London: Verso.

Mock, B. (2020). A green stimulus plan for a post-coronavirus economy. *Bloomberg CityLab*, 25 March. www.bloomberg.com/news/articles/2020-03-24/green-stimulus-plan-for-a-post-covid-19-economy

Mol, A. P. J. & Spaargaren, G. (2000). Ecological modernisation theory in debate: A review. *Environmental Politics*, 9(1), 17–49.

Moon, J. (2021). Bezos puts $1 billion of $10 billion climate pledge into conservation. *New York Times*, 20 September. www.nytimes.com/2021/09/20/business/jeff-bezos-earth-fund.html

Moran, E. F., Lopez, M. C., Moore, N., Müller, N. & Hyndman, D. W. (2018). Sustainable hydropower in the 21st century. *Proceedings of the National Academy of Sciences*, 115(47), 11891–98.

Morice, C. P., Kennedy, J. J., Rayner, N. A., & Jones, P. D. (2012). Quantifying uncertainties in global and regional temperature change using an ensemble of observational estimates: The HadCRUT4 data set. *Journal of Geophysical Research: Atmospheres*, 117, D08101.

Morton, A. (2021). Australia puts fossil fuel company front and centre at COP26. *The Guardian*, 3 November. www.theguardian.com/australia-news/2021/nov/03/australia-puts-fossil-fuel-company-front-and-centre-at-cop26

Morton, T. (2013). *Hyperobjects: Philosophy and ecology after the end of the world*. Minneapolis, MN: University of Minnesota Press.

Moser, S. C. (2014). Communicating adaptation to climate change: The art and science of public engagement when climate change comes home. *Wiley Interdisciplinary Reviews: Climate Change*, 5(3), 337–58.

Moser, S. C. & Ekstrom, J. A. (2010). A framework to diagnose barriers to climate change adaptation. *Proceedings of the National Academy of Sciences*, 107, 22026.

Moss, J. (2020). *Australia: An emissions super-power*. Kensington: UNSW. https://climatejustice.co/wp-content/uploads/2020/07/Australia-_-an-emissions-super-power.pdf

Motion, J. (2019). Undoing art and oil: An environmental tale of sponsorship, cultural justice and climate change controversy. *Environmental Politics*, 28 (4), 727–46.

Mouffe, C. (2018). *For a left populism*. London: Verso.

Mower, J. & Bradner, T. (2020). Shell to resume oil and gas exploration in Alaska Arctic offshore. *S&P Global*, 17 September. www.spglobal.com/platts/en/market-insights/latest-news/natural-gas/091720-shell-to-resume-oil-and-gas-exploration-in-alaska-arctic-offshore

Mukherjee, S., Mishra, A. & Trenberth, K. E. (2018). Climate change and drought: A perspective on drought indices. *Current Climate Change Reports*, 4(2), 145–63.

Najam, A. (1999). World business council for sustainable development: The greening of business or a greenwash? In H. O. Bergson, G. Parmann & O. B. Thommesen (eds.), *Yearbook of international co-operation on environment and development 1999/2000*. London: Earthscan, pp. 65–75.

Nalau, J., Becken, S. & Mackey, B. (2018). Ecosystem-based adaptation: A review of the constraints. *Environmental Science & Policy*, 89, 357–64.

NASA. (2021). 2020 tied for warmest year on record, NASA analysis shows. *NASA Media Release*, 15 January. www.nasa.gov/press-release/2020-tied -for-warmest-year-on-record-nasa-analysis-shows

Nash, R. F. (2014). *Wilderness and the American mind*. New Haven, CT: Yale University Press.

National Academies of Sciences Engineering and Medicine. (2016). *Attribution of extreme weather events in the context of climate change*. Washington, DC: The National Academies Press.

Neslen, A. (2018). Flooding and heavy rains rise 50% worldwide in a decade, figures show. *The Guardian*, 22 March. www.theguardian.com/environ ment/2018/mar/21/flooding-and-heavy-rains-rise-50-worldwide-in-a-dec ade-figures-show

Nestlé. (2017). *Agroforestry: Our natural climate solution*, 15 May. www .youtube.com/watch?v=dGTxdpz4QTE

Neubacher, A. (2012). Interview with Richard Branson: 'Climate change is a huge opportunity'. *Spiegel International*, 21 June. www.spiegel.de/inter national/business/richard-branson-discusses-climate-change-business- opportunities-a-839985.html

Newburger, E. & Jeffery, A. (2020). As coronavirus restrictions empty streets around the world, wildlife roam further into cities. *CNBC News*, 10 April. www.cnbc.com/2020/04/10/coronavirus-empty-streets-around- the-world-are-attracting-wildlife.html

Newell, P. & Paterson, M. (2010). *Climate capitalism: Global warming and the transformation of the global economy*. Cambridge: Cambridge University Press.

Newell, R. & Dale, A. (2015). Meeting the climate change challenge (MC3): The role of the internet in climate change research dissemination and knowledge mobilization. *Environmental Communication*, 9(2), 208– 27.

Ni, V. & Davidson, H. (2021). Death toll rises and thousands flee homes as floods hit China. *The Guardian*, 21 July. www.theguardian.com/wo rld/2021/jul/20/heavy-flooding-hits-central-china-affecting-tens-of- millions

Nissan. (2010). *Nissan Leaf polar bear*, 10 September. www.youtube.com /watch?v=VdYWSsUarOg

NOAA. (2021). *Trends in Atmospheric Carbon Dioxide*. https://gml .noaa.gov/ccgg/trends/data.html

Nobel Prize. (2018). *Press release: The prize in economic sciences 2018*. www.nobelprize.org/prizes/economic-sciences/2018/press-release/

Nolan, C. (2014). *Interstellar*. Warner Bros Pictures.

Norgaard, K. M. (2011). *Living in denial: Climate change, emotions and everyday life*. Cambridge, MA: MIT Press.

NSW Government. (2021). *Future of gas statement*. Sydney: State of NSW. www.nsw.gov.au/sites/default/files/2021-07/Future%20of%20Gas%20S tatement.pdf

Nyberg, D. (2021). Corporations, politics, and democracy: Corporate political activities as political corruption. *Organization Theory*, 2(1), 263178772098261.

Nyberg, D., Ferns, G., Vachhani, S. & Wright, C. (2022). Climate change, business and society: Building relevance in time and space. *Business & Society*, 61(5), 1322–52.

Nyberg, D., Spicer, A. & Wright, C. (2013). Incorporating citizens: Corporate political engagement with climate change in Australia. *Organization*, 20(3), 433–53.

Nyberg, D. & Wright, C. (2013). Corporate corruption of the environment: Sustainability as a process of compromise. *The British Journal of Sociology*, 64(3), 405–24.

Nyberg, D. & Wright, C. (2016). Performative and political: Corporate constructions of climate change risk. *Organization*, 23(5), 617–38.

Nyberg, D. & Wright, C. (2022). Climate-proofing management research. *Academy of Management Perspectives*, 36(2), 713–28.

Nyberg, D., Wright, C. & Kirk, J. (2018). Dash for gas: Climate change, hegemony and the scalar politics of fracking in the UK. *British Journal of Management*, 29(2), 235–51.

Nyberg, D., Wright, C. & Kirk, J. (2020). Fracking the future: The temporal portability of frames in political contests. *Organization Studies*, 41(2), 153–74.

O'Malley, N. (2020). Union boss and environmentalist bury the hatchet in the Hunter. *Sydney Morning Herald*, 19 September. www.smh.com.au/e nvironment/climate-change/union-boss-and-environmentalist-bury-the-hatchet-in-the-hunter-20200918-p55x41.html

O'Neill, S. J., Boykoff, M., Niemeyer, S. & Day, S. A. (2013). On the use of imagery for climate change engagement. *Global Environmental Change*, 23(2), 413–21.

O'Toole, K. & Coffey, B. (2013). Exploring the knowledge dynamics associated with coastal adaptation planning. *Coastal Management*, 41 (6), 561–75.

Odell, S. D., Bebbington, A. & Frey, K. E. (2018). Mining and climate change: A review and framework for analysis. *The Extractive Industries and Society*, 5(1), 201–14.

OECD. (2020). Governments should use COVID-19 recovery efforts as an opportunity to phase out support for fossil fuels, say OECD and IEA. *OECD Press Release*, 5 June. www.oecd.org/newsroom/governments-should-use-covid-19-recovery-efforts-as-an-opportunity-to-phase-out-support-for-fossil-fuels-say-oecd-and-iea.htm

OECD. (2021). *Focus on green recovery*. www.oecd.org/coronavirus/en/th emes/green-recovery

Oliveira, A. M., Beswick, R. R. & Yan, Y. (2021). A green hydrogen economy for a renewable energy society. *Current Opinion in Chemical Engineering*, 33, 100701.

Oreskes, N. & Conway, E. M. (2010). *Merchants of doubt: How a handful of scientists obscured the truth on issues from tobacco smoke to global warming*. New York: Bloomsbury.

Orlowski, J. (2012). *Chasing ice*. Submarine Deluxe.

Orlowski, J. (2017). *Chasing coral*. Netflix.

Osaka, S. (2021). Why a landmark experiment into dimming the sun got canceled. *Grist*, 8 April. https://grist.org/science/who-gets-to-decide-if-we-study-solar-geoengineering-after-the-scopex-project-canceled/

Otto, D. (2017). Lived experience of climate change – a digital storytelling approach. *International Journal of Global Warming*, 12(3–4), 331–46.

Parkinson, G. (2018). Solar, wind and batteries are killing market for new gas plants. *Renew Economy*, 9 April. https://reneweconomy.com.au/solar-wind-batteries-killing-market-new-gas-plants-57621/

Parkinson, G. & Mazengarb, M. (2019). BHP sees early end for thermal coal, plugs in to electric future. *Renew Economy*, 23 May. https://reneweconomy .com.au/bhp-sees-early-end-for-thermal-coal-plugs-in-to-electric-future-70246

Parry, I., Black, S. & Vernon, N. (2021). *Still not getting energy prices right: A global and country update of fossil fuel subsidies*. Washington, DC: International Monetary Fund.

Pascale, S., Kapnick, S. B., Delworth, T. L. & Cooke, W. F. (2020). Increasing risk of another Cape Town 'day zero' drought in the 21st century. *Proceedings of the National Academy of Sciences*, 117(47), 29495–503.

Pearse, G. (2007). *High & dry: John Howard, climate change and the selling of Australia's future*. Camberwell: Viking.

Pearse, G. (2012). *Greenwash: Big brands and carbon scams*. Collingwood: Black.

Pearse, R. (2016). The coal question that emissions trading has not answered. *Energy Policy*, 99, 319–28.

Peluso, N. L. & Watts, M. (eds.). (2001). *Violent environments*. Ithaca, NY: Cornell University Press.

Peoples, C. D. (2010). Contributor influence in congress: Social ties and PAC effects on US House policymaking. *The Sociological Quarterly*, 51(4), 649–77.

Perumal, K. (2018). 'The place where I live is where I belong': Community perspectives on climate change and climate-related migration in the Pacific island nation of Vanuatu. *Island Studies Journal*, 13(1), 45–64.

Peter, D. & Neville, K. J. (2011). Mindbombs of right and wrong: Cycles of contention in the activist campaign to stop Canada's seal hunt. *Environmental Politics*, 20(2), 192–209.

Pielke Jr, R., Prins, G., Rayner, S. & Sarewitz, D. (2007). Lifting the taboo on adaptation. *Nature*, 445, 597.

Pinkse, J. & Gasbarro, F. (2019). Managing physical impacts of climate change: An attentional perspective on corporate adaptation. *Business & Society*, 58(2), 333–68.

Pollin, R. (2018). De-growth vs a green new deal. *New Left Review*, 112, 5–25.

Poole, R. (2010). *Earthrise: How man first saw the earth*. New Haven, CT: Yale University Press.

Porter, M. E. & Kramer, M. R. (2011). Creating shared value. *Harvard Business Review*, 89(1/2), 62–77.

Potter, W. (2011). *Green is the new red: The journey from activist to 'eco-terrorist'*. San Francisco, CA: City Lights.

Powell, D. E. & Draper, R. (2020). Making it home: Solidarity and belonging in the #NoDAPL/Standing Rock encampments. *Collaborative Anthropologies*, 13(1), 1–45.

Powers, R. (2018). *The overstory*. New York: W. W. Norton.

Pyne, S. J. (2020). The pyrocene comes to Australia: A commentary. *Journal and Proceedings of the Royal Society of New South Wales*, 153(477/478), 30–35.

Ramesh, R. (2009). Maldives ministers prepare for underwater cabinet meeting. *The Guardian*, 8 October. www.theguardian.com/world/2009/oct/07/maldives-underwater-cabinet-meeting

RAN. (2020). *Banking on climate change: Fossil fuel finance report 2020*. San Francisco, CA: Rainforest Action Network.

Rapley, C. & MacMillan, D. (2015). *2071: The world we'll leave our grandchildren*. London: John Murray.

Raymond, L. (2020). Carbon pricing and economic populism: The case of Ontario. *Climate Policy*, 20(9), 1127–40.

Rea, N. (2018). Olafur Eliasson hauls 30 icebergs to London, inviting the public to contemplate the devastating effects of climate change. *Artnet News*, 11 December. https://news.artnet.com/art-world/olafur-eliasson-ice-watch-london-1416811

Readfearn, G. (2020). Great Barrier Reef's third mass bleaching in five years the most widespread yet. *The Guardian*, 7 April. www.theguardian.com

/environment/2020/apr/07/great-barrier-reefs-third-mass-bleaching-in-five-years-the-most-widespread-ever

Reeve, K. E. (2008). *NGOs & climate change campaigns: Understanding variations in motivations and activities of environmental and development organizations*. Master in City Planning Theses, Department of Urban Studies and Planning, Massachusetts Institute of Technology. https://dspace.mit.edu/handle/1721.1/45425

Rhodes, C. (2022). *Woke capitalism: How corporate morality is sabotaging democracy*. Bristol: Bristol University Press.

Ricketts, A. (2020). 'We have the right to be arrested and processed according to law': The power of effective police liaison at the Bentley Blockade. *Journal of Australian Studies*, 44(3), 384–400.

Ritchie, H. (2019). Who has contributed most to global CO_2 emissions? *Our World in Data*. https://ourworldindata.org/contributed-most-global-co2

Roberts, D. (2020). Microsoft's astonishing climate change goals, explained. *Vox*, 30 July. www.vox.com/energy-and-environment/2020/7/30/21336777/microsoft-climate-change-goals-negative-emissions-technologies

Robertson, J. (2017). Drew Hutton, how he galvanised the Greens and his unlikely alliance with Alan Jones. *The Guardian*, 23 June. www.theguardian.com/environment/2017/jun/23/drew-hutton-how-he-galvanised-the-greens-and-his-unlikely-alliance-with-alan-jones

Robinson, K. S. (2020). *The ministry for the future*. London: Little Brown.

Rockström, J., Steffen, W., Noone, K. et al. (2009). A safe operating space for humanity. *Nature*, 461(7263), 472–75.

Rosewarne, S., Goodman, J. & Pearse, R. (2013). *Climate action upsurge: The ethnography of climate movement politics*. London: Routledge.

Royal Society. (2009). *Geoengineering the climate: Science, governance and uncertainty*. London: The Royal Society.

Safi, M. & Harvey, F. (2021). COP26: Where does the world go from here? *The Guardian*, 15 November. www.theguardian.com/news/audio/2021/nov/15/cop26-climate-deal-where-world-from-here-podcast-focus

Safi, M. & Nasheed, M. (2021). COP26: What would success look like for a country vanishing under water? *The Guardian*, 29 October. www.theguardian.com/news/audio/2021/oct/29/cop26-what-would-success-look-like-for-a-country-vanishing-under-water-podcast

Salim, W., Bettinger, K. & Fisher, M. (2019). Maladaptation on the waterfront: Jakarta's growth coalition and the Great Garuda. *Environment and Urbanization ASIA*, 10(1), 63–80.

Samenow, J. (2021). Death Valley had planet's hottest 24 hours on record Sunday amid punishing heat wave. *Washington Post*, 12 July. www.washingtonpost.com/weather/2021/07/12/death-valley-record-heat-earth/

Sampathkumar, M. (2017). Trump's EPA head Scott Pruitt on Irma: Now is not the time to talk about climate change. *Independent*, 9 September. www .independent.co.uk/news/irma-trump-epa-scott-pruitt-climate-change-not-the-time-to-talk-about-it-a7937376.html

Sanderson, T. (2016). I'm proud of my daughter and the other brave Heathrow protesters: Here's why. *The Guardian*, 26 January. www.theguardian.com/ commentisfree/2016/jan/25/heathrow-protesters-plane-stupid

Santos. (2019). Chief executive officer's address 2019 annual general meeting. *Santos Media Release*, 2 May, www.asx.com.au/asxpdf/201905 02/pdf/444sf493jwbkwx.pdf

Savodnik, P. (2009). How Russia learned to stop worrying and love the warm. *The National*, 19 June. www.thenationalnews.com/arts-culture/h ow-russia-learned-to-stop-worrying-and-love-the-warm-1.493994

Sawyer, S. (2010). Human energy. *Dialectical Anthropology*, 34(1), 67–75.

Saxifrage, B. (2019). Fossil fuel burning leaps to new record, crushing clean energy and climate efforts. *National Observer*, 31 July. www.national observer.com/2019/07/31/opinion/fossil-fuel-burning-leaps-new-record-crushing-clean-energy-and-climate-efforts

Saxifrage, B. (2020). Global fossil fuel burning breaks record in 2019. *National Observer*, 16 July. www.nationalobserver.com/2020/07/16/opin ion/global-fossil-burning-breaks-record-2019-canadians-top-1

Schiermeier, Q. (2013). Did climate change cause Typhoon Haiyan? *Nature*, 11 November. www.nature.com/news/did-climate-change-cause-typhoon -haiyan-1.14139

Schifeling, T. & Hoffman, A. J. (2019). Bill Mckibben's influence on U.S. climate change discourse: Shifting field-level debates through radical flank effects. *Organization & Environment*, 32(3), 213–33.

Schiffman, R. (2017). Why it's time to stop punishing our soils with fertilizers. *Yale Environment 360*, 3 May. https://e360.yale.edu/features/ why-its-time-to-stop-punishing-our-soils-with-fertilizers-and-chemicals

Schlosberg, D. & Collins, L. B. (2014). From environmental to climate justice: Climate change and the discourse of environmental justice. *Wiley Interdisciplinary Reviews: Climate Change*, 5(3), 359–74.

Schultz, K. & Sharma, B. (2019). Rising temperatures could melt most Himalayan glaciers by 2100. *New York Times*, 4 February. www .nytimes.com/2019/02/04/world/asia/himalayas-glaciers-warming.html

Schwietzke, S., Griffin, W. M., Matthews, H. S. & Bruhwiler, L. M. P. (2014). Natural gas fugitive emissions rates constrained by global atmospheric methane and ethane. *Environmental Science & Technology*, 48(14), 7714–22.

Scott, E. (2021). Hilariously, mining giant Adani wants individuals to step up and fight climate change. *Junkee*, 11 June. https://junkee.com/adani-climate-change/297969

Scott, I. (2020). A Mann for our times. *The Brilliant*, 1 October. https://the
brilliant.com.au/case-studies/a-mann-for-our-times/

Scurr, I. & Bowden, V. (2021). 'The revolution's never done': The role of
'radical imagination' within anti-capitalist environmental justice activism.
Environmental Sociology, 7(4), 316–26. https://doi.org/10.1080/232510
42.2021.1916142

Sedjo, R. & Sohngen, B. (2012). Carbon sequestration in forests and soils.
Annual Review of Resource Economics, 4(1), 127–44.

Selk, V. & Kemmerzell, J. (2021). Retrogradism in context: Varieties of
right-wing populist climate politics. *Environmental Politics*. https://doi
.org/10.1080/09644016.2021.1999150

Serrao-Neumann, S., Harman, B., Leitch, A. & Low Choy, D. (2014). Public
engagement and climate adaptation: Insights from three local governments
in Australia. *Journal of Environmental Planning and Management*, 58(7),
1196–216.

Setzer, J. & Higham, C. (2021). Global trends in climate change litigation:
2021 snapshot. London: Grantham Research Institute on Climate Change,
London School of Economics and Political Science, London. www
.lse.ac.uk/granthaminstitute/wp-content/uploads/2021/07/Global-trends-
in-climate-change-litigation_2021-snapshot.pdf

Sheppard, K. (2016). State attorneys general pledge to crack down on climate
fraud. *Huffington Post*, 29 March. www.huffingtonpost.com.au/entry/at
torneys-exxon-probe_n_56fab959e4b0a372181b113d?ri18n=true

Shwom, R., McCright, A. M., Brechin, S. R. et al. (2015). Public opinion on
climate change. In R. E. Dunlap & R. J. Brulle (eds.), *Climate change and
society: Sociological perspectives*. Oxford: Oxford University Press, pp.
269–99.

Siefter, A. (2017). Eight things we learned from Scott Pruitt's EPA
confirmation hearing. *Media Matters*, 20 January. https://mediamatters.o
rg/blog/2017/01/20/eight-things-we-learned-scott-pruitt-s-epa-confirm
ation-hearing/215070

Singh, M., Oliver, M., Haroon, S. & Zhou, N. (2019). Global climate strike:
Greta Thunberg and school students lead climate crisis protest – as it
happened. *The Guardian*, 21 September. www.theguardian.com/environ
ment/live/2019/sep/20/climate-strike-global-change-protest-sydney-
melbourne-london-new-york-nyc-school-student-protest-greta-thunberg-
rally-live-news-latest-updates

Skovgaard, J. & van Asselt, H. (2019). The politics of fossil fuel subsidies and
their reform: Implications for climate change mitigation. *WIREs Climate
Change*, 10(4), e581.

Slaven, M. & Heydon, J. (2020). Crisis, deliberation, and Extinction
Rebellion. *Critical Studies on Security*, 8(1), 59–62.

Slawinski, N., Pinkse, J., Busch, T. & Banerjee, S. B. (2017). The role of short-termism and uncertainty avoidance in organizational inaction on climate change: A multi-level framework. *Business & Society*, 56(2), 253–82.

Slezak, M. (2016). Environmental groups could lose charity status for encouraging civil disobedience. *The Guardian*, 4 May. www.theguardian .com/australia-news/2016/may/04/environmental-groups-could-lose-charity-status-for-encouraging-civil-disobedience

Smee, B. (2018). Great Barrier Reef Foundation seeks another $400m with corporate push. *The Guardian*, 12 October. www.theguardian.com/envir onment/2018/oct/12/great-barrier-reef-foundation-seeks-another-400m-with-corporate-push

Smiley, L. (2018). Private firefighters and five-star hotels: How the rich sit out wildfires. *The Guardian*, 20 September. www.theguardian.com/world/201 8/sep/20/private-firefighters-wildfire-insurance-climate-change-capitalism

Smith, B. (2020). Microsoft will be carbon negative by 2030. *Microsoft*, 16 January. https://blogs.microsoft.com/blog/2020/01/16/microsoft-will-be-carbon-negative-by-2030/

Smith, P., Bustamante, M., Ahammad, H. et al. (2014). Agriculture, forestry and other land use (AFOLU). In IPCC (ed.), *Climate change 2014: Mitigation of climate change. Contribution of working group III to the fifth assessment report of the intergovernmental panel on climate change.* Cambridge: Cambridge University Press, pp. 811–922.

Smith, P. & Howe, N. C. (2015). *Climate change as social drama: Global warming in the public sphere.* New York: Cambridge University Press.

Smith, T. F., Choy, D. L., Thomsen, D. C. et al. (2014). Adapting Australian coastal regions to climate change: A case study of south east Queensland. In B. Glavovic, M. Kelly, R. Kay & A. Travers (eds.), *Climate change and the coast: Building resilient communities.* Boca Raton, FL: CRC Press, pp. 269–84.

Snaith, E. (2019). Greta Thunberg thanks OPEC chief for complaining about 'threat' of climate activists. *Independent*, 5 July. www.independent.co.uk /environment/greta-thunberg-opec-climate-change-campaigners-oil-sector-mohammed-barkindo-a8990011.html

Solnit, R. (2021). Ten ways to confront the climate crisis without losing hope. *The Guardian*, 18 November. www.theguardian.com/environment/ 2021/nov/18/ten-ways-confront-climate-crisis-without-losing-hope-rebec ca-solnit-reconstruction-after-covid

Somerville, P. & Burton, M. (2019). Degrowth: A defence. *New Left Review*, 115, 95–104.

Sovacool, B. & Linnér, B.-O. (2016). *The political economy of climate change adaptation.* London: Palgrave Macmillan.

Spash, C. L. (2016). This changes nothing: The Paris agreement to ignore reality. *Globalizations*, 13(6), 928–33.

SPREP. (2021). World leaders told – 'we are not drowning, we are fighting'. *Secretariat of the Pacific Regional Environment Programme*, 2 November. www.sprep.org/news/world-leaders-told-we-are-not-drowning-we-are-fighting

Standaert, M. (2021). Despite pledges to cut emissions, China goes on a coal spree. *Yale Environment 360*, 24 March. https://e360.yale.edu/features/despite-pledges-to-cut-emissions-china-goes-on-a-coal-spree

Steffen, A. (2016). Predatory delay and the rights of future generations. *Medium*, 30 April. https://medium.com/@AlexSteffen/predatory-delay-and-the-rights-of-future-generations-69b06094a16

Steffen, W., Broadgate, W., Deutsch, L., Gaffney, O. & Ludwig, C. (2015). The trajectory of the Anthropocene: The great acceleration. *The Anthropocene Review*, 2(1), 81–98.

Steffen, W., Richardson, K., Rockström, J. et al. (2015). Planetary boundaries: Guiding human development on a changing planet. *Science*, 347(6223), 1259855.

Steffen, W., Rockström, J., Richardson, K. et al. (2018). Trajectories of the Earth system in the Anthropocene. *Proceedings of the National Academy of Sciences*, 115(33), 8252–59.

Steiger, R., Scott, D., Abegg, B., Pons, M. & Aall, C. (2019). A critical review of climate change risk for ski tourism. *Current Issues in Tourism*, 22(11), 1343–79.

Stephens, J. C. & Surprise, K. (2020). The hidden injustices of advancing solar geoengineering research. *Global Sustainability*, 3(e2), 1–6.

Sterling, T. (2015). Engineering firm sees climate change opportunity in cities. *Reuters*, 4 December. www.reuters.com/article/us-climatechange-summit-arcadis-idUSKBN0TM1XB20151203

Stern, N. (2007). *The economics of climate change: The Stern Review*. Cambridge: Cambridge University Press.

Sternfels, B. (2021). Why do we serve high-emissions companies? Because that is where the emissions are. *McKinsey*, 27 October. www.mckinsey.com/about-us/media/why-do-we-serve-high-emissions-companies-because-that-is-where-the-emissions-are

Stevens, F. (2016). *Before the flood*. National Geographic.

Stevens, P. (2013). History of the international oil industry. In R. Dannreuther & W. Ostrowski (eds.), *Global resources: Conflict and cooperation*. Houndmills: Palgrave Macmillan, pp. 13–32.

Stober, E. (2019). First nations suicide rate 3 times higher than for non-indigenous people: Statscan. *Global News Canada*, 30 June. https://globalnews.ca/news/5448390/first-nations-suicide-rate-statscan/

Stockholm Environment Institute, International Institute for Sustainable Development, ODI, E3G & United Nations Environment Programme. (2020). *The production gap report: 2020 special report*. Stockholm: SEI. http://productiongap.org/2020report

Stoddard, I., Anderson, K., Capstick, S. et al. (2021). Three decades of climate mitigation: Why haven't we bent the global emissions curve? *Annual Review of Environment and Resources*, 46(1), 653–89.

Streeck, W. (2011). The crises of democratic capitalism. *New Left Review*, 71, 5–29.

Streeck, W. (2016). *How will capitalism end? Essays on a failing system*. London: Verso.

Stuart, D., Gunderson, R. & Petersen, B. (2020a). *Climate change solutions: Beyond the capital-climate contradiction*. Ann Arbor, MI: University of Michigan Press.

Stuart, D., Gunderson, R. & Petersen, B. (2020b). Overconsumption as ideology: Implications for addressing global climate change. *Nature and Culture*, 15(2), 199–223.

Stuart-Smith, R. F., Otto, F. E. L., Saad, A. I. et al. (2021). Filling the evidentiary gap in climate litigation. *Nature Climate Change*, 11(8), 651–55.

Suliman, S., Farbotko, C., Ransan-Cooper, H. et al. (2019). Indigenous (im)mobilities in the Anthropocene. *Mobilities*, 14(3), 298–318.

Sumaila, U. R. & Tai, T. C. (2020). End overfishing and increase the resilience of the ocean to climate change. *Frontiers in Marine Science*, 7, 523.

Supran, G. & Oreskes, N. (2017). Assessing ExxonMobil's climate change communications (1977–2014). *Environmental Research Letters*, 12(8), 084019.

Supran, G. & Oreskes, N. (2021). Rhetoric and frame analysis of ExxonMobil's climate change communications. *One Earth*, 4(5), 696–719.

Surane, J. (2020). Citi vows to stop working with thermal coal-mining companies. *Bloomberg Green*, 21 April. www.bloomberg.com/news/articles/2020-04-20/citi-vows-to-stop-working-with-thermal-coal-mining-companies

Swyngedouw, E. (2013). Apocalypse now! Fear and doomsday pleasures. *Capitalism Nature Socialism*, 24(1), 9–18.

Szabo, J. (2022). Energy transition or transformation? Power and politics in the European natural gas industry's trasformismo. *Energy Research & Social Science*, 84, 102391.

Szczepanski, M., Sedlar, F. & Shalant, J. (2018). Bangladesh: A country underwater, a culture on the move. *onEarth*, 13 September. www.nrdc.org/onearth/bangladesh-country-underwater-culture-move

Tabuchi, H. & Fountain, H. (2017). Bucking Trump, these cities, states and companies commit to Paris accord. *New York Times*, 1 June. www.nytimes.com/2017/06/01/climate/american-cities-climate-standards.html

Taylor, M. & Watts, J. (2019). Revealed: The 20 firms behind a third of all carbon emissions. *The Guardian*, 9 October. www.theguardian.com/environment/2019/oct/09/revealed-20-firms-third-carbon-emissions

Taylor, M., Watts, J. & Bartlett, J. (2019). Climate crisis: 6 million people join latest wave of global protests. *The Guardian*, 28 September. www.theguardian.com/environment/2019/sep/27/climate-crisis-6-million-people-join-latest-wave-of-worldwide-protests

Teachout, Z. (2014). *Corruption in America: From Benjamin Franklin's snuff box to Citizens United*. Cambridge, MA: Harvard University Press.

TFCD. (2017). *Recommendations of the Task Force on Climate-related Financial Disclosures*. New York: TFCD. www.fsb-tcfd.org/wp-content/uploads/2017/06/FINAL-2017-TCFD-Report-11052018.pdf

Thompson, L. G. (2010). Climate change: The evidence and our options. *The Behavior Analyst*, 33(2), 153–70.

Thunberg, G. (2019a). If world leaders choose to fail us, my generation will never forgive them. *The Guardian*, 24 September. www.theguardian.com/commentisfree/2019/sep/23/world-leaders-generation-climate-breakdown-greta-thunberg

Thunberg, G. (2019b). *No one is too small to make a difference*. London: Penguin.

TigerSwan. (2017). Internal TigerSwan situation report: DAPL sitrep 233, 4 May. www.documentcloud.org/documents/3940287-Internal-TigerSwan-Situation-Report-2017-05-04.html

Toadvine, T. (2018). Eco-destruction: Derrida and environmental philosophy. In M. Fritsch, P. Lynes & D. Wood (eds.), *Groundworks: Ecological issues in philosophy and theology*. New York: Fordham University Press, pp. 50–80.

Tollefson, J. (2018). First sun-dimming experiment will test a way to cool earth. *Nature*, 563(7733), 613–15.

Toro, T. (2012). Yes, the planet got destroyed (cartoon). *The New Yorker*, 88(37), 43.

Trenberth, K. E., Cheng, L., Jacobs, P., Zhang, Y. & Fasullo, J. (2018). Hurricane Harvey links to ocean heat content and climate change adaptation. *Earth's Future*, 6(5), 730–44.

Treuer, G. A. (2018). The psychology of Miami's struggle to adapt to sea-level rise. *Bulletin of the Atomic Scientists*, 74(3), 155–59.

Troianovski, A. (2020). A historic heat wave roasts Siberia. *New York Times*, 25 June. www.nytimes.com/2020/06/25/world/europe/siberia-heat-wave-climate-change.html

Tschakert, P., Das, P. J., Shrestha Pradhan, N. et al. (2016). Micropolitics in collective learning spaces for adaptive decision making. *Global Environmental Change*, 40, 182–94.

Turner, G. (2016). Celebrities and the environment: The limits to their power. *Environmental Communication*, 10(6), 811–14.

Umbach, F. & Yu, K.-H. (2016). *China's expanding overseas coal power industry: New strategic opportunities, commercial risks, climate challenges and geopolitical implications*. London: European Centre for Energy and Resource Security.

UNEP . (2020). *Global climate litigation report: 2020 status review*. Nairobi: UNEP. https://wedocs.unep.org/bitstream/handle/20.500.11822/34818/GCLR.pdf

UNEP. (2021). *Adaptation gap report 2020*. Nairobi: United Nations Environment Programme.

United Nations. (2021a). *Inequality – bridging the divide*. www.un.org/en/un75/inequality-bridging-divide

United Nations. (2021b). A matter of life or death: At COP26, vulnerable countries tell developed nations it's time to keep their promise on climate finance. *UN News*, 8 November. https://news.un.org/en/story/2021/11/1105222

United Nations. (2021c). The waters are literally lapping at our ankles – adaptation day at COP26. *UN News*, 8 November. https://news.un.org/en/audio/2021/11/1105212

United States District Court – District of North Dakota. (2018). *Energy Transfer Equity v. Greenpeace International*. https://ccrjustice.org/sites/default/files/attach/2018/08/88%20etp%20v%20gp%20et%20al%20order%20denying%20gp%20mtd.pdf

Urry, J. (2008). Climate change, travel and complex futures. *British Journal of Sociology*, 59(2), 261–79.

Vale, L. J. (2014). The politics of resilient cities: Whose resilience and whose city? *Building Research & Information*, 42(2), 191–201.

van der Zee, B. (2022). More than 400 weather stations beat heat records in 2021. *The Guardian*, 7 January. www.theguardian.com/world/2022/jan/07/heat-records-broken-all-around-the-world-in-2021-says-climatologist

Van Huijstee, M., Pollock, L. E. O., Glasbergen, P. & Leroy, P. (2011). Challenges for NGOs partnering with corporations: WWF Netherlands and the Environmental Defense Fund. *Environmental Values*, 20(1), 43–74.

van Renssen, S. (2018). The inconvenient truth of failed climate policies. *Nature Climate Change*, 8(5), 355–58.

Van Veelen, B. (2018). Negotiating energy democracy in practice: Governance processes in community energy projects. *Environmental Politics*, 27(4), 644–65.

Vicedo-Cabrera, A. M., Scovronick, N., Sera, F. et al. (2021). The burden of heat-related mortality attributable to recent human-induced climate change. *Nature Climate Change*, 11(6), 492–500.

Victor, D. G., Hults, D. R. & Thruber, M. (eds.). (2012). *Oil and governance: State-owned enterprises and the world energy supply.* Cambridge: Cambridge University Press.

Vivid Economics. (2020). *Greenness of stimulus index: An assessment of COVID-19 stimulus by G20 countries in relation to climate action and biodiversity goals.* London: Vivid Economics. www.vivideconomics.com /wp-content/uploads/2020/09/GSI_924.pdf

von Schuckmann, K., Cheng, L., Palmer, M. D. et al. (2020). Heat stored in the Earth system: Where does the energy go? *Earth System Science Data*, 12(3), 2013–41.

Voosen, P. (2021). Key Antarctic ice shelf is within years of failure. *Science*, 374(6574), 1420–21.

Vorrath, S. (2021). Sun Cable welcomes Singapore plan to import 4GW of electricity by 2035. *Renew Economy*, 26 October. reneweconomy.com.au /sun-cable-welcomes-singapore-plan-to-import-4gw-of-electricity-by -2035/

Wainwright, J. & Mann, G. (2018). *Climate leviathan: A political theory of our planetary future.* London: Verso.

Walenta, J. (2020). Climate risk assessments and science-based targets: A review of emerging private sector climate action tools. *WIREs Climate Change*, 11(2), e628.

Walker, G. & Devine-Wright, P. (2008). Community renewable energy: What should it mean? *Energy Policy*, 36(2), 497–500.

Wallerstein, I. (2004). *World-systems analysis: An introduction.* Durham, NC: Duke University Press.

Walsh, B. (2012). Exclusive: How the Sierra Club took millions from the natural gas industry – and why they stopped. *Time*, 2 February. https://s cience.time.com/2012/02/02/exclusive-how-the-sierra-club-took-millions -from-the-natural-gas-industry-and-why-they-stopped/

Wang, Q. & Yang, X. (2020). Imbalance of carbon embodied in south-south trade: Evidence from China-India trade. *Science of The Total Environment*, 707, 134473.

Weart, S. (2011). The development of the concept of dangerous anthropogenic climate change. In J. S. Dryzek, R. B. Norgaard & D. Schlosberg (eds.), *Oxford handbook of climate change and society.* Oxford: Oxford University Press, pp. 67–81.

Webber, S. (2013). Performative vulnerability: Climate change adaptation policies and financing in Kiribati. *Environment and Planning A: Economy and Space*, 45(11), 2717–33.

Webber, S. (2016). Climate change adaptation as a growing development priority: Towards critical adaptation scholarship. *Geography Compass*, 10(10), 401–13.

Weed, J. (2018). Why tourists are chasing glaciers. *Gulf News*, 10 March. https:// gulfnews.com/business/tourism/why-tourists-are-chasing-glaciers-1.2185080

Westervelt, A. (2021). Big oil's 'wokewashing' is the new climate science denialism. *The Guardian*, 9 September. www.theguardian.com/environ ment/2021/sep/09/big-oil-delay-tactics-new-climate-science-denial

Wilkinson, M. (2020). *The carbon club: How a network of influential climate sceptics, politicians and business leaders fought to control Australia's climate policy*. Sydney: Allen & Unwin.

Williams, A. P., Abatzoglou, J. T., Gershunov, A. et al. (2019). Observed impacts of anthropogenic climate change on wildfire in California. *Earth's Future*, 7(8), 892–910.

Williams, R. (2019). 'This shining confluence of magic and technology': Solarpunk, energy imaginaries, and the infrastructures of solarity. *Open Library of Humanities*, 5(1), 1–60.

Wise, R. M., Fazey, I., Stafford Smith, M. et al. (2014). Reconceptualising adaptation to climate change as part of pathways of change and response. *Global Environmental Change*, 28, 325–36.

Wissman-Weber, N. K. & Levy, D. L. (2018). Climate adaptation in the Anthropocene: Constructing and contesting urban risk regimes. *Organization*, 25(4), 491–516.

World Bank. (2012). *Thai flood 2011: Rapid assessment for resilient recovery and reconstruction planning*. Bangkok: World Bank. https://open knowledge.worldbank.org/handle/10986/26862

World Bank. (2015a). *Preparing for carbon pricing: Case studies from company experience Royal Dutch Shell, Rio Tinto, and Pacific Gas and Electric Company*. Washington, DC: International Bank for Reconstruction and Development/The World Bank. http://documents1.worldbank.org/curated/e n/392401468127153795/pdf/939440WP0201500ers0385391B00PUBLI C0.pdf

World Bank. (2015b). *Salinity intrusion in a changing climate scenario will hit coastal Bangladesh hard. The World Bank: News*, 17 February. www .worldbank.org/en/news/feature/2015/02/17/salinity-intrusion-in-changing -climate-scenario-will-hit-coastal-bangladesh-hard

Wright, C. & Nyberg, D. (2012). Working with passion: Emotionology, corporate environmentalism and climate change. *Human Relations*, 65 (12), 1561–87.

Wright, C. & Nyberg, D. (2015). *Climate change, capitalism and corporations: Processes of creative self-destruction*. Cambridge: Cambridge University Press.

Wright, C. & Nyberg, D. (2017). An inconvenient truth: How organizations translate climate change into business as usual. *Academy of Management Journal*, 60(5), 1633–61.

Wright, C. & Nyberg, D. (2022). The roles of celebrities in public disputes: Climate change and the Great Barrier Reef. *Journal of Management Studies*. https://doi.org/10.1111/joms.12800

Wright, C., Nyberg, D. & Bowden, V. (2021). Beyond the discourse of denial: The reproduction of fossil fuel hegemony in Australia. *Energy Research & Social Science*, 77, 102094.

Wright, C., Nyberg, D., De Cock, C. & Whiteman, G. (2013). Future imaginings: Organizing in response to climate change. *Organization*, 20(5), 647–58.

Wright, C., Nyberg, D. & Grant, D. (2012). 'Hippies on the third floor': Climate change, narrative identity and the micro-politics of corporate environmentalism. *Organization Studies*, 33(11), 1451–75.

Wu, X., Lu, Y., Zhou, S., Chen, L. & Xu, B. (2016). Impact of climate change on human infectious diseases: Empirical evidence and human adaptation. *Environment International*, 86, 14–23.

WWF. (2021). *Announcing WWF's new partnership with the Bezos Earth Fund*, 17 November. www.youtube.com/watch?v=u6BlNdkfLWI

Yusoff, K. (2010). Biopolitical economies and the political aesthetics of climate change. *Theory, Culture & Society*, 27(2/3), 73–99.

Index

Printed in the United States
by Baker & Taylor Publisher Services